FIRST SHOT

FIRST
SHOT

The Untold Story of the Japanese Minisubs that Attacked Pearl Harbor

John Craddock

McGraw-Hill

Camden, Maine • New York • Chicago • San Francisco • Lisbon
London • Madrid • Mexico City • Milan • New Delhi • San Juan
Seoul • Singapore • Sydney • Toronto

1 2 3 4 5 6 7 8 9 DOC DOC 9 8 7 6 5

© 2006 John Craddock

Library of Congress Cataloging-in-Publication Data
Craddock, John.
  First shot : the untold story of the Japanese minisubs that attacked
Pearl Harbor / John Craddock.
    p. cm. 940.5426
  Includes bibliographical references and index. C
  ISBN 0-07-143716-9 (hardbound : alk. paper)
  1. World War, 1939–1945—Naval operations—Submarine. 2. World War,
1939–1945—Naval operations, Japanese. 3. Midget submarines—Japan.
4. World War, 1939–1945—Pacific Ocean. 5. Japan. Kaigun—History—
World War, 1939–1945. I. Title.
  D783.6.C73 2005 $4|07$
  940.54'26693—dc22   SEBCO BKS
                          1495   2005026408

Maps on pages viii–ix by International Mapping Associates.
All photos courtesy Naval Historical Foundation unless otherwise noted.
Drawing of midget submarine Jim Sollers.

For

Bo F. Craddock,
Colonel, AUS (Retired)
and
Ernest E. Lycan, USMC,
veteran of Guam
and Iwo Jima

Contents

Photos may be found following page 74.

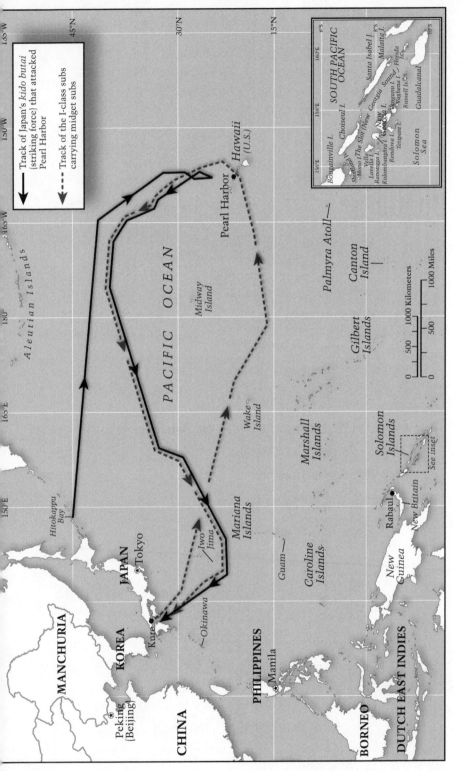

The path to war.

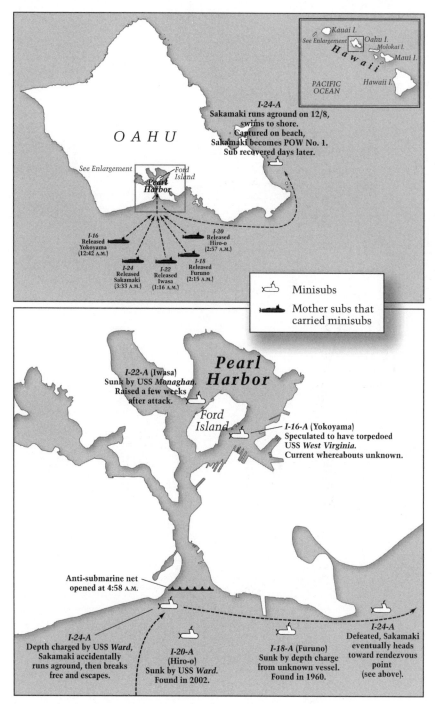

Map of Oahu shows the approximate locations of the I-class submarines when they launched their midget subs to attack the U.S. Navy. The precise launch times are taken from Japanese military records. The enlargement of Pearl Harbor shows what is known of the midget subs' involvement on December 7, 1941.

FIRST SHOT

The Search

IN NOVEMBER 2000 the world's most successful underwater explorer, Robert Ballard, embarked on a mission to find a long-lost World War II Japanese submarine. Ballard for years had enjoyed a celebrity reputation for locating sunken ships and cracking open their archeological treasure chests; he'd made a media name for himself in particular by finding what others overlooked. The *Titanic* and *Bismarck* discoveries had established Ballard as the world's top undersea Argonaut.

This time the vessel Ballard sought was only 79 feet long and about 6 feet wide. This "midget"—indeed a shrimp by submarine standards—was less than one-tenth the length of the *Titanic*. The little Japanese sub was thought to have sunk somewhere off the coast of Oahu on December 7, 1941, the first Japanese casualty in the sneak attack on Pearl Harbor. The sub's historic significance rested on its unusual fate. A tired old World War I–era American destroyer, the USS *Ward*, was patrolling the mouth of Pearl Harbor that morning. Alerted to the presence of what seemed impossible—an enemy midget sub trying to sneak into the harbor—the *Ward* shot at and apparently hit the vessel more than one full hour before the air attack began, then reported the incident to Pearl Harbor headquarters in one of the most famous unheeded warnings in history: "We have attacked[,] fired upon and dropped depth charges upon submarine operating in defensive sea area." The time was 6:53 A.M.

The grim significance of the report would not sink in until 7:55, when waves of Japanese airplanes, red suns painted on their wings, descended with a vengeance on the harbor. Military personnel and civilians gaped as the enemy aircraft—Zeros, Kates, and Vals—strafed, bombed, and torpedoed America's "indomitable" fleet of more than a hundred ships. The dawning comprehension came too late—2,403 people would die; 1,178 were wounded. As the attack unfolded, the exclamation of one embattled sailor to his buddy perfectly underscored America's innocence and haplessness: "I didn't even know they were mad at us."

Early on that terrible December Sunday, the first shot fired at Pearl Harbor—and thus the first shot fired in a U.S. battle in World War II—came from the U.S. Navy, not the Imperial Japanese Navy. The hit scored by the *Ward*'s No. 3 gun, however, would quickly be overshadowed by the black smoke pouring from the heart of America's Pacific armada, the horror of thousands dead—many of them trapped and drowned in capsized ships—and the grim voice of President Franklin D. Roosevelt preparing a stunned nation for a long war. As time passed, the *Ward* incident provoked unavoidable questions. Why did officers on duty at Pearl Harbor ignore the sinking of the Japanese sub? Might a one-hour warning have changed the outcome of the attack?

Since the midget sub had never been recovered, it was natural to wonder whether the event had occurred at all. False sub sightings had been routine around Oahu in 1941; Navy command on December 7 thought it more likely the *Ward* had shot a big whale. Over the years, numerous searches were undertaken to find the wreckage of the little sub, but none succeeded. It became one of the last lingering mysteries about Pearl Harbor. Men who'd been there that day in 1941 wondered for the rest of their lives what might have happened if their attack warning had ended up in the right hands at the right time. Most surviving veterans of Pearl Harbor can only visit the USS *Arizona* Memorial and grieve over the thousands of lost comrades. For the crew of the *Ward* and others involved, however, there was still something to prove and only one way to do it: find the midget sub. After almost sixty years of questions, Bob Ballard aimed to uncover the answer, and, in his words, "to write history" that no one could challenge.

A top scientist with leading-man looks and an anchorman's voice, Ballard enlisted a sizable entourage for his search. A crew from the National Geographic *Explorer* television series stood ready to record the discovery; a chronicler for *National Geographic* magazine, Priit J. Vesilind, tagged along to write the play-by-play. Stephen Ambrose, the nation's most widely read military historian and a *National Geographic* explorer-in-residence, added his expertise; calling the Hawaiian assignment "easy duty"—there would be no endless weeks of pounding on North Atlantic seas, tough conditions Ballard's previous undersea expeditions had to overcome. Ballard's equipment was as impressive as his crew. He chartered a Hawaiian-based research ship, *American Islander*, and imported his own high-tech mini-fleet: two remote-controlled underwater vehicles and two manned submersibles that had helped him succeed on other missions. Also joining Ballard were three men who had plied these same waters almost sixty years earlier. Two were American crewmen who had served on the *Ward*, eyewitnesses to their ship's firing on the midget sub and the enemy air assault that followed. The third man had a different point of view—he had been a radioman on a 300-foot Japanese submarine known as *I-16*.

On November 6, 2000, Ballard's expedition departed at the glistening first light of dawn. A calm day greeted them, with gentle swells, rolling under a clearing sky. It was the same sort of good weather that Japanese Navy commanders on December 7, 1941; had considered a "go" sign from God.

As the *American Islander* cruised toward open water, the aging *Ward* crew members—Russell Reetz (84) and Will Lehner (79)—told Ballard their accounts of the first shot. Reetz had served as a machinist on the *Ward*. He'd stood watch until almost 4:00 A.M. on December 7, then retired to his bunk. When the general quarters alarm sounded at 6:40, Reetz scrambled back up on deck and watched the action from amidships. At the same time, Lehner—a cook in the *Ward*'s mess—rushed topside to load shells for the No. 4 gun.

Reetz and Lehner—along with 82 other teenagers and twenty-somethings—had joined the Naval Reserve in the St. Paul area of Minnesota. In 1940 the Navy had shipped their entire unit to the *Ward*, a creaky destroyer known as a "four-stacker" because of its four tall smokestacks that poured out black smoke from the fire boxes below. Both men had a special stake in Ballard's search, not only for themselves but also for their fellow crewmen. Although they had received recognition for the event, the *Ward*'s extraordinary claim invited skeptics. Was it truly possible that the *Ward* spotted the enemy sub and then sank it with a crack shot? The tale bordered on the fantastic—a sea story. "No one ever believed us," Lehner said. In fact, one of the numerous military inquiries into the Pearl Harbor attack questioned the *Ward*'s report. Finding the sunken craft would erase any doubt. It would prove that those young men from Minnesota and their old ship had accomplished something extraordinary. For the crew of the *Ward*, the war wasn't over, and it wouldn't be until this sub was found. Ballard wrote that he, too, "wanted to find [the sub] and close the book."

A stoic man, Japanese radio operator Kichiji Dewa, 80, seemed distant as the *American Islander* began its search. He had served aboard a special sub squad that was part of Japan's *kido butai* (striking force): 353 aircraft on six aircraft carriers and more than twenty *I*-class submarines. The planes and warships had secretly departed from Japan on November 26; two weeks earlier, the subs had slid from Japanese harbors on their mission to form a circle around Oahu.

Each of five *I*-subs (each more than 300 feet long) had carried a secret weapon: a midget submarine. Like a baby in a backpack, each midget sub was strapped to a pedestal on the aft deck of its mother craft for the 4,000-mile journey from Japan. The plan called for the two-man midget subs to sneak into Pearl Harbor before dawn. As the air attack began, they were to fire their two torpedoes at enemy ships.

At 12:42 A.M. on December 7, Kichiji Dewa's big sub closed to within seven miles of the harbor entrance and released its midget sub. Known as *I-16-A* (or *I-16-tou*, which means *I-16*'s boat), it was painted with black enamel over a red zinc undercoat. The cigar-shaped sub was powered by batteries—33,000 pounds of them, wired in series, producing a positive charge that turned the 600-hp electric motor and propelled the craft at a top speed of 24 knots (27.6 mph). The center of the sub contained a control room packed with gear and gadgets: a gyrocompass, electric trim pump, torpedo firing mechanism, crystal radio, ship's wheel, and a tiny navigation table. The conning tower directly overhead housed a retractable 10-foot periscope that could be raised and lowered by an electric winch. The little sub carried more than 500 lead oblong weights, called pigs, which added about 6,000 pounds of ballast. Altogether the sub weighed a hefty 46 tons. Its two torpedoes weren't light, either: each measured 18.3 feet long and packed 770 pounds of explosives. Powered by pure oxygen and kerosene, they were among the most advanced in the world. The torpedoes were loaded in 18-inch bow tubes, one above the other, like a derringer, and just one of them could blow a 40-foot hole in a ship.

A radioman on *I-16*, Dewa had been assigned the additional task of maintaining *I-16-A* on the long trip from Japan. He had also worked out with the little sub's two-man crew how they would communicate by radio after firing their torpedoes, and how they would eventually rendezvous with the mother sub. He had become friends with the men, and they shared a little sake party on December 6, 1941. He had spoken the last words to the midget sub crew (a casual "take care") as they cast off. Yet, as they embarked on their mission, he had known they would never return.

After a few days aboard the *American Islander*, Ballard gently questioned the Japanese veteran about the war. As early as October 1941, Dewa had been aware that his nation would attack the U.S.. He had hated America then, believing the propaganda that the

United States wanted to destroy Japan through economic embar-
goes and lure his nation into war. After Pearl Harbor, Dewa served
on *I-16* for three more years until it sank in a battle near Saipan.
He swam for hours to reach safety.

Ballard's first search "team" consisted of his two unmanned underwater modules. Connected directly to the *American Islander*, a
tethered vehicle named *Argus* issued low-frequency sonar to locate objects. *Argus* also served as a stable underwater platform, a
kind of "middleman," (as Ballard put it) for another remotely operated vehicle. Tethered to *Argus*, *Little Herc*'s high-frequency sonar
and a high-resolution color video camera scoured the ocean floor
like a roving eyeball. Working in tandem, the remote vehicles
could stay underwater indefinitely. In addition to his high-tech
hardware, Ballard had detailed maps of the seabed made from sonar
readings compiled over the years and provided to him by the National Park Service at Pearl Harbor.

When he examined the Park Service maps, however, Ballard ran
into an unexpected problem. He saw an astounding array of possible targets—about a hundred in all. For decades the Navy had
hauled obsolete or damaged equipment and weapons out to sea and
dumped them overboard. Ballard's first impression of the ocean
floor around Pearl Harbor was that it looked like "a museum of
World War II"; his second was that it was littered with "junk."
Wrecked planes, damaged patrol boats, worn-out wire cable, left-
over concrete pilings, punctured air tanks, ancient half-tracks, jettisoned jeeps—all could show up as echo returns on sonar. That's
not to mention rock outcroppings, duly recorded as "possibles." It
dawned on Ballard that pinpointing a 79-foot submarine in an underwater junkyard would differ greatly from finding something as
large as the *Titanic* or the *Bismarck* on a relatively uncluttered
ocean floor.

The *Ward* crewmen eagerly watched the video screen on the *Islander* as the camera on *Little Herc* scanned the bottom. As the
first pieces of scattered debris appeared, the men presumed they

would soon see the midget sub. Lehner said, "This is really exciting. Everything looks like parts of it." As the days passed, however, their initial enthusiasm was assaulted by one dash of reality after another. *Little Herc* would run across some debris that looked like a torpedo, but a closer inspection would show only a piece of pipe. Over time, the veterans became more comfortable aboard ship and with each other. All Navy men at heart, they relished the chance to be at sea and on a mission. Ballard was working with slightly more than a two-week window; he had limited funds, and he had other targets scheduled for the months ahead. By day 10, he'd thoroughly covered a two-square-mile area known as "the flats." The *Ward* crewmen suggested that the *Islander* had gone out too far, and Ballard decided to concentrate closer to the harbor entrance. It was there, Ballard wrote, ". . . the *Ward* veterans were convinced...that the midget submarine was sunk. . . ." Still, they found nothing but junk. Ballard wondered if the little sub had simply broken apart, never to be recovered. Flashing back to his unsuccessful search for the Loch Ness monster (the chimerical plesiosaur forgotten by time), he wondered if this was another Nessie.

In mid-November, his search window about to close, Ballard turned to a manned submersible, *Deep Worker*, for his final attempt. Scanning the inscrutable waters around *Islander*, poring over sonar images of the littered seabed below, his crew pondered the raft of questions drifting around the lost sub. How close had this one little sub come to undermining the Japanese attack by alerting the American enemy? Surprise had been critical to Japanese success on December 7. Its early discovery by the men of the *Ward* could have changed history. Why did the Japanese even launch those little subs?

The answer to that question lay not on the sea floor, but with the architect of the Pearl Harbor attack, Isoroku Yamamoto, a man who both respected and admired the United States—and who had tasted American life firsthand.

The Samurai's Son

WITH OR WITHOUT Isoroku Yamamoto, there would have been a war between the United States and Japan. But it is also fair to say that if Yamamoto had chosen medicine or law or professional gambling (a real possibility) instead of the military as his profession, there would have been no sneak attack on Pearl Harbor, and certainly no midget sub assault.

Yamamoto took the measure of the United States for more than two decades before the war. Some of his visits to America were brief, others extended. In 1916, when he was 32, he traveled to Oregon and stayed at the Crown Point Chalet outside Portland; in 1919 he enrolled at Harvard University and remained in the U.S. until 1921; he twice took cross-country trips from the West to East coasts; and from 1926 to 1928 he was attached to the Japanese embassy in Washington, D.C.

After each visit to the United States, Isoroku Yamamoto came away more impressed; his chief biographer, Hiroyuki Agawa, wrote simply, "he liked the country." Yamamoto marveled at America's natural resources and manufacturing base. He admired its leaders, especially Abraham Lincoln. He even enjoyed American sports. During a one-day layover in Chicago on a cross-country train trip, he ventured out to Evanston to catch the Iowa-Northwestern football game (final score: Iowa 20, Northwestern 7). Yet, despite his apparent affinity for America, Yamamoto would be seen as responsible for more than 3,500 American casualties on December 7, 1941, and he would become a villain to the American people. Yamamoto appeared on the cover of *Time* magazine on December 22, 1941, in a menacing caricature with the headline: "Japan's Aggressor: Admiral Yamamoto. His was the daring execution of a brilliant treachery." (It's not known whether he ever saw the cover; Yamamoto subscribed to *Life*.) Only the bloodthirsty Japanese leader Hideki Tojo, later hanged for his war crimes, would rank higher on the Allies' most-wanted list in the Pacific.

Yamamoto's first visit to America was brief, a jaunt across the Pacific for a West Coast sightseeing trip in 1916. There's nothing in his official naval records about this trip, but his signature is definitely on the Crown Point Chalet register. He probably was taking a break from the Japanese naval war college he attended. Three years later he re-entered the U.S. to begin studies at Harvard. The 35-year-old Japanese Navy lieutenant commander was among 175 foreign students enrolled there in 1919, some seventy of them Japanese. The university made a special effort to welcome foreigners to a postwar world by holding a reception at the venerable Phillips Brooks House; later that academic year the Student Council agreed to add at least one foreign student to its board in order to encourage more interaction between foreigners and the American student body. The philosopher W. E. Hocking was designated as the faculty adviser for Japanese students.

Not all gestures and attitudes were friendly, however. In an editorial that year, the *Harvard Crimson* expressed concerns about an immigration flood to the U.S. of "the yellow race."

The record of Yamamoto's academic career and stay in the U.S. during those years remains incomplete, but some facts are clear. Though recently married, he did not bring his wife with him. He lived at 157 Naples Road in Brookline, just west of Boston and about three miles from the center of the campus in Cambridge, and listed Mrs. Sarah Clifford and Mrs. Frederick Charles Morrow, both of the same address, as contacts. He enrolled in a single class—English E—

as a special student, meaning he wasn't seeking a degree. His purpose, he wrote in his application, was "to take up English only." He met other Japanese students, in particular two who would become life-long friends: Shin'ichiro Oguma and Isamu Morimura.

That fall Harvard's football team enjoyed a great season (7-0-1) that would culminate in a Rose Bowl victory on New Year's Day. Many students were returning to campus and civilian life after World War I. Among them was James B. Conant, who had graduated with a degree in chemistry in 1914. He'd worked for the Army, specifically in the production of poison gas. In 1919, he was teaching undergraduate chemistry. In 1933, he would be named the president of Harvard, a post that would lead to his joining a secret committee with, as it turned out, life and death power over Japan. He, along with six other men, would oversee a project known as S-1, the top-secret effort to manufacture the atomic bomb.

Autumn leaves, red and yellow, swirled beneath the elms in Harvard Yard. There were a few days of unusually balmy weather— it was warm enough to play golf on November 30. A writer at the time saw it as a bad sign: "Winter is about to leap upon us." It did. The winter weather was harsh, and on February 6, 1920, the city was snowbound for the first time in more than a decade; in fact, it was the first paralyzing storm since the automobile had become commonplace. Drivers tried the streets with little success. (Imports, such as Fiats, seemed to do better than American cars.) People packed the trains and subways. The next day, February 7, with no official explanation, special student Isoroku Yamamoto withdrew from Harvard, having received one grade, a C+. The future commander-in-chief of the Japanese Navy had decided to take a detour from academic life. He would hitchhike to Mexico, where he went to look for oil wells.

As a naval officer, Yamamoto knew no modern fleet could run without stores of petroleum, even though coal-burning ships were still prevalent when Yamamoto had last served at sea. Japan had only a few places that produced oil domestically, so it imported most of its oil from other countries. Scouting potential oil sources in North America, Yamamoto ventured briefly through the Southwest U.S. (he would return there three years later), then explored Mexico. He wrote to his brother, Kihachi: "I'm now in Tampico on a tour of the oil fields. Some wells are said to produce about twenty thousand gallons of oil per day, and some have apparently been yielding continuously for thirteen years. The current price of forty gallons of crude oil is one yen [equivalent to 50 cents at the time] and the tax is one yen, which must seem incredible back home in our part of the country."

Yamamoto traveled on the cheap, so cheaply, in fact, that he attracted the attention of Mexican authorities, who wired the Japanese embassy in Washington: "A man who claims to be Yamamoto Isoruku, a commander in the Japanese navy, is traveling around the country inspecting oil fields. He stays in the meanest attics in third-rate hotels and never eats hotel food, subsisting instead on bread, water and bananas. Please confirm his identity." The embassy responded that it knew Yamamoto and acknowledged the mission.

He eventually landed at the Japanese embassy in Mexico City. The military attaché was Kenzo Yamada, who was from the same Niigata district as Yamamoto. Yamada had fought side by side in the Russo-Japanese war with Yamamoto's older brother. They shared stories about the war, which Yamamoto had also fought in, and the homeland they loved.

Then Yamamoto virtually disappeared. Almost no record exists of his travels in subsequent months. He participated in a naval conference in Washington in the summer of 1920 and returned to Japan in the summer of 1921. Some accounts say he returned to Harvard and finished his studies, but there's no record. A Harvard official speculated in a 1974 letter, responding to an author's query, that since Yamamoto wasn't a student at Harvard after February 1920, "I can only assume, if his embassy was vouching for him, that he was using Harvard as a front to cover other activities." In other words, Yamamoto was spying.

This bit of speculation by a Harvard registrar was more accurate than she guessed or than had previously been known. The three-year period before Yamamoto arrived at Harvard is usually recorded as a time when he was attending and teaching at a war college—a kind of graduate school for military officers. In fact, for about a year of that time, Yamamoto had been a student at a spy school, a Japanese version of the American CIA. In a way, Yamamoto again showed he was a forward thinker. His enrollment at Harvard would make him among the first—if not the first—of a long series of Japanese naval officers attending college in the United States and using that cover to reconnoiter American manufacturing and military installations. The ploy had become so transparent by the late 1930s that some "students" were routinely tailed by the FBI when they left campus.

Yamamoto's next U.S. excursion came in 1923, when he traveled with Admiral Kenji Ide on a Western fact-finding tour that included Europe and a quick trip across the United States—specifically with a stop in Texas, again to look at oil wells. In December 1925, he was appointed naval attaché in Washington and left Japan for his post in January 1926. He was regarded as a man on the rise in Japanese military circles.

His 1926–1928 stay in the United States bore the outward appearance of a leisurely pace, and he spent frequent holidays satisfying an urge that had become an obsession. Yamamoto loved to gamble—cards, dice, roulette, almost anything. He rarely spent a free moment without playing some sort of game—and he was good at them. In a visit to Europe, he won so much money at Monaco that he was banned from the casino, only the second person at the time to earn that "honor." He once joked to his superior, Admiral Ide: "If only you'd give me a couple of years amusing myself in Europe, I'd earn you the money for at least a couple of battleships." During his stay in Washington, he traveled by boat from New York to Cuba (Las Vegas was still a wasteland) and won big at the casinos in Havana as well.

In his last trip, in 1934, he once again traveled cross-country, beginning in Seattle and ending in New York at the Astor Hotel. He and his colleagues gambled en route, with Yamamoto winning big, as usual. A colleague once noted that Yamamoto employed the same technique in bridge, poker, or *shogi*, a traditional Japanese game similar to chess. Yamamoto liked to go on the attack.

After 1934, Yamamoto never returned to the United States, but it was clear that the country still fascinated him. Back in Japan, Yamamoto would leave copies of *Life* magazine out in his office and mark in red the articles he found interesting. He often recommended Carl Sandburg's illustrated biography of Lincoln when he wanted to enlighten others about America. He noted Lincoln's tough circumstances as a boy: "Born into poverty—there was a photo of his birthplace in Kentucky—you wouldn't see many houses like that, even in Japan." He called Lincoln a man "of real purpose," whom he respected foremost as a "champion of the emancipation of the slaves, the emancipation of women—in short, human freedom."

Strange that the man who held Lincoln in such high regard was destined to become an evil fascist to Americans—at least during World War II. Since the war, Yamamoto has often been portrayed as the "reluctant admiral," hesitant to fight America. He refused to side with what was called the "fleet" faction, a group of naval officers rabid for war, and would not align himself with the xenophobes in the Japanese Army or Navy. As time passed, this revisionism made him into a sympathetic character. Dozens of American and British military who had socialized with him during his years in the United States and at naval conferences in London remembered him as smart, sociable, and exceptionally open to Western ideas.

But that view isn't any more accurate than *Time* magazine's menacing caricature of 1941.

Isoroku Takano (he would change his name to Yamamoto at age 32) was born April 4, 1884, in Tokyo, the last child of Sadayoshi Takano, a former samurai who'd been stripped of his possessions after clan warfare left him on the losing side. The proud warrior, relegated to repairing and sharpening swords, lived with his family in a wooden shack in Nagaoka, a coastal town. His youngest son was named Isoroku, which means "56" (literally five ten six), because the father was 56 when his son was born.

Isoroku in his early years attended a Christian missionary school, though he never converted to Christianity. He learned to read the Bible and practiced his English with a missionary named Newall. The citizens of Nagaoka made extraordinary sacrifices to establish a strong education system, contributing more financial resources than they could really afford. (Even today, Nagaoka's school system is regarded as one of the best in Japan.) The idea was to match Western progress in science and technology. It was an extraordinarily well-rounded education for the late nineteenth century.

Isoroku Takano excelled at everything. Though slight of build, he became an excellent gymnast and a skilled fighter in samurai training rituals. And he was a brilliant student. Though his family had limited financial means and zero political pull, he set his sights on a career as a naval officer. When he took the entrance exam, he finished second in the nation, and in 1901 headed to the naval academy at Eta Jima, just a ferry ride from Hiroshima. At the academy, referred to as a "cold-water" school, cadets rose early for their cold showers, followed by endless days of hard physical and mental training. Takano made friends easily, but also managed to stand apart. He kept a Bible on his desk, and once a group of zealous students demanded to know why he seemed to embrace this foreign religion. He answered their questions calmly, noting that it was good to know the beliefs of other cultures to better understand them. Then he turned on the other students and drove them out of his room. Do not trifle with Isoroku Takano, he seemed to be saying. Soon he was regarded as a leader.

He graduated seventh in his class on November 14, 1904, and having specialized in gunnery, he signed on as a gunnery officer on the *Nisshin* on January 3, 1905, reporting just in time for a war. The Japanese and Russians were in competition over which nation would dominate Asia. The spoils of the contest were to be China, Korea, Manchuria, and, to a lesser extent, Southeast Asia.

On the morning of May 27, 1905, the Japanese fleet was in Tsushima Strait, between Korea and southwest Japan. Takano on the *Nisshin* stood watch before retiring at 4:00 A.M. A few minutes afterward a fleet of Russian ships was spotted. Later that day, at 1:45 P.M., a battle finally erupted. The Japanese ships outmaneuvered the enemy and sank or damaged the entire Russian fleet, sending thousands of Russian crewmen to their deaths. During the battle, there was an explosion on the *Nisshin*. No one could determine for certain whether the ship was hit by a Russian shell or whether a gun on the ship overheated from firing and exploded. In any case, Takano was wounded, shrapnel having peppered his body and torn a chunk of flesh from his thigh. The most severe injury was to his left hand. As he described it, ". . . two fingers on my left hand had been snapped off and were hanging by the skin alone." He wrapped up his hand and stayed at his battle station, and though he was later treated for his wounds, he lost his middle and index fingers. (The disfigurement would lead to his being referred to in the geisha district as "Eighty Sen"; a manicure cost 1 yen, but with eight fingers, Takano would pay only 80 percent.) Takano received a letter of commendation from Admiral Heihachiro Togo on May 30, 1905.

Yamamoto's name change came in 1916, after he had earned the rank of lieutenant commander and entered graduate/spy school. On occasion, clans in Japan would find themselves with no male offspring and thus no bloodline male leaders. One such clan was named Yamamoto. Isoroku, a promising young naval officer, was the youngest in his family and had an older brother and three older half-brothers, placing him at the bottom of his family hierarchy. He was approached by the Yamamoto clan to assume its name and become its new leader, the hope being that he would father sons to carry on a proud family name in Japanese history. So in 1916 Isoroku Takano became Isoroku Yamamoto. The change undoubtedly elevated Isoroku's status, but no one could have predicted the fame Isoroku in turn would bring to the Yamamoto clan.

In 1918, after returning from the West, Yamamoto married a woman named Reiko from Wakamatsu, a one-time stronghold of the Yamamoto clan. The match was the first step in meeting his obligation to the clan, and a few years later, the agreement was fulfilled when a son was born. Yamamoto was not at home for the birth, but wrote a curious letter to his wife: he asked if his new son had all his fingers.

An avid student of English, Yamamoto would become a key player in the decades of negotiations aimed at limiting the naval arsenals of the world's three primary naval powers. Along with Japan, two English-speaking countries—Great Britain and the United States—met in the 1920s in Washington. The so-called 5:5:3 pact brokered there left Japan in an inferior position for building new ships. Great Britain and the U.S. were allowed an equal tonnage of naval ships, while the Japanese were relegated to 60 percent of that amount. As the decade passed, an increasingly power-hungry Japanese government, determined to dominate Asia, came to regret and resent the pact, and Yamamoto, too, considered it a slap at Japan's national pride. Japanese officials wanted to abrogate the treaty—but didn't want to say so publicly and risk looking like aggressors to the rest of the world. When more conferences were held in London in the 1930s, Japan adopted a clever stance promoted by Yamamoto: all three nations should abolish all aircraft carriers and other war-waging ships. There wasn't an ounce of sincerity to it, but this debate stratagem threw opponents off guard and won respect for Yamamoto as a negotiator for his country's interests. One American official commented, ". . . it's Yamamoto who's beginning to have an edge on us."

After the day's disarmament debates were set aside, Yamamoto could be found at dinners and cocktail parties. He ran easily in those circles, playing bridge with naval staffs of the British and Americans (he usually was a winner) and shopping at London's stores, where he treated himself to fashionable luxuries like a snakewood walking stick. He was often invited for holidays in the country, once going to Prime Minister Ramsay MacDonald's estate outside London for the weekend. Later he visited the home of former Prime Minister David Lloyd George, who, in his advanced years, had poor eyesight. Lloyd George asked if he could touch Yamamoto's face, a moment that stuck with the Japanese naval officer. He said Lloyd George's hairy hand felt like "a bear's paw."

During the 1934 conference the debate over ship tonnage found the Japanese and British oddly aligned. Neither country wanted the United States to be amassing an unrestricted armada, or as the British representative said, exercising "the American national character." The Americans countered that tonnage and security weren't the same thing, and that the 5:5:3 ratio presented no threat to Japan. Yamamoto's retort received widespread publicity: "If America's five is no threat to Japan's three, then surely Japan's five should present no threat to America's five?" In another widely quoted line, when asked at a state dinner why he didn't agree with the 5:5:3 ratio he replied, "I am smaller than you but you don't insist I eat three-fifths of the food on my plate. You allow me to eat as much as I need."

By 1935, the talks had collapsed and the parties engaged in bilateral maneuvering amid fears that the cap on warships would be removed altogether. The English naval chief of staff met privately with Yamamoto, but no agreement could be reached. It didn't really matter. All the while the Japanese were secretly planning to build a modern naval force that would be unequaled in the Pacific. Just after Yamamoto's last-minute talks with British officials fell through, keels were laid for two behemoth battleships, *Yamato* and *Musashi*, at 72,000 tons each. The ships were twice as big as the largest British battleship, so big in fact that they couldn't pass through the Panama Canal. Any battleships the United States might build to match them would impose strategic limitations on America's "two-ocean" navy, a drawback certainly not lost on the Japanese.

Traditional Imperial Navy men were hell-bent on bigger battleships, but Yamamoto (though trained in gunnery) viewed the world differently and made his case for what he believed would be his Navy's future. He'd long before latched on to the value of an aerial force. While in the U.S. he'd followed the story of Charles A.

Lindbergh's nonstop flight across the Atlantic and listened to the debate provoked by General Billy Mitchell of the U.S. Army Air Service, who predicted that the next war would be won by the nation that dominated the air. As the big battleship designs continued, Yamamoto visited one of the naval architects, whom he knew well, and told him, "I'm afraid you'll be out of work before long. From now on, aircraft are going to be the most important thing in the navy . . . big ships and big guns will become obsolete." He was prophetic. Much later, during World War II, there would be a saying in the Imperial Navy that "the three great follies of the world were the Great Wall of China, the Pyramids, and the battleship *Yamato*." (In an ironic twist, the *Yamato* would serve as Yamamoto's flagship during the Battle of Midway.)

In fact, between his stints as an arms negotiator from the mid-1920s to the mid-1930s, Yamamoto had clearly been training himself for the next war. He gained the rank of second in command at the Navy's aviation corps headquarters in Kasumigaura, where he didn't just bark orders at pilots—Yamamoto himself learned to fly during this period (though he was well beyond the prime age for a pilot). In 1928 he captained an aircraft carrier, the *Akagi*, the ship that would later attack Pearl Harbor. He earned another promotion in 1930, this time to head the aerodynamics division of the Japanese military. Yamamoto expressed dissatisfaction with the manufacturing standards of Japanese aircraft contractors and ordered them to develop innovative designs for his review. Among the plans that crossed his desk was a set submitted by Mitsubishi, an industrial conglomerate. The design came from an engineer who'd previously worked for the Sopwith aircraft company in Great Britain. During the early years of the war the final product line—called the Zero—would own the skies over the Pacific. (The Zero model was named for the zeroes in its birth year—2600 by the old Japanese calendar [1937 by the Gregorian calendar].) Besides this famous class of fighter plane, Yamamoto also put in orders for torpedo planes and a line of long-range bombers; the bomber would come to be known—and feared—as "the Betty."

Besides expanding his nation's air force, Yamamoto lobbied for more aircraft carriers. Two battle cruisers were converted to carriers, and light carriers soon started to come off the production line—*Ryujo* was ready in 1927. The training of pilots on these carriers was also well underway by then, and Yamamoto expressed his view that the men who died in training flights should be highly honored for their sacrifices; these tests helped naval aviators gain the skills necessary to lead their nation into war. To Yamamoto, their deaths meant as much as or more than bravery on the field of battle.

It's a simple fact that the man who negotiated arms limitations and voiced public doubts about attacking the United States (he told the head of the government in 1940, Prince Fumimaro Konoe, "to avoid war with America") would be the engineer of a ruthless attack plan he had been working on for almost twenty years. It's also a matter of record that after World War I, Japan's Imperial Defense Policy targeted the United States as its primary enemy. Russia was second, though to the Navy, it was no contest: "[T]he . . . enemy is always America," the Defense Policy stated. Japan viewed the United States as an obstacle to its plan to control East Asia; war between the two nations at some point seemed inevitable to Japanese leaders.

As for Yamamoto, his hesitation to strike America was more a matter of degree than genuine reluctance. As the Japanese empire expanded, there were only two military factions: xenophobic and less xenophobic. In that atmosphere, "reluctant" warriors were viewed suspiciously. As Yamamoto moved up the ranks, there were plots against his life because the extremist Japanese military viewed his interest in America and Great Britain as suspicious, and in those days young military officers didn't hesitate to hunt down and shoot "running dog" traitors. Attacks by these radicals struck down even the highest Japanese officials.

The "February 26 Incident" of 1936 was among several such assassination plots. Japan's lord privy seal, finance minister, and inspector general of military education were killed, and the lord chamberlain, Kantaro Suzuki, was wounded. The perpetrators, a military group, also attacked the prime minister's house, misidentified his brother-in-law for the prime minister, and killed him, too. Yamamoto was peripherally involved when he sent a doctor to aid Suzuki. After that incident, the rebel soldiers were hunted down and either shot or forced to commit ritual suicide. Martial law was imposed, and the extreme right wing of the Army came to hold greater sway over the government. Eventually the head of the military would become the most powerful person in Japan.

After he became a Navy vice minister in December 1936, Yamamoto received regular death threats, many in the form of formal declarations (biographer Agawa called them *farragoes*, or jumbled messes) written on scrolls of handmade paper, "the gist of which was that Heaven was going to punish Yamamoto . . . via them." As the threats escalated, Yamamoto was given an escort of bodyguards. He was told there was a bounty of 100,000 yen on his head. Small anti-Yamamoto groups had formed, and they said they had stores of dynamite just for him. In fact a man was arrested while lying in wait with explosives on the banks of the Sumida River. There was even a saying around the naval ministry: "Whatever you do, don't accept a lift in the vice-minister's car." But the threats didn't much disturb Yamamoto; the biggest irritation was that they interfered with his regular visits to a mistress.

A change in government in 1939 ended Yamamoto's tenure as a Navy vice minister, but he quickly earned another promotion, this time to commander of the combined fleet, which gave him power over virtually everything that either floated (from carrier groups to submarines) or flew. The post required Yamamoto to go to sea. This was widely regarded as a strategy to protect his life. His aides said they "felt a sense of relief as they watched the limited express [train] with Yamamoto on board draw out of the station without . . . incident . . . ." He would be the commander of 40,000 men, but even then, the military atmosphere was charged. One of Japan's top-gun pilots said openly, "Yamamoto's got no guts. He's too fond of England and America. Something of a coward, I'd say." The speaker was Lieutenant Commander Mitsuo Fuchida, who would lead the air raid on Pearl Harbor.

In 1940, as American and Japanese negotiations continued over a variety of issues, Japan forged an open agreement with Germany and Italy known as the Tripartite Pact. If one nation declared war or was attacked, the other two would join in and declare war as well. The Japanese Army had pressed for the agreement since 1939, for it was aimed at one nation only—the United States. The Army believed the show of fascist unity would keep the U.S. from trying to halt the Japanese troops in China, which Japan had invaded in 1934.

Yamamoto opposed the pact. Five years earlier, he had already shown skepticism about Germany's Nazi Party. On his way home from London in 1935, he had been asked by Nazi party officials to meet with the German Navy minister and Hitler himself. In Berlin, Yamamoto had called on the Navy official but had little to say, and he had avoided the meeting with Hitler. Though 1935 was only Hitler's third year in office, Yamamoto had already been suspicious of the radical German agenda and did not want to give the appearance that Japan was in league with such an extremist. By 1940, however, the Japanese Army approved of Hitler's way of doing things. It took the German Army just over three hours to capture Denmark that year, and Japan's fascists had their way and welcomed the Axis union with German and Italy.

Yamamoto's objection to the Tripartite alliance was that it would likely lead to a cutoff of oil and scrap metal from Britain and America, which supplied about 80 percent of Japan's needs for these materials. Further, by forcing Japan into a war against the United States, the alliance might leave Germany or even the Soviet Union as the dominant power in the postwar world. Yamamoto simply didn't want to fight Germany's Pacific war. Nonetheless, the Navy fell in line, and further opposition from Yamamoto and what was being called the Navy's "left wing" was silenced. More protests would have ended badly. Said one official, ". . . (T)here'd have been a danger of his being killed."

• • •

As Japan marched through China and expanded its so-called Greater East Asian Co-Prosperity Sphere, the likelihood of war with America increased. No one knew when the conflict might begin, but after the Tripartite Pact was concluded Yamamoto began seriously to flesh out the idea of an attack on Hawaii. This should have come as no surprise. According to his biographers, it was around April or May of 1940 when Yamamoto started to believe an attack on Hawaii could actually become reality. Other evidence shows that he was intimately familiar with the store of literature about Japan attacking Hawaii, and certainly he became acquainted with the plan while at war college. The primary target of the attack, however—the U.S. Navy's Pacific fleet—didn't arrive at Pearl Harbor until 1940.

At that point, something clicked for Yamamoto, but he had to overcome the entrenched and antiquated views of his peers and superiors before he could proceed further. For many years, the official working plan to instigate war against the United States was to attack the Philippines (a U.S. territory). The assumption was that the U.S. fleet would come to the rescue, the Japanese would wage war using the Marianas Islands as bases, and the subsequent all-out battle would decimate America's Navy.

On January 7, 1941, Yamamoto rewrote Japanese strategy. In "Views on Preparations for War," he unveiled his plan of attack on Hawaii. In this nine-page document sent to the Navy minister, he wrote that international turmoil made it "obvious that the time has come for the Navy, and the Combined Fleet in particular, to go ahead with arming and training itself, and possibly drawing up a plan of operations, on the assumption that war with America and England cannot be avoided." His plan, he added, conformed largely to verbal comments he'd made in November 1940. The plan had four sections, with a special note emphasizing that "the outcome must be decided on the first day."

In the end, almost everything would go according to Yamamoto's plan—but only after he overcame monumental objections within the Navy. He and his tacticians ground away at draft after draft, with one of the main contributors an officer referred to as "Madman Genda" because he had long advocated the "crazy" idea that aircraft should lead the attack. As a follow-up at some later point to the attack on Pearl Harbor, Yamamoto also wanted to explore the idea of landing troops on Hawaii and taking all the U.S. Navy's officers there as POWs. He considered their value extremely high because he knew firsthand that ". . . there was no shortcut to training a naval officer."

When Yamamoto's Pearl Harbor plan landed in Tokyo for review, the head of the Navy General Staff and two other top division and staff officers unanimously opposed it. Yamamoto sent a captain to discuss the operation, and a violent argument ensued. The consensus in Tokyo was that it was too great a gamble. Nonetheless, officials agreed to give it a test in map maneuvers in late summer.

Meanwhile, Japan in 1941 had struck a deal with the new German-controlled Vichy government of France to "co-defend" French Indochina (Vietnam). In real terms this meant the French would acquiesce when the Japanese invaded, which they did on the day the document was signed, July 29. In response, the American government upped the stakes: Japanese assets in the U.S. were frozen and a ban was imposed on oil exports and all scrap metal. This was exactly what Yamamoto had feared, and the precise point he had raised when he opposed the Tripartite Pact. The squeeze on resources—especially petroleum—hit the Navy hardest. It supposedly left Japan with about a four-month oil supply unless it found other sources. Japanese public reaction to the U.S. embargo was a national temper tantrum that amounted to: How dare you! (In fact, the public had again been deceived. The Imperial Navy had stockpiled 5.5 million tons of oil in a strategic reserve; in a normal year, the Navy used about 2 million tons.)

Working far behind the political scene, Yamamoto had his war plans well underway. He had the carrier *Akagi* training at a place called Kagoshima Bay, a spot picked for its similarity to a Hawaiian landmark—Pearl Harbor. At first, maneuvers testing Yamamoto's plan of attack showed that the outcome might not be exactly what the Combined Fleet admiral had wished: Japan's naval losses would almost equal those of the American Navy. Opposition to the Hawaiian campaign mounted. One top officer said, "It was like putting one's head in the lion's mouth." Yamamoto would not budge. He circulated rumors that he might retire as head of the Combined Fleet. He cajoled his colleagues and warned them that the threat to Yamata (the home islands) would come directly from the American force in Hawaii. He said, ". . . the other side has brought a great fleet to Hawaii to show us that it's within striking distance of Japan . . . conversely . . . we're within striking distance too . . . . America has put itself in a vulnerable position. If you ask me, they're just that bit too confident." (Ironically, his statement reflected the exact sentiment of the commander at Pearl Harbor at the time; Admiral James O. Richardson was replaced by Admiral Husband Kimmel, after persistently expressing his doubts to Washington about concentrating U.S. naval forces so far from the mainland.)

Slowly, more officers started to side with Yamamoto, who wasted no time in training pilots and commanders on how to execute a sneak attack on ships anchored in a harbor. Biographer Agawa points out that Yamamoto's eventual success in winning people over came from the personal magnetism he exuded. He'd been seen as a natural leader since his days at the naval academy, and now he held his ground, urging his colleagues to be willing to "go against the grain." More and more, they came around, and even those against the attack toned down their opposition or simply kept silent. By September, Yamamoto was ready to meet the prime minister. The topic: war or peace.

Prime Minster Fumimaro Konoe still held out hope for a summit between Franklin D. Roosevelt and himself. When the question arose whether the Navy would be ready if peace talks failed, Yamamoto offered his standard answer. He could keep the enemy occupied for 18 months, but after that, all bets were off. How this message was perceived came under scrutiny after the war, and is one of the rare instances when Yamamoto was seen as too brazen. Konoe was regarded as inexperienced in government, and Yamamoto's estimate that he could "give them hell for a year or a year and a half" has since been criticized. "Why didn't Yamamoto come out and say that the Navy wasn't able to take on America . . . ?" asked a fellow officer. Another wrote, "the Navy should have insisted straightforwardly that it could not agree to the war with America." This after-the-fact criticism is about as close as Japanese contemporaries ever came to accusing Yamamoto of being the aggressor. A few weeks later, under pressure from the military, Konoe resigned and his government was replaced—the maniacal General Hideki Tojo assumed leadership. Compared to some of Tojo's genocidal ideas of wiping out entire races of people to secure Japan's influence, Yamamoto's hit-and-run attack plan suddenly seemed more mainstream.

As late as November, Yamamoto still had doubts whether his force was ready. His worries filtered down the ranks to air commander Fuchida, who asked for a meeting with Yamamoto. Fuchida requested a full fleet maneuver with six carriers participating. On November 4, the mock attack force took off—Betty bombers, dive bombers, torpedo bombers, and Zeros—and over a few days, carried out their tasks successfully. It was during these exercises that the "Imperial HQ Navy Section Order No. 1" was handed down, officially ordering Yamamoto to carry out the plan for a sneak attack. In essence his plan had gone up the chain and come back down virtually unaltered, though the plot to capture American naval officers was set aside for another day. By the day the imperial order was received, Yamamoto already had an attack manual ready for distribution.

One loose end of the operation remained: how would the submarine force be employed at Pearl Harbor? In early maneuvers, the Japanese plan called for twenty-seven *I*-class subs to head out early to Oahu; also penciled in were five midget subs that would sneak into Pearl Harbor to torpedo ships. As the attack plan progressed, the submarine mission remained vague, in part because, if the air plan succeeded, the subs would be unnecessary.

Two midget sub proponents arranged an appointment with Yamamoto. Lieutenant Naoji Iwasa and Lieutenant Saburo Akieda worked as test pilots on the subs and believed their vessels should be part of the great attack. They argued that the technologically advanced subs could deliver a totally unexpected death blow. From the start, however, it was obvious the subs could not be transported into battle the same way they were being carted around Japanese seas: loaded onto a converted seaplane tender and dropped off by crane. The subs' limited range of a hundred miles or so made it impossible to drop them off anywhere near Pearl Harbor without their tender being spotted.

Another drawback made the midget subs unacceptable for their mission, at least in Yamamoto's eyes. The crews had been recruited as part of a "special attack force," which was a euphemism for "suicide squad." Yamamoto wouldn't have it. He refused to send out men and machines simply to waste them in battle. If the officers couldn't devise plans to sneak closer to Pearl Harbor without being detected and also recover the sub crews, the midget subs were out.

Two other specialists were brought in: Commander Toshihide Maejima and Lieutenant Keiu Matsuo. Enthusiastic, they also saw the subs as perfectly suited for a sneak attack—they were small, agile, and especially hard to detect at night; though built originally for open-water attacks, the subs, they agreed, "can do so much more damage to an enemy on his doorstep . . . ." The midget sub strategists came back to Yamamoto with the proposal to strap the little subs to big subs and creep within striking distance of Pearl Harbor. Then Matsuo and Maejima solved the recovery problem. Through intelligence gathered by spies in Hawaii, they picked the small, remote island of Niihau (southwest of Oahu) as a safe place for the subs to rendezvous after the attack. The island was populated by natives who spoke only Hawaiian, which made them unlikely to sound an alarm if they saw anything. The deep waters off Niihau were perfectly suited to hide the big subs while they waited for the midget subs to arrive. Yamamoto agreed that if the test runs proved successful, the little subs were in.

In the final imperial orders issued, the big *I*-subs were ordered to patrol outside the harbor "to attack enemy warships which may have escaped." Prior to the attack, the subs would do reconnaissance. If, along the way, the subs encountered any stray foreign ships that might later blow the main fleet's cover, the subs could sink the unlucky vessel without warning.

As for the midget subs, they were ordered to "carry out surprise attacks . . . after the flights of planes have attacked Oahu." That's all the instruction they received from the imperial order.

For all the extraordinary planning that made Pearl Harbor a success from Japan's point of view, the last-minute inclusion of the midget subs has never been easily explained. Even with the question of how to retrieve the subs addressed, the plan still left open the actual military impact the subs would have. Somehow, the midget subs seemed more like a toy in a war game than a weapon in a life-or-death mission.

Perhaps the inclusion was a nod from Yamamoto to his gambler's instinct to totally surprise an opponent with the unexpected and also, perhaps, a personal flamboyance he occasionally showed. From the gambler's side, the midget subs were the derringer up the sleeve, the perfect weapon to spring on an unsuspecting foe. His friend from Harvard, Morimura, also noted that Yamamoto had an unpredictable side. He once crossed a busy street in Japan while throwing cooked beans in the air and catching them in his mouth; he was 51. He had been known to entertain friends (even U.S. naval acquaintances in Washington) by suddenly doing handstands and then walking on his hands. As a top officer in Japan, he was reported leaving an important dinner and walking down the street for some distance doing a very good imitation of Charlie Chaplin's Little Tramp. When both of his old Harvard classmates (Morimura and Oguma, who had become prominent businessmen) wanted to visit Yamamoto on his flagship *Nagato*, they asked as a joke if they could bring geishas. Yamamoto played along and said of course. They showed up with about ten women, paraded onto the commander of the Combined Fleet's ship for lunch, and sent a shock through the headquarters compound. Maybe when it came to the little subs it was just a whim that struck him: The attack of the midget submarines. Why not?

With peace negotiations stalled and war plans set, the Japanese forces gathered in two places. The subs headed out in early November from a secluded harbor at Kure, and the main fleet—called *kido butai* (striking force)—left during the final days of November from the Kuril Islands in northern Japan. Seals and walruses lounged on the beach as the ships awaited their orders. The big ships had unloaded everything unnecessary—such as personal items—and loaded up with arms, ammunition, and food. They also took on thousands of drums of oil, anticipating that rough seas might prevent refueling from tankers. So many drums were stuffed on board that they were tied down on deck.

Crews were totally confused about where they were going. Because the fleet would steer through the North Pacific in winter, the planes were lubricated with freeze-proof grease on their rudders and flaps, and crewmen were issued winter wool uniforms. They also were given tropical uniforms. As Agawa writes, they "could only scratch their heads in bewilderment." On the morning *Akagi* was to leave, Yamamoto stood on the flight deck and toasted the crew and officers with a cup of sake. When the ship left port, rain and snow blew across its deck. A crewman wrote he felt like a samurai sent out to seek revenge. Of course, he had been sent by Yamamoto, a samurai's son.

Yamamoto was confident. He spent a few days with his mistress in Tokyo and waited until the crucial day when he would radio the fleet at sea that the attack was to proceed. On shore, he and his staff had a ceremonial meal of dried chestnuts, dried shellfish, and seaweed; the names of the foods stood for "fight," "win," and "be happy"; all were washed down with sake before the group partied on into the next morning with local geishas. The radio message to *kito buati* (a final "go" order) was necessary because some held a faint hope that a settlement could be reached with the American government. Controversy arose early in the planning when Yamamoto warned the fleet leaders that they might be on their way to battle and suddenly be ordered to turn around and come home. Some of the headstrong leaders carped that they couldn't stop once they'd gone that far, but Yamamoto challenged their bravado. He told them if they couldn't obey the order, they should resign on the spot. No one did.

On December 1, a conference was held at the Imperial Palace. It was on that day that Japan took the irrevocable step and made the formal decision to wage war on Britain, Holland, and the United States. The emperor himself was at the meeting, but did not speak. On December 3, Yamamoto in full-dress uniform met with the emperor at his palace (such meetings were called "crossing the moat") and received a more personal order. The emperor told Yamamoto that, "Since you have trustworthy experience in many years' of training of the fleets, we expect you will satisfy our desires by displaying our authority and force through victory over the enemy." That night Yamamoto went home for dinner, an event so rare it stunned his wife and four children. His presence was so out of the ordinary, in fact, that he had to climb over a wall to get into his own house. His family later reported that he seemed preoccupied.

On the Thursday night before the attack on Pearl Harbor, Yamamoto put on civilian clothes (a blue suit) and, carrying a parcel in which he had packed his dress uniform, boarded the train from Yokohama Central station. His destination was Hiroshima and his flagship *Nagato*, from which in a few days he would direct the attack and listen to the reports of his mission's success. Train rides on crowded coaches weren't normal for people of Yamamoto's status, but he apparently wanted to blend in and see his country still relatively tranquil, the last peaceful journey he would ever take.

• • •

By then the submarines had closed to within a few hundred miles of Oahu, and the crews were preparing their midget subs, testing for leaks, and writing what they knew would be their last letters home. One pilot would compose a poem expressing his feelings that if these brave crewmen must fall like cherry blossoms, "Let them fall!"

Fall they would.

Why the midget subs were included in the attacks can be traced to the basic usefulness of underwater craft in warfare. They're hard to spot. Subs for centuries have been the best stealth fighters. Twentieth-century technological advances, especially those made by the Japanese, would allow tiny subs carrying huge torpedo payloads to sneak close to the biggest ships in the world and deliver a mortal blow. Or, at least, that was the plan.

The Smallest Subs

GORDON PRANGE, the author of the voluminous *At Dawn We Slept*, probably wrote the best single line describing the midget subs. He noted that they were "the epitome of the Japanese preoccupation with smallness and precision—the mechanical counterpart of a bonsai tree."

The basic blueprint for small submarines—or any sub, for that matter—can be traced back 500 million years to the Cambrian Period, and the design remains virtually unchanged, even today. The chambered nautilus, first cousin to an octopus, routinely rises 1,000 feet in the evening to feed at the surface of the sea and lowers itself back to the bottom when it has had its fill. It often lives among towers of coral, and as it travels up the colorful walls, the nautilus looks for food and tries to avoid turtles and triggerfish that want to eat it. The nautilus propels its ascent by filling the chambers within its calcium-carbonate shell with gases (a mixture of nitrogen and the inert gas argon), which it manufactures itself. When it wants to descend, the little one-foot-wide cephalopod fills its chambers (read: ballast tanks) with water, and down it goes.

Throughout history inventors stretched their imaginations to find some way humans might stay submerged: records tell of glass barrels dropping to the ocean floor and underwater rowboats sculling beneath the surface; designs of sub prototypes—were drawn 500 years ago by Leonardo da Vinci, who could foresee the usefulness of an underwater vessel, as he could so many things (automobiles included).

The first submarine used in war, the *Turtle*, was built by an American colonist, David Bushnell of Connecticut. Like all early subs, it was small; its mission during the Revolutionary War was to sneak close and attack the British fleet. After a few test runs, Bushnell (a Yale graduate) somehow persuaded Sergeant Ezra Lee to climb aboard and set his sights on the British frigate HMS *Eagle*, which was anchored in New York Harbor. The sub was launched on September 7, 1776, armed with a 150-pound explosive charge on a timer; Lee was supposed to attach the package to the *Eagle* by screwing a hole into its hull. The mission failed because no one took into account that the *Eagle* had a copper-plated hull, and Lee couldn't penetrate the shield with his drill bit. The *Turtle* was spotted by the British, who pursued Lee, but soon backed off when he detached his bomb and triggered the explosive charge. He managed to slip away unharmed. The *Turtle* made no encore appearance, but the sub made a leap forward in submersible design because it was among the first submersibles to use ballast to control buoyancy, though the method was definitely crude. The *Turtle* didn't have ballast tanks—it let water directly into the craft until the vessel began to sink, and the water was expelled by a hand pump when the pilot wanted to surface. This required two brass breathing tubes with float valves to keep water from entering when the *Turtle* slipped too far below the surface.

The first sub believed to carry the name *Nautilus* was designed in the early nineteenth century by the American Robert Fulton, who would six years later, in 1806, invent the steamboat. French-financed, the *Nautilus* had room for three crew members, and was powered by a hand-turned propeller located at the rear. Fulton also equipped the sub with a folding sail for propulsion on the surface. Successfully tested in France in 1800, it reached a depth of 25 feet.

War prompted the next leap in submarine technology. The CSS *H. L. Hunley*, a Confederate Civil War submarine, about half the size of the Japanese midget subs, holds the distinction of being the first sub to sink a ship in war. Horace L. Hunley, a wealthy sugar-cane baron from Mobile, Alabama, and a team of engineers cut an iron water boiler in half, lengthened it, and put it back together, adding metal fins, a rudder, and a propeller. Powered by eight men turning a hand crank, its top speed was 4 miles per hour. It was transported to Charleston, South Carolina, from Alabama by train in August 1863 and prepared for its first and last mission. It was the end product of a series of tests that cost the lives of dozens of people. Forty-one men died during the *Hunley's* many trial runs, including Horace L. Hunley himself, who drowned while serving as captain on October 15, 1863. The boat was fished out of Charleston Harbor three weeks later and refitted for service.

On the night of February 17, 1864, Lieutenant G. E. Dixon and a crew of eight men cranked their way through the harbor in the *Hunley*, their target the USS *Housatonic*. The Union warship was blockading the harbor, and the South desperately needed to break the Union stranglehold on supplies. The *Housatonic* was a 207-foot long, 1,400-ton steamer made of wood and copper. Its crew were expecting a submarine attack—reports about the *Hunley* were carried as wartime gossip in the local newspaper, the *Charleston Daily Courier*—but by the time the Union sailors spotted the *Hunley* creeping along just beneath the surface of the water, it was too late—they couldn't aim their cannons fast enough. The submarine slipped under the side of the warship and with an explosive spear extending from its nose, set off an explosion. It sank the *Housatonic* but also destroyed the *Hunley*, killing all on board.

The second *Nautilus* gained attention in 1870. Shaped like a cigar, it was 232 feet long, with a maximum width of 26 feet and a total weight of 1,500 tons. Made from 2-inch-thick steel plates, the craft was double-hulled and could dive routinely to 1,000 fathoms (6,000 feet). Its parts were fabricated all over the world: the keel in France, the screw in Glasgow, the hull in Liverpool, the engine by Krupp in Germany, the instruments in New York. The assembly took place in secret on a desert island. The launch, too, was made in secret, under the close eye of its owner and architect, Captain Nemo. The sub—fabricated in the mind of author Jules Verne in his novel *20,000 Leagues Under the Sea*—captured the imaginations of readers throughout the world. Although the a craft was almost too fantastic—even by fiction's standards—much of it would be a reality fifty years later.

The hard-luck Irishman John Holland designed the first *real* modern submarine. An immigrant to the United States, Holland found his only source of funds for sub building in the U.S. branch of the Fenian Brotherhood, an Irish revolutionary group that wanted a sub to attack British ships. Holland turned to the Fenians after sending his designs to U.S. Navy officials who told him they weren't interested but then later reproduced the plans, without permission, in a book about sub design. Holland ran through several prototypes, including the Fenian Ram, and by 1896 came up with a sub that was powered by a gasoline engine while on the surface and by battery-powered electric motors underwater, allowing it to reach speeds of 8 knots on top and 5 knots submerged. It also had a single torpedo tube that fired a self-propelled torpedo. The *Holland VI* was purchased by the U.S. Navy and put into commission in 1900, marking the birth of the United States' submarine force.

The *Holland VI* passed sea trials in time to fight in the Spanish-American war, but the U.S. government lacked confidence in the boat. It was small. At 53 feet 10 inches in length, it was similar in size to the Japanese midget submarines to be built forty years later, but the *Holland VI* was beamier at 10 feet 3 inches, and it displaced 74 tons. The United States fleet of one would soon be surpassed by another country. The Japanese bought the next five Holland-class boats, which gave them the world's largest submarine force. But the vessels didn't arrive in time for use in the Russo-Japanese war, so they remained untested in battle.

As World War I approached, subs grew bigger and faster. The German Navy was building U-boats (*Unterseeboots*) that measured more than 100 feet, twice the size of Holland's "electric boat." But in a sort of parallel, reverse evolution, the Italians began to think small. Lieutenant Commander Raffaele Rossetti, in particular, worked on the idea of strapping two men to a kind of submersible bobsled with a steering and propulsion system and torpedoes. The men would attach the torpedo to a ship, then retreat on the sled. From each branch of the Italian Navy chain of command, Rossetti's idea received a resounding *no*. Undeterred, he purloined parts from scattered divisions of the Navy and experimented with how to power the craft, settling on a gas engine and enlarged propellers. Somehow, he secretly secured two torpedoes with 375-pound warheads and constructed a working weapon. Commanders who had once scoffed now saw an opportunity.

As World War I wound down, the port of Pola was still being blocked by Austrian ships in the Aegean Sea. Rossetti chose a crewmate, a young naval surgeon named Raffaele Paolucci (whether a need for his surgery skills was anticipated is unclear); their assignment was to blow up the *Viribus Unitis*, a battleship. Time was working against the extraordinarily determined seamen—the Armistice could be signed any day.

Racing against peace, the sub, named *Mignatta*, was launched on November 1, 1918. The crew found the battleship, and at 4:30 A.M. attached a torpedo with a magnetic strap and a 2-hour timer. As they escaped, the men—whose heads poked above the water—could see they'd been spotted. Rather than have their craft captured, they armed the other explosive charge, pushed the sub away, and started swimming, wearing rudimentary camouflage—basically plant foliage. A motorboat closed in and fished out the strange-looking men, who were taken back to the *Viribus Unitis*. This wasn't exactly where Rossetti and Paolucci wanted to be as the timer clicked closer to 6:30. They concocted a story about how they had parachuted into the harbor, but knowing that the *Viribus Unitis* would be the victim of a bomb, they soon confessed. The captain ordered everyone to abandon ship (including the two saboteurs) and waited. Nothing happened. The angry crew of the ship returned, ready to string up the two Italians. At 6:20 the bomb blew and the ship listed 20 degrees; fifteen minutes later the *Viribus Unitis* turned turtle and sank. The captain went down with the ship.

The *Mignatta*, on its own now, cruised along on the harbor currents until it nestled beside the ocean liner *Wien*, which was serving as a dormitory for German submarine crews. The other 2-hour timer worked perfectly, the warhead exploded, and down went the *Wien*. The two blasts together may have taken as many as four hundred lives.

As for Rossetti and Paolucci, both men survived the blast and were held on an Austrian prison ship, but only for four days. On November 5, the Armistice was signed, the Italians occupied the port of Pola, and both men were freed. The success of the mission earned Rossetti and Paolucci medals and money—the government gave them 1.3 million lira in gold. Remarkably, the men distributed some of the money to widows of men killed on the *Viribus Unitis*.

The success, if it could be called that, gave birth to a legacy. The Italian Navy began looking for ways to improve on its basic minisub model, and soon plans emerged to upgrade the *Mignatta*. The modifications would create a "miniature submarine with entirely novel features," or so wrote the designer, who envisioned two men sitting astride the sub, which he called an "underwater aeroplane"; they'd be protected as they flew through the ocean by a curved plastic screen. Their luminescent gauges would allow them to operate at night yet still be invisible to the enemy. Wearing dive suits with air tanks, they could take the sub down to depths of more than 60 feet. As with the *Mignatta*, this new sub's crew would drop off its torpedo and scurry away. The description sounds more like an underwater motorcycle—a sort of submersible wave runner, fully armed.

A dozen vessels were built to fill the first order. The Italian's new Maiale-class sub looked like an oversized splinter. Measuring 24 feet long and only 21 inches wide, it carried a 6-foot-long warhead that weighed 660 pounds. It also acquired an unusual nickname. During a test, when one of the craft sank, an engineer exclaimed, "That swine got away." From then on, it would be known as the "pig." The strange vehicle later did a fair amount of damage in World War II, sinking four ships and damaging nine others, including the battleship *Queen Elizabeth*. The "pig" patrolled mainly in the Gibraltar area.

The Italians also led the way in the West in developing more conventional midget sub technology—as well as pursuing some crazy, "outside the box" ideas. The Italian Navy faced two situations midget subs might address: harbors to defend and harbors to penetrate. In the 1930s the Italians designed and built a 50-foot sub with both gas and electric engines that carried a crew of two and two torpedoes, and also featured a highly unusual addition. Attached to it were "caterpillar tracks," like those on a tank, so the sub could literally climb out of the water and over anti-submarine nets, which were erected to keep subs from entering a harbor. When the sub reached the top of a net, the crew would fill the ballast tanks with water, and the weight would allow the teetering craft to plunge over to the other side and not be spotted. While this vessel never entered a harbor in combat, it proved that the Italian Navy had no lack of imagination.

Other World War II–era little Italian subs included the CA class, designed specifically to infiltrate and attack targets within New York Harbor. Besides inflicting material damage, the attack was to be a psychological blow to America and would siphon off military resources from the European front to defend the harbor. Italian strategists also envisioned the use of frogmen, who would be towed behind the sub. Then, once inside the harbor, the frogmen would depart the sub with handheld explosives and seek out their own targets. The Italian navy built the prototype, conducted trials, and devised a way to piggyback the sub to America on a larger sub, the *Leonardo da Vinci*. The mission was a go, but the *Leonardo* sank after being depth-charged by the British. Germany declined to lend a U-boat for this mission and the war was over before efforts to equip other subs were completed. The prototype would never be put to use.

The early successes of Italy's fleet of small underwater craft prompted Winston Churchill to pursue the same course. "Please report what is being done to emulate the exploits of the Italians in Alexandria harbour and similar methods of this kind . . . . Is there any reason why we should be incapable of the same kind of scientific aggressive actions the Italians have shown? One would have thought that we would have been in the lead." The memo came in one of his famous "Action This Day" missives.

The British Navy hopped to it, and soon, using photographs of a Maiale ("pig"), fashioned a vessel called the *Chariot*. The prototype, built of wood, measured 25 feet in length and could carry a 600-pound warhead. As in the Italian model, the warhead was attached to the front of the sled and two riders sat astride the submersible toward the back. It used batteries to power a 2-hp motor at speeds of 3 to 4 knots. Able to travel about 18 miles over 6 hours, the sub could enter harbors and return to its mother craft.

Outfitting the pilots came through trial and error. They ended up wearing thick rubberized suits and scuba tanks from which they breathed pure oxygen. The engineers didn't realize that there was such a thing as oxygen poisoning. In early trials the vessels worked well, but a pilot was lost when he passed out while putting his charge in place. Oxygen poisoning was the most likely cause. The Chariots did finally fulfill their mission of blowing up a ship in the Mediterranean, but the British also lost a T-class sub in the process. One commander complained: "If [the operation] only resulted in the sinking of a light cruiser . . . then the prolonged use of T-class submarines for Chariot work and the loss of one of them, seems a disproportionate price to have paid."

Another British effort, the Welman subs, came about the same time. They were a product of the British Special Operations Executive, set up in an old hotel and filled with some of Britain's most inventive minds and a least a few eccentrics. The group came up with the useful (a portable telephone) and the useless (an exploding turd). The Welman would come closer to turd than telephone.

Colonel John Dolphin can take credit for this class of one-man subs. They were designed to attack ships in harbors, drop off agents in enemy territory, and scout out hostile locations. The project came together like an amateur musical. The prototype sub employed an electric motor straight from a London bus and ran on a 40-volt battery. The pilot sat in a seat taken from an Austin automobile; the steering stick came from a Spitfire airplane, and the bilge was vented by foot pump. Two ballast tanks were cleared with compressed air and filled via a lever operated by hand. The craft stayed underwater with the aid of a 300-pound weight, which had to be shifted to keep the craft level. Early estimates were that the Welman could drop to 300 feet below the surface, but that figure was revised when an unmanned test craft imploded at 100 feet. There was no periscope, but instead four windows. Underwater, the pilot—who wore a face mask hooked to an oxygen tank— steered blindly, relying on a gyro compass (also from a Spitfire), a depth gauge, and a prayer.

Strapped to the vessel was a 1,200-pound warhead. The plan was for the Welman to approach a ship, attach the bomb by magnet, and, using a long screwing mechanism, arm the bomb by screwing the rod in and then release the Welman from the explosive by detaching the rod. To offset the weight loss, the pilot would have to shift the big weight forward. A 5-hour fuse would give the Welman time to head home at its designed pace of 3 knots.

Testing included a trial run by an upper-crust admirer of the Welman, Admiral Louis Mountbatten, who was almost drowned when a window blew out. Sturdy or not, the craft received the go-ahead for production, and 150 were ordered. Work began at a Morris car plant; the final number manufactured came to 100. By then, some sanity seemed to have filtered up the chain of command when Mountbatten was sent to India and was no longer able to champion the craft. The Welman-class subs figured in only one operation. Four of them were towed to Norwegian waters and set loose on a German repair dock used for U-boats. One vessel was captured without doing any damage, and the other three were ditched by the crews, who went ashore and hid until the Norwegian underground came to the rescue. The Welman's service officially ended on February 15, 1944.

The Germans too were inspired by what seemed liked the latest trend in sub warfare, specifically the efforts made by the Italians and the British. They had in fact captured a Welman in Norway, and though late to the game, brought on line three vessels that would impact the Allies, though not in quite the way anyone anticipated.

The initial craft was named *Neger*, a play on *Mohr* (German for "Moor")—the last name of the man who developed the vessel. It was a straight over-and-under design. On top was a vessel 22 feet in length, shaped like a torpedo; underneath it was a German G7e torpedo, which was about the same length. The initial Neger-class subs couldn't really dive, but later models could stay submerged for brief periods. The pilot sat in a cockpit in the bow with a shield in front. His equipment consisted of a steering mechanism, a waterproof wrist compass, and a rod on the front—similar to the front sight on a rifle—that was used for aiming the torpedo. A handle released the torpedo underneath, though occasionally the torpedo didn't drop and delivered both the payload and the operator to oblivion. Also, the cockpit design made it hard to see, especially if oil was smudging the front screen, which was often the case; if the pilot were to crack the hatch to take a peek, the vessel would flood. The casualty rate for the Neger and its sister model (Moloch) was 60 to 80 percent.

Another German model that saw action was the Biber. Launched near Normandy in August 1944—two months after the D-Day invasion—it was intended to seek out British ships and wreak havoc. Historian Paul Kemp, truly the world's midget sub expert, described the "debut" as being carried out in "a singularly unsuccessful fashion," a dubious honor in light of all the previous catastrophic small-sub failures.

Powered by a gasoline motor, the 18-foot-long sub carried two G7e torpedoes on either side; they fit into indentations on the sub's port and starboard sides. This sub had a conning tower with windows and a nonretractable periscope that only faced forward. To disguise the periscope, a bird's nest of sticks was put on top so that if the periscope came near the surface, it would look like a little raft of debris. This sub's chief operational defect came from the lack of adequate exhaust for the gas engine, which produced carbon monoxide and caused the deaths of at least a dozen pilots.

In late August off the coast of France, the Biber fleet set out, all 18 of them, on their way to make their assault on British shipping. Remarkably, all 18 returned to base, but there was a good reason for this unprecedented success: apparently none of them ever fired a torpedo or did anything else but make a round trip. There's zero mention made in British records of any action involving these little subs during that period.

Assignment 2 was supposed to be an attack at the British Channel Islands, but the idea was dropped when the task of transporting so many subs was fully weighed. Also, the tides and currents there would have tested the pilots' navigation skills in such shaky craft.

The subs finally were stationed near Antwerp in December 1944. They had to make a 40-mile voyage to arrive at their targets: British ships. Of 18 subs sent out in late December 1944, four were caught as they were being towed, one hit a mine, and one returned damaged. The other 12 simply disappeared. It's suspected that the carbon monoxide did in the pilots.

At a base in Holland, about a dozen of the fleet were destroyed when a G7e accidentally exploded and blew up the surrounding Bibers at the dock. Another accident followed in March, with 14 sunk and nine put out of action. By late 1945, the number of Bibers destroyed through accidents was at least 40. Further plans for the subs included an assault on the Suez Canal. The idea was to airlift a Biber to the Great Bitter Lake, from where it would enter the canal. The Biber would sink a ship and block the canal, delivering a crucial blow to the Allies' oil supplies. The plan never came together.

The big mission for the Bibers came in early 1945. U-boats were fitted with the little subs on the outside. The initial plan was to sneak within 40 miles of the target of Kola Inlet, an Allied stronghold in the Barents Sea. The little subs were to attack Allied ships, then retreat and lie still underwater until the parent sub reappeared. But trouble started even while the subs were being transported when the vibration rattled them so much that pipes started to spring leaks. Efforts to fix the problem failed, and the final major Biber assault came to an end. It didn't matter. The night they were scheduled to enter the harbor, the main targets had left.

Near the start of the Germans' small-sub assault, the British found Bibers abandoned here and there, and it worried them. They could envision a fleet of these attackers sneaking in and doing real harm. They allocated resources, including special RAF units and Navy ships, specifically to seek out midget subs in the summer of 1944. As a distraction, the German subs proved successful, but only with the aid of an overactive British imagination.

The development of the Japanese midget submarine goes back to some innovative thinking among military planners in the early 1930s. Japanese strategists recognized a primary weakness of torpedoes, especially those fired at long range: they often missed. To address the problem, engineers designed a small submarine that could sneak close to a target and fire at close range.

Bristling from the limitations imposed by naval treaties, the Japanese started building their midget subs in secret in 1932. They first saw the subs as a part of a defensive plan that would thwart the American invasion of their home islands, an assault they viewed as an inevitability because of what they perceived as the West's imperialist character. The subs could not only defend harbors but also sneak out to sink American battleships as they drew close enough to fire their big guns and fulfill what the Japanese believed was America's plan—to force Japan into war and annihilate the Japanese people.

The prototype had several flaws. The sub's batteries used hydrochloric acid and expelled a gas that could be deadly. The prototype was hard to steer, and the periscope wasn't long enough—the sub showed on the surface when the pilot wanted to take a look around. Japanese engineering addressed the issues: a conning tower was added with an extendable periscope housed in it, and the ventilation was improved. By December 1934, the sub was not only operational but reached a surface speed of 24.85 knots, probably the standing record for a battery-powered midget sub. The sub could dive safely down to more than 300 feet and wouldn't be in real trouble unless it fell below 600 feet. These were amazing depths for such a small craft.

Ballast malfunctions, however, plagued the little sub. When the main ballast tank was blown and the sub surfaced, the bow floated while the stern lay underwater. It looked like a whale that couldn't quite breach. An emergency ballast tank was added under the control room to level off the sub. The other ballast issue came when the sub fired its torpedoes. A water intake valve was designed to open when the torpedoes shot out of their tubes; it theoretically would let water in to offset the weight loss when the torpedo fired. But the valve wasn't wide enough, and when a torpedo was fired, the sub tended to bob to the surface. This would become a signature flaw of the Japanese midget subs—an uncontrollable hiccup.

Various torpedoes were tried, with the oxygen-powered weapon (called Type 97) winning out because it was lighter. The torpedoes were loaded in an unusual way: there were no bow caps on the torpedo tubes, so the torpedoes were shoved into the tubes tail first from the outside. The torpedoes were fired by air pressure, which caused concern among sub pilots because the air sent up a stream of bubbles, giving away the location of the supposedly stealth weapon.

Of all Japan's military secrets, the midget sub was probably the best kept. The subs were specifically fabricated in three parts so they could be assembled in a closely guarded plant on an island that was even more closely guarded. No workers, military or otherwise, were allowed to have a camera. Trains passing by had their window curtains pulled as they approached the naval base. Tests of the subs were conducted in areas cleared of local fishing traffic.

What came off the production line looked impressive. The initial batch of 20 Type HAs were made from ultra-hard, cold-rolled steel and reinforced with welded angle-iron frames. The hull was coated with red zinc-chromate primer and liquid tar to prevent corrosion, then painted with black enamel. The key payload: two 18-foot-long torpedoes, stacked one above the other in the torpedo room, which made up the bow section of the sub and which could be unbolted. The subs ran on 192 two-cell batteries wired in series to generate enough power for the 600-hp electric motor in the sub's stern section. With no generator, the sub had to recharge its batteries either when it docked or by connecting to the "mother" ship carrying it, a process that took nine hours. The center section of the sub contained a control room, with the conning tower and periscope directly overhead. From there—in what was destined to become the death seat—the pilot guided the sub. Other features included a 32-inch radio antenna, wire cutters fore and aft for anti-submarine nets, and a telephone plug-in connection between the little sub and the mother ship, so a last word could be exchanged.

The midget subs secretly waited for war long after Japan had notified the world that it was withdrawing from the League of Nations and abandoning all naval treaties. Over time, the strategy for employing the little subs would transform from mainly defensive (protecting the homeland) to both defensive and offensive. After all, the sub's chief strength was surprise: the enemy would not be prepared to defend against a small craft sneaking into harbors. Also, these subs definitely would try to make round trips—initial training exercises included retrieval maneuvers. The Japanese outfitted a seaplane tender, the *Chiyoda*, that actually carried the midgets in its hold, packing in twelve subs and successfully delivering and recovering them. The ship dropped them off, then scooped them up, like a retriever. The problem with the tender, however, was that it was easy to spot, and the subs would have to be released hundreds of miles from their targets to maintain the element of surprise. The midget subs, powered by batteries, could only go so far.

As the plans for a sneak attack on Pearl Harbor progressed, strategists toyed with different roles the midget subs might play. Nothing definite had been decided even as late as August and early September. The final "go" came about October 12 after overcoming Yamamoto's objections. Officials settled on the idea of putting a cradle on *I*-class submarines, a solution that would allow the midget subs to be transported from Japan to Hawaii undercover, then delivered undetected just a few miles from the channel leading to Pearl Harbor. The extra weight concerned some officers, but the addition wasn't that much of a stretch. Some large subs already were capable of carrying hangars on their decks for collapsible seaplanes.

In their final training for midget submarine duty, the two-man Japanese crews were told their mission would involve three specific roles: if encountered, the little subs could attack an enemy ship immediately; they could sneak up on a ship in Pearl Harbor and attack; or they could stand ready to be a "trump card" if circumstances dictated.

Secretly deploying the midget subs several hours before the sneak attack was a big risk—if spotted, the subs could alert the enemy. The Japanese commanders took the gamble because they couldn't foresee how successful their air strategy would be. They brimmed with confidence in front of their troops, but worried behind closed doors. "We thought the chance of the air assault being successful was only about 50-50," said Vice Admiral Shigeru Fukudome.

As the war continued, other small subs were developed by the Japanese, but they would improve very little from the pilots' perspective. Each one would be a death trap. Among the most famous was the Kaiten or "heaven shaker." After considering different ways to transport the weapon, the Imperial Navy again chose a big sub to carry the smaller craft. At 48 feet in length and 8 tons in weight, the Kaiten was basically all torpedo with an enclosed cockpit. Designed after the "Long Lance" (Type 93) torpedo, the Kaiten could be steered by the pilot, but the gyro course was preset by the mother sub; the pilot's job was to control the depth (18 feet was standard) and keep it pointed in the right direction. The "heaven shaker" was extremely fast—it could hit 40 knots—and a devil to steer. In a test, one craft headed straight to the bottom at 30 knots, killing the pilot and destroying the craft. In theory the pilot was supposed to escape from a hatch at the top as he approached the target, but this was a ruse. Even if an operator was certain the torpedo was on target and if he could slip out of the sub at 50 yards, it wouldn't have mattered much. The weapon had a 3,400-pound warhead. If the torpedo hit, the shock wave would have killed the pilot anyway.

This weapon, part of the kamikaze tradition, actually worked and sank Allied ships. It might have been invaluable in some rearguard action later in the war, but by then the Japanese military had started to crumble, and women and children were being trained to use pointed sticks to kill Americans.

In the end, midget subs generally turned out to be more lethal to their operators than they ever were to the enemy, a fact proved on December 7, 1941.

The First Shot

A ROUTINE MISSION to deliver lumber, cigarettes, guns, basket-balls, footballs, fishing rods, and cigars to naval personnel would—in a sense—unwittingly lead America straight into World War II. The voyage of the 21-year-old supply ship USS *Antares* from Pearl Harbor, Hawaii, to Canton Island—a distant and virtually forgotten outpost 1,900 miles from Hawaii—began about midday on November 3, 1941. The mission called for the *Antares* to pick up a *lighter* (an open barge used for loading and unloading supplies) at Palmyra Island during its return trip, and tow the barge back to Pearl Harbor. Its arrival date would be the morning of December 7.

After Navy maneuvers around Hawaii in 1940, President Franklin D. Roosevelt ordered the U.S. Navy's Pacific Fleet not to return to San Diego but to stay at Pearl Harbor, massing in a single harbor the best-armed flotilla the world had ever seen. It was an undisguised warning shot across Japan's bow.

The Navy also started digging in on islands like Palmyra (annexed as a U.S. territory in 1898) and Canton, where the United States, Great Britain, and Pan American Airways—which built an airstrip and hotel there—all laid some claim to ownership. The military idea back then was to keep the fleet at Pearl Harbor and the surrounding islands ready for . . . something.

If war broke out in the Pacific, the U.S. lineup looked strong, at least in terms of its big ships. The Navy had eight aircraft carriers in 1941, with five assigned to the Pacific; it also had 16 battleships, eight of them anchored at Pearl Harbor. Most of the American carriers were built after 1934, and even though some of the battleships were ancient, they were built to last.

While the Navy's first string was packed with power, many of its second- and third-tier ships were well worn. The *Antares* was typical among the older service vessels (called M16s). It was built in 1920 by a private contractor (part of the U.S. Shipping Board program). Shipbuilding in the United States had declined in the 1920s under post–World War I treaties to limit naval power; construction fell off even further in the 1930s, when the nation was ravaged by the Depression. During that time, the Navy began shopping the private sector for ships and tried to convert them for military use rather than contract out the work of building them. It was cheaper. Initially christened the *Nedmac*, the Navy acquired the vessel in 1921 and rechristened it the *Antares*—named after a star in the Scorpion constellation that the ancient Greeks dubbed "brighter than Mars." The *Antares* didn't exactly bring bright stars to mind, however. It was battleship gray, 401 feet long, reached a top speed of only 11.5 knots, and groaned in rough seas. It was especially adept at pulling heavy loads like barges weighing many tons—essentially a draft horse of a ship, slow but powerful.

The *Antares* reached Canton Island on November 17, just in time to witness the Pan Am hotel burning up, triggering a series of explosions as cases of booze caught fire. On the *Antares*, Attilio Edward Chiappari, a signalman second class whom everyone called "Til," saw the fire break out and then spread. "I could see they weren't putting out the fire," he said. To help, some crew members took a boat in—Canton had no docks. "We carried what we called a hurdy-gurdy and strung a hose to it," Chiappari said. The hurdy-gurdy was a generator that operated a water pump. They also scooped up some of the undamaged bottles of booze. It was the most excitement the sailors had seen in months. The alert eyes of "Til" Chiappari, a five-foot-seven sailor of Italian descent with brown eyes and dark brown hair, would later prove extremely valuable to his ship—and offer him a brief chance to change history.

Heavy squalls set in and delayed unloading. The *Antares* steamed around at a half speed of about 6 knots and waited for the seas to calm. During that time, dozens of passengers boarded and left the ship, some of them civilian construction workers leaving one ship to wait to be assigned to another. The USS *Selfridge*, a destroyer, delivered one D. L. Whitson, mess attendant second class, to the *Antares*, where he was put in solitary confinement for five days and fed only "bread and water" for a disciplinary violation.

The *Selfridge* and *Antares* would soon meet again. It was on the way back to Pearl Harbor that the *Antares* attracted a stalker—a submarine of "unknown origin." The *Antares* attempted radio contact, but received no response. The sub was in fact Japanese and on a definite mission. As part of its planned attack on Pearl Harbor, the Japanese had sent out submarines (all *I*-class) to reconnoiter the Pacific and specifically to sink ships fleeing Pearl Harbor after the attack on December 7. No shots were to be fired beforehand. The subs had left Japan in early November, with nine of them rendezvousing and refueling in the Marshall Islands. Most of the subs were so technologically advanced they could travel 10,000 miles before they'd need to refuel again. The big I-subs carrying midget subs didn't need to refuel on their course, which took them between Wake Island and Midway. The Japanese submarine fleet surrounded Oahu. Twelve approached the island from the north, and fourteen closed in from the south; one sub, *I-10*, made a loop even farther south than the rest of the fleet and ended up east of the island. Altogether, there were twenty-seven *I*-class subs in and around Hawaii by early December, waiting like wolves for their prey to run.

The *Antares* notified command at Pearl Harbor about the unidentified sub. More and more sub sightings had been recorded around Hawaii that fall, but no one in charge interpreted the increase as a serious threat. Many seemed to be false alarms. Soon the *Selfridge* rejoined the *Antares* and ran an anti-submarine screen—meaning it accompanied the supply ship and watched out for potential trouble. The *Selfridge* was a more modern ship—a Porter-class destroyer built in 1933 and equipped with a new technology—sonar. The destroyer previously had done duty tagging along with President Roosevelt on his yachting trips off the East Coast before it journeyed west in 1937 to join the Pacific Fleet.

The Japanese sub tracked the *Antares* to Hawaii. Fireman Third Class William Ellis could see it from the deck. Enlisting in the Navy in February 1941 when he was almost 18, he'd crewed on the *Antares* since the summer. "We were in rough seas all the way back, but the submarine stayed with us," said Ellis, a stocky Missouri boy with sandy hair. "It appeared every night. The destroyer also stayed and screened for us, because that darn sub tailed us all the way."

On December 5 the *Selfridge*, a much faster ship than the *Antares*, was released from its anti-sub screening mission, and pulled ahead toward Pearl Harbor. At this point, the safety of the *Antares* fell to two minesweepers on patrol: the USS *Crossbill* and USS *Condor*. They formed as unlikely a pair of protectors as could be imagined.

Built in 1937, with a double-decker cabin far forward and a bow-to-stern swoop, the *Condor* looked more like a trawler. In fact, that was exactly what it was before the Navy acquired it in 1940 and armed it with one .30 caliber machine gun. Its sister, the *Crossbill*, was no better. It too had been a commercial fishing boat (christened the *North Star*) hauling purse seines off America's northwest coast, mainly fishing for tuna. The converted fishing boats had taken up weekend watch as the *Antares* chugged back toward its Pearl Harbor destination at about 9.8 knots, pulling a 500-ton steel barge.

William Ellis came up from his berth at about 3:45 A.M. on the morning of the 7th. He was looking forward to weekend liberty, even if it was already Sunday. He and his friends would hit the bars, maybe a cathouse, or maybe get another tattoo. "I was just eighteen years old, and my shipmates, every one of my friends, was tattooed. So I was as stupid as those guys."

He could see the lights of Honolulu and Pearl Harbor. At some time between 6:00 and 6:30, the *Antares* approached the entrance of the channel. Ellis had come up from the boiler room to trim the vents; these controlled the flow of air down into the compartments below. Usually they could be adjusted with "reach rods" from below, but on this morning, one was broken. Ellis was on top to adjust the vents by hand.

"Til" Chiappari was on the 4 to 8 watch, too, looking over the starboard side just as dawn broke. "I saw something like a buoy," he said. "It was narrow at the top. And I thought, 'What the hell is that?' " He went to the flying bridge to take a better look through the telescope. The captain, Commander L. C. Grannis, was on a wing of the bridge. Even at 1,500 yards away, the object was easy to identify with the telescope because it had guide wires running fore and aft from the conning tower and a periscope shooting at least 5 feet above the tower.

"That's a sub," Chiappari told the captain at 6:30. "That's not one of ours."

"How do you know?" Grannis asked.

"Til" Chiappari had joined the Navy in 1934. He had served in the seas around China and was aware of the carnage that was already taking place in Asia. He'd even visited Japan. He felt in his gut one thing was certain: "I knew we were going to war." Chiappari of course wasn't aware that the Japanese had built a secret weapon midget submarine, but no friendly subs should have been submerged in that area, and he had never seen one like this. His gut feeling about the war told him all he needed to know. He explained his reasoning to Grannis and repeated, "That's not ours."

Ellis looked up from his job on the vents and saw the captain, signalman, and radioman in a mad scramble. "The bridge just went goofy," he said. At 6:37 Grannis told Chiappari to signal a destroyer in the area, the USS *Ward*, for help. The *Antares* itself was utterly defenseless. Though it had plied the Pacific for months, it had never been outfitted with a gun.

The first day of command on the USS *Ward* for Lieutenant William Outerbridge began on December 5, 1941, when he replaced Lieutenant Commander Hunter Wood Jr. and headed out for the *Ward's* weekend patrol to guard the entrance to Pearl Harbor. On his second full day in command, Outerbridge would enter World War II wearing a life jacket over his pajamas and ordering the first American shot fired at what, he hoped and prayed, was the enemy.

Through the early morning of the 7th, the *Ward*, a Wickes-class destroyer, was running lazy "figure eight" patterns at the mouth of the harbor. The *Ward* had picked up ping contacts on its sonar, and also hours earlier had received signals from the *Condor* that something suspicious was moving around in a defensive area as early as 0342. The *Condor* contacted the *Ward* at 0359:

"Sighted submerged submarine on westerly course, speed 9 knots . . . . Approximately 0350 it appeared to be heading for the entrance."

"Roger that *Condor*. We will investigate."

At 0435, the *Ward* signaled back. "No contact on unidentified sub."

Built in 1918, the *Ward* should have been in a scrap pile. In *Battle Report*, a book commissioned by the Navy, the *Ward* had been classified as "over age" since July 24, 1934, and described as ". . . on the decrepit side." Recommissioned in 1941 because of the shortage of naval vessels, the *Ward* had more in common with sailing ships than modern-day warships. The berths and mess areas were crammed into one space. The head was a "sluice" with seawater constantly running through it and wooden seats hinged over the top.

Besides being old, the *Ward* had another handicap. Most of the crew manning the ship were raw recruits with no experience at sea; most had not even attended Navy boot camp. About 70 percent of the men were Naval Reservists from Minnesota whose training had been at the Minnesota Boat Club on the banks of the Mississippi, plus cruising during the summer on the Great Lakes and leading ship parades on holidays. These men left Minnesota for San Diego, transferred straight to the *Ward*, and headed to Hawaii. Among them was Fireman First Class Ken Swedberg, a five-foot-ten, 19-year-old with wavy brown hair and blue eyes. Warm weather duty sounded great to him. He remembered the day (January 23, 1941) he left St. Paul by train: "It was 20 below zero," he said.

After the *Antares*'s signal was received by the *Ward*, the destroyer crew soon spotted a midget sub, most likely *I-20-A*. The little sub had been launched from its mother sub at 2:57 A.M., with Ensign Akira Hiroo and Petty Officer Second Class Yoshio Katayama aboard. With a 600-horsepower electric motor, the little sub could reach speeds of 19 knots submerged and hit a nifty 24 knots on the surface, making it among the fastest warships around. At those speeds, however, it would run out of power in an hour or so. But if it stayed at 2 to 4 knots, it had a 100-mile range. The *I-20-A* patrolled the outer edge of the harbor channel, apparently looking for just the right opportunity, which it found when the *Antares* appeared. The anti-torpedo nets blocking the harbor would be opened for the slow-moving ship. It would be like falling in behind some tired plow mule heading toward the barn.

The "decrepit" *Ward*, and a largely teenage crew would seem unlikely heroes to come to the rescue, but as it turned out, the ship and men stood tall. That's in large part because the ship had a captain whose nickname was "Wild Willie." Lieutenant William W. Outerbridge, a slightly built man with haunting dark eyes, the son of a British sea captain and an American nurse, had graduated from the U.S. Naval Academy in 1927. Unlike his green crew, W. W. Outerbridge was a fourteen-year Navy veteran. Said an admiring Russell Knapp, then a 22-year-old boatswain's mate on the *Ward*, "Wild Willie was something else. He was gung ho."

There was some chance that the *I-20-A* could have been a friendly sub—it might have been a secret American prototype unknown to these patrol ships and young crews. Outerbridge never hesitated in his attack, however: from the time the *Ward* spotted the midget until it fired the first shot was at most five minutes. He didn't check with command at Bishop Point on Oahu. He called for general quarters. The order rang out: "All hands man your battle stations. Man all guns. Prepare depth charges. Prepare to ram." His plan—in no particular order—was to shoot it, ram it, and blow it up. As Knapp would say later of Outerbridge with a smile, "Shoot first and ask questions later. That's what the old man did."

At this point, there entered a new player, this time from the air. Ensign William Tanner and his crew of two manned a Catalina No. 14-P-1, a PBY seaplane. Part of Patrol Squadron 14, they were on routine anti-submarine duty, leaving from Kaneohe Naval Air Station at 0600. They had dawn patrol on December 7. The plane was cruising at about 1,000 feet and surveying south of Pearl Harbor when it spotted the *Antares* with something following the ship. Tanner turned his plane to investigate, thinking it probably was just a buoy. But as he swept in from another angle, he could see the conning tower of what seemed to Tanner a very small submarine.

On board the *Ward*, the ship was a madhouse. Lieutenant Outerbridge had been asleep on a makeshift bunk in the chart room. He rushed to the bridge in his pj's and also threw on a blue-and-white kimono, along with his life jacket and a tin helmet. Boatswain's Mate Knapp, among the first to spot the sub, headed to his gun on the galley deck even before general quarters was sounded. All four of the *Ward*'s main guns were manned. The *Ward* charged hard, at a speed of more than 15 knots, and as it closed in to 100 yards, it made a fast turn to port. As it did, the bow gun fired but the shell flew over the conning tower. The quick turn, said Swedberg, "raised the starboard side of the ship and these 4-inch guns were not made to fire at close range." Essentially, the gun couldn't aim any lower. That left the second shot to the gun on the galley deck, where Knapp stood. He actually had to rouse the aimer, who somehow managed to stay curled up and asleep right under the gun. The sub was now less than 75 yards away. The gun fired its 4-inch shell, and it looked like a direct hit just below the conning tower.

At about the same time the *Ward* was firing, Tanner in his PBY found he was too close to arm and drop its depth charges, so he dropped smoke pots to mark the little sub's position. (Because of his perspective from the plane, Tanner was among the few to notice the unusual size of the midget sub. Ellis aboard the *Antares* said, "I believed this was a big submarine, not a small one.")

The shots from the *Ward* unleashed a full-scale attack on the little sub. The *Ward* spun around and in a nifty maneuver came across the top of the sub and started dumping depth charges—four of them in a diamond pattern— as the sub was disappearing. They were rigged to explode at 100 feet. The water heaved from the explosions. The PBY added two more depth charges from the air for good measure. With one direct shell hit and the multitude of explosions, the little sub sank to the bottom.

Conflicting accounts emerged about what surfaced after the *Ward* had opened fire. Tanner from above could see the water had been churned up and that it looked discolored, but there was no flotsam or debris that he noticed. Nearer to the scene, Ellis said, "You could see the debris and bodies. The ocean was full of stuff from the sub." That statement never appeared in an official report. Outerbridge reported an oil slick.

As the water calmed, a thought nagged at Outerbridge: was that really an enemy sub? Tanner said he too worried about the same thing: "Had we killed our own people?" Outerbridge threw off his doubts and immediately sent a message to the radio station at Bishop Point. The first report, sent at 0650, said, "We have dropped depth charges upon sub operating in defensive sea area." Then Outerbridge thought he should be more specific. The message at 0653 said, "We have attacked[,] fired upon and dropped depth charges upon submarine operating in defensive sea area." Tanner sent a message at the same time to his command, Fleet Air Wing One: "Sank enemy sub one mile south of Pearl Harbor." He was ordered to stay in the area until further instructions. The *Ward* headed out to stop a motorized sampan crossing a restricted zone.

With three messages sent to headquarters alerting the men in charge that the enemy was literally at the gate, the command response proved amazingly lackadaisical—a yawn on a lazy Sunday morning. Why no one acted on the news of a Japanese sub trying to sneak into Pearl Harbor, or anticipated that more hostile action might follow, has been the subject of study and debate for decades.

Admiral Husband E. Kimmel, commander-in-chief of the Pacific Fleet, knew a surprise attack was a possibility. The sneak attack scenario was spelled out in the Martin-Bellinger report distributed in March 1941 to top government officials. According to the report, the priorities of a Japanese assault would be: (1) A surprise submarine attack on ships in the operating area. (2) A surprise air attack on Oahu, including ships and installations in Pearl Harbor. (3) A combination of these two.

Further, a "heightened state of alert" (now a familiar phrase to twenty-first-century Americans) had gone into effect on November 27, prompted by the impasse in negotiations between the governments of the United States and Japan. The message sent to Kimmel from the Naval Chief of Operations, Admiral Harold Stark, seemed clear: "This dispatch is to be considered a war warning."

A detail-oriented Navy veteran, Kimmel for months had evaluated Pearl Harbor's vulnerability. His conclusion: the Navy was as ready as it could be, based on the intelligence he and his staff received. The consensus among U.S. officials was that the Japanese would strike at the Philippines; or, then again, they might strike north at the Russian port of Vladivostok or at the Aleutians, as Franklin Roosevelt wrote in 1941 to Winston Churchill. In truth, everyone but the Japanese was guessing.

Kimmel ordered that at least 25 percent of all officers and 50 percent of the enlisted men stay aboard their docked or anchored ships at all times. He thought, and so did most of the traditional military, that a submarine attack indeed seemed the most likely, meaning ships in the harbor were safe behind the anti-submarine nets across its entrance. Air strikes might occur as a distraction or as part of an amphibious assault on Hawaii, or as part of a sabotage campaign. The Navy also considered its ships secure from one other threat: torpedoes dropped from aircraft. The water at Pearl Harbor in most places was just 30–40 feet deep. It was believed that torpedoes carrying 450-pound warheads could not be dropped from aircraft in such shallow water and hit their targets—they'd stick in the mud or veer off course. What the intelligence experts did not know was that the Japanese had rigged their Thunderfish torpedoes so they wouldn't dip very far below the surface (about 10 to 20 feet). Japanese engineers put wooden fins on the torpedoes to break the fall; the fins fell off after splashdown. It turned out that the wave-skimming Japanese torpedo planes had little problem with the shallow depths of Pearl Harbor: of the thirty-six torpedoes dropped, twenty-five scored hits.

Intelligence failed on numerous other fronts. While rumors and theories still abound about what the government knew before December 7, apparently no spy for the United States ever uncovered the specific plan for the Pearl Harbor attack. Cryptographers had cracked the Japanese diplomatic code, but in December 1941 the Japanese Navy's military code remained largely unbroken (though to what extent has never been resolved). U.S. officials regularly read the messages Tokyo sent to the Japanese diplomats in Washington and around the world, but it ultimately did them little good. The Japanese military did not tell embassy officials in Washington about the planned attack on Pearl Harbor. On the night of December 6, when President Franklin Roosevelt broke away from a White House dinner party and violin concert and reviewed the decoded orders from Tokyo that told Japanese embassy personnel in Washington to destroy documents, he drew the right conclusion. "This means war," he exclaimed, according to a lieutenant in the room. But there were two key words Roosevelt did not find in the dispatches: Pearl Harbor.

Another lapse concerned the Japanese fleet that went "missing" before the attack. In this case, the Navy analysts had just enough intelligence information to come to the wrong conclusion. In prior Japanese military movements into French Indochina and other strategic areas, Japanese aircraft carriers stayed close to the main home islands; the Japanese government would not leave the heart of the nation exposed to retaliation. In late November 1941, there was again a military buildup to the south in Indochina. Navy intelligence assumed the carriers were staying home, as they had done twice before that year, in February and July. Of course, six carriers and a fleet of more than twenty ships were actually steaming toward Oahu, and even when just 230 miles north of the island, the fleet was never spotted by reconnaissance flights or even a passing ship at sea. About half of the military's PBYs had been shipped to Guam and Midway, where the military anticipated enemy action. As one observer aptly put it, "Too much geography, too few planes."

Add to the intelligence gaps these other components:

Kimmel ordered that the military's radar be on alert from before dawn to 7:00 A.M. each day, correctly anticipating an early-morning raid of some sort. Unfortunately, the radar didn't work well. Continual problems positioning the radar and training personnel plagued the Pearl Harbor defensive effort from the start. The motorized units that turned the dishes broke down frequently. There were so many bogus readings that on December 7, a radar operator who saw a large number of planes approaching Oahu at 7:02 more or less shook his head. He later testified that the blips certainly had seemed "out of the ordinary," and in fact he did call the information command center, but no one was available. An inexperienced lieutenant still in training called back at 7:20 and said the planes were probably U.S. aircraft returning from a mission. "Don't worry about it," was his order.

The internal communications system at Pearl Harbor, which depended almost completely on the local telephone system, was laughable. Here is a verbatim description from an officer in charge of how the various units funneled their information into central command "For Army bombardment information . . . we had no means of direct communication, except through the Pearl Harbor,

Ford Island, [and] Hickam Field telephone exchanges . . . . It was very difficult to communicate with General Division, who had command of all fighter aircraft . . . . Our only direct means was the telephone through Pearl Harbor Exchange. In addition to that we had two or three . . . teletype page printer circuits . . . but . . . not all outlying stations were continuously manned." Overall, the response teams operated, as one officer phrased it, "like a volunteer fire department."

Then there is the almost inexplicable fumbling after the midget sub incident. The message was encoded as a by-the-book precaution, then had to be decoded before it reached Kimmel's staff just a few miles away. Kimmel didn't see anything until 7:40. In later testimony he said he was waiting for further verification of the *Ward*'s report. He noted that before he would take drastic action, he wanted more proof, adding that there had been a "number of such [submarine] contacts." He didn't want to act too hastily. More to the point, Boatswain's Mate Knapp of the *Ward* said, "The brass didn't believe (us)."

While there were in fact numerous false submarine contacts (usually whales) before December 7th, the *Ward*'s message was not just about a possible sighting of Moby Dick—it reported an all-out attack directed at the enemy. When a request for reconfirmation was sent to the *Ward*, the ship radioed what it was doing at the moment—pursuing the suspicious sampan. It did not repeat (for a third time) the midget sub attack message.

Lieutenant General Walter C. Short, the top Army man in Hawaii, was not told of the midget sub sinking until after the air attack on Pearl Harbor. He said in later testimony if he had known he would have ordered a full alert. Perhaps he would have. But in retrospect, most of the preparations by the Army and Navy were half measures, based in large part on the belief that the simple presence of the massive U.S. fleet of more than ninety ships in one place would be a deterrent in itself. The Japanese saw it quite differently—for them, it was an opportunity. Both Kimmel and Short were relieved of command in December 1941. Short retired that month. Kimmel was demoted, but he unofficially started that process himself a little early—he tore the stripes from his uniform as the ships at Pearl Harbor smoldered.

The first bullets that hit the *Antares* came from a low-flying Japanese fighter at about 8:00 A.M. The old ship had wooden hatches that were taken apart piece by piece when it was loaded and unloaded. The bullets came zipping through the wood and rattling below deck, where William Ellis was about to take a shower. "The guys started running topside to find out what's going on. As soon as the last guy got up the ladder, about ten of them came flying back down because, boy, the planes were hot and heavy coming in. They were going right over us." Also below deck was "Til" Chiappari, who was brushing his teeth when he heard a "thump, thump, thump." He thought it was the ship's old engine firing up. He calmly finished brushing his teeth, "then I hung up my towel. By then I knew it was machine gun fire, and I ran like hell down to a lower deck!" There was no general quarters sounded because there had never been a general quarters drill on the *Antares*. The *Antares* crew up top had a good view—a little too good—of the attack. Bombs hit all around and shell fragments crashed near the defenseless ship. The captain started to look for safe harbor for his slow-moving ship and headed to the docks at Honolulu, pulling in at 11:47. By then the Japanese planes were long gone.

On the *Ward*, the ship caught the sampan that was trying to run away. The lone man aboard was waving a white towel. It was about then that the executive officer of the day looked toward Pearl Harbor, turned to Outerbridge, and said. "They are making a lot of noise over there this morning, captain." Outerbridge thought they were blasting to build a new road. Then he saw the planes. Though he had sunk the *I-20-A* only an hour before, he was stunned that there were Japanese planes over Pearl Harbor. "I had no idea the air attack was going to follow," he said in later testimony.

The *Ward* soon came face to face with the Japanese air force. A dive bomber targeted the ship, but the bomb hit 300 yards away.

That was too close for Outerbridge. The old four-stacker revved up and went into evasive maneuvers. That was about all the ship could do. Its big guns, which earlier that morning had proved they couldn't aim low enough at close range, also couldn't aim high enough to hit a plane. All that was available were .30 caliber water-cooled machine guns, which stopped working because the water jackets were clogged by salt water. Said Knapp, "We expected the whole Jap fleet, and all we had was an old four-stacker with a jammed machine gun." But the *Ward* was a lucky ship. No other planes attacked.

The rest of the day the *Ward* sounded for enemy subs with its sonar and dropped all its depth charges, reloading at West Lock on Oahu in the afternoon. Over three days, the *Ward* dropped 170 depth charges and finally had to be rationed because Outerbridge kept asking for more. He said that while the *Ward* didn't visually spot any more subs, it had "good metallic contact," the kind of pings that only a sub produces. These probably were the Japanese *I*-subs waiting for ships to emerge from the harbor. No other sub kills were reported by the *Ward*.

"Wild Willie" Outerbridge went on to have a distinguished career. He left the *Ward* to command the USS *O'Brien*, a destroyer, and fought throughout the South Pacific. He won the Navy Cross for sinking the *1-20-A* and would later command the USS *Los Angeles*, one of the Navy's premier cruisers. His relationship with the *Ward* would include one last chapter. The *Ward* ran anti-submarine patrols and, after a switch in armament, became a sharpshooting craft to be reckoned with. (The original "first shot" gun was removed and shipped to Minnesota, the home of so many *Ward* crew members; the gun sits today in the Capitol Approach area in St. Paul.) Right after the Battle of Guadalcanal, the *Ward* fended off a Japanese air attack and downed three planes. Two American ships were lost in the conflict. On June 16, 1943, the *Ward* was again attacked by air; it shot four Japanese aircraft and slipped away unscathed.

However, the *Ward*'s luck ran out in 1944 on her most famous anniversary, December 7. At Ormoc Bay, Leyte in the Philippines, a Japanese kamikaze bomber dove into the *Ward*'s hull, and the ship caught fire. The blaze couldn't be controlled, and the now bat-tle-tested crew abandoned ship. To make sure the *Ward* wouldn't present a danger if it exploded, the ship was sunk by gunfire. The shots came from the USS *O'Brien* under the command of "Wild Willie" Outerbridge. His comment: "It had to be done."

The *Antares* was luckier, supplying sailors all over the Pacific. It did have one strange and close encounter involving another type of midget sub much later in the war. By that time the little subs (called Kaitens) had evolved into a new design and become the vehicle for suicide missions—what the Japanese called "body crashing"—or essentially human torpedoes. On June 28, 1945, the sub *I-36* launched an attack on the *Antares* just southeast of the Marianas Islands. The Kaitens missed their target, and the *Antares* was rescued by a destroyer (the *Sproston*), survived the entire war, and was sold to a scrap yard in 1947.

"Til" Chiappari still thinks about his plodding old ship, and in particular a question he asked on the bridge on December 7, 1941, just after the midget sub was attacked. It was a moment, even at age 87 in 2003, he could never quite put behind him. He asked Commander Grannis, the captain, whether he should notify the Pearl Harbor Shore Signal Tower that an enemy submarine had been sunk. Because it was his job to operate the signal blinker, the message would have been picked up immediately by the signal receiver at Pearl Harbor. The news would have been in some-body's hands almost instantly. "I asked the captain, 'Should I send a message?' "

Grannis thought for minute and said, "No, don't bother. The *Ward* will do it."

The time was 6:47. "Til" Chiappari would never forget. Maybe it would have made a difference. He said he thinks of his friends who died that day, and all he can do is wonder: "What if?"

· · ·

That same "what if" question has been officially posed and pondered thousands of times since that December 7. The first wave of congressional investigations into Pearl Harbor began forty-eight hours after the Japanese bombs and torpedoes fell and continued virtually nonstop until 1948. (This puts in perspective efforts by the George W. Bush administration to delay, for being premature, congressional investigations into the 9/11 World Trade Center attack.) Altogether there have been eleven government inquiries into the events leading to Pearl Harbor, with one in-depth hearing as late as 1995. Also, the U.S. Senate passed a resolution during the Clinton administration proposing that Kimmel and Short be absolved of blame for being unprepared. (The resolution died in the U.S. House.)

Lieutenant Commander Edwin T. Layton, later to earn the rank of rear admiral, would carry a burden similar to that of Chiappari, but added to Layton's burden were the souls of all who died that day. He had the distinction of being the Navy's chief intelligence officer at Pearl Harbor. He would not take the fall for the intelligence failure, however. His boss, Kimmel, would and that fact would forever haunt Layton. He knew better.

A few days before, on December 2, 1941, Admiral Kimmel asked Layton where the six "missing" carriers of the Japanese Navy might be. Layton had submitted a report to Kimmel with the note "Homeland waters?" as his best guess. The meeting took place in Kimmel's office, which he had moved from the USS *Pennsylvania* to the second story of the submarine headquarters overlooking the harbor.

"You don't know where the carriers are?" Kimmel asked.

"No, sir," Layton replied.

"You haven't any idea where they are?"

"No, sir."

"You mean to say that you, the intelligence officer, don't know where the carriers are?"

"No, sir, I don't."

"You mean they could be coming around Diamond Head, and you wouldn't know?"

To that Layton could only say, "Yes, sir, but I hope they'd have been sighted by now."

Kimmel then said, "I understand." He had a kidding look, Layton would write, as if to say, "How could anyone lose six aircraft carriers?"

The truth was that Eddie Layton had a very good idea about how and where the Japanese would attack. He also had at least an inkling about when. After a party on the evening of December 6, he yelled out to no one in particular, "Wake up, America!"

For decades Layton kept relatively quiet about intelligence matters before the Pearl Harbor attack. When he turned 80 he decided to set the record straight. His handwritten accounts would come to form a voluminous book about both the attack itself and the recriminations that followed; Layton was a key witness at five congressional hearings, some of them secret. *"And I Was There"* was published posthumously, with the aid of coauthors Captain Roger Pineau of the Navy, historian John Costello, and Layton's widow, Miriam. She recalled how he kept his memories alive over the years by reminiscing, but only with a tight family circle or close Navy friends. He'd signed an oath as an intelligence officer not to reveal the secrets he knew. Then in 1977, another Navy man, President Jimmy Carter, released top-secret documents, and Layton felt he no longer had to honor his pledge. His store of knowledge and pent-up anger would fill 600 pages.

Eddie Layton was a slender, bespectacled teenager of 17 when he applied to the Naval Academy at Annapolis. He was so skinny, in fact, he had to stuff himself with bananas to gain enough weight to be eligible for the academy. His slight frame made him perfect for what he called the radiator gang—guys who swapped stories inside while the athletes butted heads outside. He liked acting and even played a drag role in a play when he was a midshipman, something his classmates razzed him about for years. Layton, however, saw it as giving him a chance to practice deception, something that would help him excel in the field where he became an expert—intelligence, in particular, Japanese intelligence. By 1939, he had done two tours of duty in Japan, become fluent in the language, and gone to work in Washington for the ONI (Office of Naval Intelligence).

Assigned as chief intelligence officer for the Pacific Fleet in 1940, he sensed a serious problem in early 1941. It wasn't what he knew—it was what he didn't know. For months he and Kimmel were on the list to receive classified reports on Japanese activity; then, starting in July 1941, intelligence all but stopped. He asked a former colleague who worked with him in Tokyo, Commander Arthur McCollum, director of Far East intelligence in Washington, to find out why. McCollum wrote back what Layton described as a "Dear Eddie" letter that said in essence the intelligence was, as Layton wrote, "none of Pearl Harbor's business."

In fact, the intelligence brass was deeply paranoid about information leaks. One slip had already occurred: an aide to President Roosevelt accidentally mislaid a file of deciphered Japanese diplomatic messages; soon after, a rumor surfaced on Washington's embassy row that the U.S. could crack Japanese diplomatic codes. Intercepts also showed that the Japanese themselves were questioning whether their codes had been broken. The answer Japan never learned in wartime: absolutely.

The Navy's OP-20-G focused on deciphering messages sent from Japan to its diplomats around the world, a bit of eavesdropping American intelligence services had performed off and on since 1917. By the 1930s, the Japanese had caught on, in large part because of a revealing and embarrassing 1931 book by American codebreaker Herbert O. Yardley. Japanese diplomats then came to rely on an encryption machine, similar to the famous "Enigma" used by the Germans. Cipher machines work like this: a machine encodes a message into a series of letters or numbers or both; the message is sent using Morse code or even via cablegram; a receiving machine at the other end, set the same as the sending machine, decodes the message. The enemy could pick up the Morse code or even see the cablegram, but it would make no sense without the cipher machine to interpret the jumble of letters and numerals.

The cipher wheel itself dates back to the fifteenth century, but it came into general use during the Civil War. One simple version even became commonplace in American households: the radio show *Captain Midnight* popularized the secret decoder ring (with a cipher wheel) during the late 1930s and the 1940s. Germany's Enigma became the uber-machine of its day by using multiple mechanized wheels, making possible code variations that ran to a staggering 10 trillion.

The Japanese diplomats used a cipher machine (called Purple by the United States), and the intercepting machine the United States made was referred to as Magic. It was a fitting name, for U.S. intelligence had secretly crafted a duplicate of the Purple machine from scratch. (The Germans' Enigma machine had been sold on the commercial market in the 1920s and 1930s for use by governments and businesses. When the British band of code-breaking geniuses set to the task, they had a good head start because they knew how the machine worked.) The Purple machine was an unknown that even utilized a different type of wheel system from Enigma. A truly bright civilian cryptanalyst named Larry Clark figured out that the machine had a stepping switch like those used in telephone exchanges. The Navy's team built two of the machines for a cost of $684.65. (When a Japanese Purple machine was captured in 1945, it was found to be almost a perfect match for the one U.S. intelligence had built.)

With its own homemade machines, from the fall of 1940 on the military could read every diplomatic dispatch sent to and from the Japanese embassies. The content of these messages, when made known after the Pearl Harbor attack, shocked men like Layton. He referred to them as pieces of a jigsaw puzzle that would have given him a clearer picture of Japanese strategy. What follows is a sampling of key messages, starting on November 5, 1941, and continuing to December 6. American intelligence officials in Washington were privy to them, but intelligence personnel in Hawaii were not. To put the messages in context: Tokyo was sending detailed instructions to its Washington diplomatic team about how to negotiate a proposed agreement (referred to as the *modus vivendi* or temporary arrangement) between the United States and Japan. President Roosevelt still thought some sort of peace treaty was possible, while the Japanese diplomats were being pressed to come to a speedy resolution.

November 05, 1941
#736
(of utmost secrecy)
Because of various circumstances, it is absolutely necessary that all arrangements for the signing of this agreement be completed by the 25th of this month . . . .

Another message, from November 11:

. . . the United States is still not fully aware of the exceedingly criticalness of the situation here. The fact remains that the date set forth in my message #736 is absolutely immovable under present conditions.

Then on November 15:

Please, therefore, make the United States see the light so as to make possible the signing of the agreement by that date.

The reason for this emphasis on some sort of resolution by a November 25 deadline looks obvious enough on its face: some action was planned after that date. Historian Roberta Wohlstetter reviewed diplomatic messages sent before November 1941 and found that while they had a sense of urgency, the strict November 25 deadline was unprecedented. Unbeknownst to the United States, of course, the Japanese fleet was set to sail on November 26 from the Kuril Islands for Hawaii. (The Japanese submarines were silently launched from Kure Island on a course of 9 degrees East and other locations several days earlier.)

On November 28, after the deadline had passed, messages from Tokyo changed in tenor. One was sent that praised the diplomats' efforts but acknowledged that the negotiations had in fact failed. It also instructed the diplomatic corps as follows:

However, I do not wish you to give the impression that the negotiations are broken off. Merely say to them that you are awaiting instructions and that, although the opinions of your Government are not clear to you, to your own way of thinking the Imperial Government has always made just claims and has borne great sacrifices for the sake of peace in the Pacific . . . .

Some of the diplomats were receiving direct instructions via telephone (also intercepted) urging them to stall.

On December 2, Tokyo sent a message worldwide for its embassies to destroy their code books and machines, except in Washington, which was advised to burn all its telegraphic codes, except two, and to keep one cipher machine operating.

The Japanese government's subsequent messages to Honolulu, Seattle, Portland, Los Angeles, Panama, Vancouver, Ottawa, and Havana cautioned the embassies to: "Be especially careful not to arouse suspicion of those outside . . . . [This information] is preparatory to an emergency situation and for your information alone. Remain calm."

By December 3 the Japanese striking force was 1,000 miles from Hawaii. The crew could hear Honolulu radio KGMB broadcasting music that would soon carry a generation of Americans to war. That same day, the attack fleet received the crucial message from Tokyo: "12-08 Climb Mount Niitaka Repeat 12-08," the signal that the attack was a go. (December 8 would be December 7 east of the international date line.) Niitaka was the highest mountain in the Japanese empire, a difficult one to scale but not insurmountable.

By then the United States had also intercepted an especially telling message from Tokyo advising its diplomats in Berlin to inform Hitler and other top leaders that "there is extreme danger that war may suddenly break out between the Anglo-Saxon nations and Japan through some clash of arms and add that the times of the breaking out of this may come quicker than anyone dreams."

Another type of decoded diplomatic message usually came in a simpler form (the J-19 and PA-K2 codes) and took second position behind the Purple intercepts. That didn't mean they were less important, especially when viewed in retrospect. The chief Japanese spy in Honolulu was sending back to Tokyo the layout of ships anchored at Pearl Harbor. Tokyo was asking for specific information ". . . with regard to warships and aircraft carriers, we would like to have you report on those at anchor . . . tied up at wharves, buoys and in docks."

A later dispatch from Tokyo to Honolulu advised the spy to "make your 'ships in harbor' report . . . at a rate of twice a week." Then on November 20, the spy was told to investigate the "Hawaiian military reservation," in order to expand the knowledge about military forces around Pearl Harbor.

When these latter three messages, all decoded in Washington, came to light after December 7, they threw Layton into a fit of disbelief and anger. He, the chief intelligence officer, had not even been given these low-priority intercepts dealing directly with Hawaii, the key area for which he was responsible. He believed this critical intelligence, bottled up in a bureaucratic power play and guarded with a paranoiac fear, could have alerted leaders in the Pacific to stand ready for an immediate assault. Then again, maybe not.

Even the late-breaking messages Hawaii did receive from Washington didn't sound a very loud alarm. For example, Kimmel, Layton, and other officers did learn a few days before December 7 that Japanese diplomats had been ordered to destroy their code books. It didn't arouse a tremendous wave of concern, for at the very same time, the United States was ordering Guam and other outposts to destroy their code books.

Even the famous "war warning" on November 27 went on to name the Philippines and Borneo as probable targets for the first outbreaks. The war warning message from Naval Operations in Washington was written by Admiral Richmond Kelly Turner, the Navy's head of war planning. In Layton's eyes, Kelly Turner was incompetent and a bully. He was the man who ordered that a tight lid be kept on vital decoded Japanese messages and summarily judged what was important, what wasn't, and who should see the intelligence. After the sneak attack he denied any culpability, loudly proclaiming that Kimmel and crew at Pearl Harbor "had enough information." By the end of the war, Layton believed much of the blame for not knowing about the surprise attack at Pearl Harbor should have fallen on Turner, an officer whose quick temper earned him the nickname "Terrible." Layton knew firsthand that the officers who made the line decisions at Pearl Harbor had been denied key information. At the end of the Pacific War, Layton—then a captain and a respected intelligence officer—would confront the fiery Turner on the USS *Missouri* on the day Japan officially surrendered. In the officers' mess Turner was ranting about Kimmel and the congressional hearings still ongoing in Washington. "They ought to hang him from the yardarm," Turner said of Kimmel. Layton had had enough. He said to Turner, "If you'd done what you should have, we wouldn't have had a Pearl Harbor." Turner rushed at Layton, grabbed at him, and screamed, "Are you calling me a liar?" The men were pulled apart, but Layton always wondered what might have happened to a captain who took a poke at an admiral.

Perhaps the most remarkable section of Layton's 600-page lament is often overlooked, in part because he made no effort to hide it. It was a personal "what if" demon he never could shake. To sharpen his skills in Japanese, Layton had translated an article published in 1934 by the Japanese naval expert Shinsaku Hirata. Titled "When We Fight" (Layton noted the "when" as opposed to "if"), the article describes how a cowering American Navy at Pearl Harbor would suffer from a Japanese attack of "a fast striking force of cruisers and aircraft." Hirata continued: "[W]hether such a surprise raid could be organized only the Japanese Naval General Staff knows." He also pointed out that the Americans themselves engaged in a fleet exercise off Hawaii some years before, with a carrier striking force sending flights of planes, effectively executing a sneak attack, and "theoretically destroying the major naval base." In essence the U.S. itself had demonstrated the feasibility of a carrier sneak attack against itself in the 1930s.

Layton's interest in the plan didn't stop there, however. He was so impressed he submitted his English translation of Hirata's work to several American magazines in October 1940 under the pen name Tomomasa Emura. In his cover letter he wrote, "Whether or not it is a preview of Japanese–American naval warfare is a matter for history to determine." All he received in return were rejection slips.

Navy officials weren't any more prescient than magazine editors. Layton actually showed the translated article to Kimmel and another officer after a rumor circulated in early 1941 that Pearl Harbor might be a target. The rumor came from a credible source: Joseph C. Grew, the veteran U.S. ambassador to Japan. Yet the trail of information was a little shaky: a Peruvian embassy chauffeur heard it; he told a maid in the American embassy he was dating, and she passed it along to Grew. In February 1941, the verdict from Washington and Pearl Harbor was unanimous: the chances of a sneak attack: slim and none, respectively.

Layton wrote on the second page of Chapter 1 in his book that on December 3 when he was quizzed by Kimmel about the possible carrier locations, he should have mentioned again the article they had discussed earlier in the year. He said he had forever "kicked himself in the pants" for not saying anything. In truth, the head of fleet intelligence at Pearl Harbor had the Hirata's blueprint for the attack translated in his office, but no one quite made the connection.

Actually, the literature predicting a Pearl Harbor attack was even more extensive than Layton knew. A British journalist and former spy named Hector Bywater outlined the attack plan in a 1929 novel *The Great Pacific War*, and there's convincing evidence Japanese military officials studied it thoroughly. Yamamoto taught the book in his war-college classes. An earlier book—*Fantasy on the Outbreak of a Japanese-American War*—published by Japan's National Military Affairs Association in 1913 was considered a sort of companion text. The central ideas of Japan waging a Pacific War against the United States and Hawaii serving as the opening campaign site had germinated for decades before 1941. The books also reinforced the Japanese belief that the Hawaiian

Islands (40 percent of its population being Japanese) belonged more to Japan than the United States.

The mystery of the failure to anticipate the attack on Pearl Harbor becomes a little easier to understand when considered from Layton's perspective. Decoded messages in hand or not, the possibility of the Japanese coming across the ocean without being spotted and launching an attack seemed preposterous enough for almost everyone to dismiss the idea without too much hesitation. In the military, a hunch isn't a fact. There was even a racial element as well. Captain Forrest Biard, a code-breaker at Oahu's famous Hypo station, noted that there was an "attitude that there was no severe threat to the great United States by the little yellow men with supposedly poor eyesight." Many in the military believed the Japanese were cross-eyed and couldn't possibly hit a target from the air.

That the reaction to the midget sub's sinking in the early morning of December 7 was slow seems even less surprising under the circumstances. Michigan Senator Homer Ferguson phrased it well at a hearing in 1943: "You mean that our intelligence was such that we didn't even know that Japan had these small submarines?"

Afraid so.

As for intelligence officer Layton, on December 11 he would actually meet a midget sub commander in person. Kazuo Sakamaki, who would become P.O.W. No. 1.

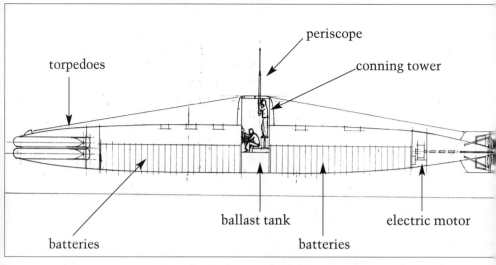

Despite measuring nearly 80 feet in length, a Japanese midget sub provided little room for its crew. The batteries required to propel the stealthy vessel occupied nearly every open space within the hull.

Crewmembers of the old destroyer USS *Ward* proudly surround a deck gun on their ship. These young men in their teens and twenties believed their "first shot" fired at a midget sub on December 7, 1941—more than an hour before the air attack began—was a direct hit. Over the years, underwater searches failed to turn up any evidence of the sunken sub.

More than 1,000 men from the battleship USS *Arizona* died during the sneak attack on Pearl Harbor. In Japan, midget subs were publicly credited with sinking the *Arizona*, but airmen who actually bombed the battleship insisted they'd struck the death blows.

This is the view Japanese pilots had just after they dropped their bombs and hit the powder magazine of the USS *Arizona*.

This picture was taken from a "Kate" bomber as it was flying away from Battleship Row. Tracks in the water (center) may have been left by torpedoes speeding toward their targets. Explosive shock waves are spreading from the USS *West Virginia* and the battleship *Oklahoma*. The image within the circle is widely believed to be a Japanese midget sub (see enlargement below).

This enlargement shows a rectangular object sitting atop a dark, linear structure. This is believed to be *I-16-A*, piloted by Yokoyama. The plumes of water behind the object are most likely "rooster tails" formed by the action of shock waves striking the sub's propeller. Based on this photograph, some experts believe that the USS *West Virginia* was torpedoed by the midget sub.

By 8:25 A.M. on December 7, 1941, the battleship USS *West Virginia* was already sinking, and desperate rescue efforts were underway.

In drydock, the destroyer USS *Shaw* was bombed during the second wave of attacks and its forward magazine exploded. The blast severed the bow of the ship. Amazingly, the Shaw was repaired and went on to serve in the South Pacific campaign.

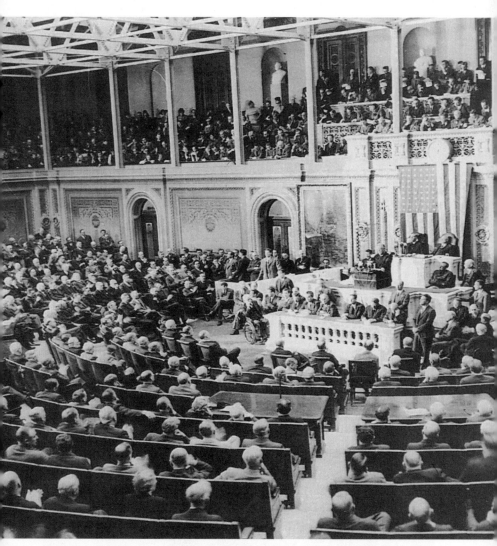

On December 8, 1941, President Franklin Roosevelt appeared before a joint session of Congress. The nation heard a resolute president declare that "since the unprovoked and dastardly attack by Japan on Sunday, December seventh, 1941, a state of war has existed between the United States and the Japanese Empire."

After running aground on December 8, the midget sub known as *I-24-A* sat helplessly in the surf off Bellows Army Air Field on Oahu. U.S. soldiers used a rope to tie the sub's bow to a tree.

A faulty gyrocompass (pictured to the right of the ship's wheel) doomed the mission of *I-24-A*. When the captured sub was being inspected by the U.S. Navy, the compass was given a few taps, and it worked fine.

This detailed map found on *I-24-A* confirmed the worst fears of American intelligence officials. Japanese spies on Hawaii helped supply vital information, such as landmarks, so that the crews on the midget subs could navigate their way into Pearl Harbor at night.

This midget sub managed to sneak into Pearl Harbor on December 7, and fire its torpedoes, but both missed. The little sub fell victim to depth charges dropped by the destroyer USS *Monaghan*, which also rammed the little sub. It was raised from the harbor just a few weeks after the attack. The picture clearly shows the dimpled "washboarding" effect caused by the depth charges.

Discovered in 1960, this midget sub was among the five that attacked Pearl Harbor. It was found in about 75 feet of water. The sub was hauled to shore by the U.S. Navy and eventually shipped to Japan. Refurbished, it sits now at Eta Jima, once the home of the Japanese Naval Academy.

Midget sub crewmembers were considered "hero gods" in Japan, and a portrait on silk of the men who died in the sneak attack on Pearl Harbor was commissioned to honor them. Though there were 10 crewmen, only nine are pictured. Kazuo Sakamaki, the captain of *I-24-A*, was captured and therefore disgraced in Japanese eyes. His portrait was not included.

As a young Japanese naval officer, Isoroku Yamamoto lived in the United States for several years and attended Harvard University. The chief architect of the sneak attack on Pearl Harbor, he promoted the innovative idea of launching airplanes from aircraft carriers to deliver the first strike.

Fluent in English, Yamamoto (center) was a key negotiator in the international naval conferences convened during the 1920s and 1930s. The conferences were held to set limits on the warship tonnage of the primary naval powers—Great Britain, the United States, and Japan. The Japanese chafed at the restrictions and broke off talks after a conference in London in 1934. (BETTMANN/CORBIS)

The retreating Japanese left behind these remnants of war at Guadalcanal, illustrating how thoroughly they'd been defeated on a vital island in the Pacific. Pictured are a damaged midget sub and the cargo ship, *Yamazuki Maru*.

Sakamaki's sub served an unlikely land-based mission after its capture. It toured the United States in the U.S. Treasury Department's effort to drum up sales of war bonds. (BETTMANN/CORBIS)

The First Prisoner of War

THE FIVE MIDGET SUBS that attacked Pearl Harbor inspired the Japanese nation and fueled the euphoric belief that it was only a matter of time before the Pacific War would be won. A civilian witness to the attack, Takao Okuna, could have spoken for the majority of Japanese when he said that ". . . we'd done it at last. . . . All the feelings of inferiority of a colored people from a backwards country, towards white people from the developed world, disappeared in that one blow." News that the little subs were an integral part of the assault surfaced just a few days after December 7. From there the legend grew. The Japanese Imperial Navy office of public relations expanded the story, gave the subs credit for sinking the USS *Arizona*, and played up their heroic mission—while also acknowledging (erroneously) that all midget sub hands were lost. According to the Japanese Navy publicists, who spread their propaganda worldwide via Associated Press wire stories, "the annihilation of the United States Pacific Fleet," led by the midget subs, "threw . . . the whole Japanese nation into a crucible of indescribable excitement." In 1942 a fictional newspaper serial about the midget subs (written by one of the nation's top literary figures, Toyoo Iwata) and a movie (complete with hokey sub models zipping around underwater) further convinced the Japanese people that a death blow had been delivered to the American Navy.

The newspaper serial ran from August to December (think Charles Dickens' nineteenth-century newspaper serials, plus falling cherry blossoms) and was later published as a book. All Japan buzzed about the miniature marvels and the brave men who manned them. Titled *Kaigun* (or *Navy*), the story had a melodramatic plot: two young men—one rich, one poor—grow up together and become lifelong friends. Both take the physical exam to enter the Navy, but the privileged one doesn't make it. Instead he becomes a naval artist. His friend takes command of a midget sub in the top-secret "special underwater navigation" unit.

The sub commander is part of the assault on the American Navy on December 7 and leads the battle that ends with a huge explosion. The midget subs and an overwhelming Japanese force vanquish the U.S. fleet. The artist paints a picture to memorialize the scene, but learns after the fact that his friend was the submarine hero who perished. While seemingly not that tantalizing a tale, it fed Japanese imaginations and glorified the military credo of "discipline, training, loyalty, self-sacrifice, and boldness." The public responded. Memorials to the dead midget sub crew members sprang up around Japan; people flocked to makeshift shrines leaving flowers and gifts to honor these new "hero-gods," a religious designation that put them in a pantheon above mere humans and edged into the realm of the emperor himself. Their sacrifice proved that Japan could prevail against any other nation, for only the Japanese could blend such strong character traits with technological brilliance. From a propaganda standpoint, the midget subs became the epitome of the war effort and gave the nation a major morale boost. That these subs were almost total military failures would not become known in Japan until years later.

The little submarines did surprise the American military. Few U.S. service personnel had ever heard of a midget sub, much less seen one in the water ready to attack. Rumors surfaced before December 7 about some sort of secret craft being built in Japanese shipyards, but no one in the U.S. military could foresee a fleet of stealth midget subs ready for war. By 1941, Japan had twenty of them set to launch.

After years of preparation, the Japanese left as little as possible to chance. When the ocean liner *Taiyo Maru* approached Honolulu's Pier 8 on November 5, 1941, on board were two men listed on the passenger manifest as doctors. They were in fact the two officers (Keiu Matsuo and Toshihide Maejima) who helped develop the midget sub attack strategy to win over Yamamoto. As their ship cruised past Pearl Harbor, the two spies stood at the railing, their eyes searching for details—navigational landmarks, ship locations, anti-submarine nets. The men submitted a lengthy questionnaire to the local spymaster, Takeo Yoshikawa; he answered their questions and drew maps of Pearl Harbor, all smuggled in newspapers onto the ship and ready for review in Japan by November 15.

On November 18, five big subs (*I-16, I-18, I-20, I-22,* and *I-24*) with their midget cargoes tucked aboard left Kure, Japan around midday. After exiting the narrow channel, they fanned out about 20 miles apart to make the journey. The subs would come close enough during the early part of the voyage to send blinker signals, but they all maintained radio silence. The mother subs didn't submerge until they reached the American-controlled Wake Island area; from then on, they switched to the routine of staying underwater by day and surfacing at night.

Inside the subs, excitement ran high. The crews of the mother subs anticipated the battles to come, while the midget sub men checked and rechecked their equipment. Being submerged for 12 hours proved a good way to test the little subs. One sprang a leak, another had a torpedo jam. Rough seas and darkness made work on the surfaced boats precarious. The midget sub crew members tied ropes to themselves; Ensign Kazuo Sakamaki on *I-24* was swept overboard but was saved from drowning by his tether.

The submariners had a plan for releasing the midget subs, but little time to practice the routine. Each little sub was strapped tightly on the mother sub's aft deck for the voyage, then when ready to launch, all the cables but two were removed, and the midget sub took air in its tanks for buoyancy. As the mother sub slowly submerged and moved forward, the little sub through its breakaway telephone connection signaled the mother sub crew to cut the remaining cables. The midget sub then drifted the opposite way, flipped on its engine, lowered its buoyancy, and slipped below the surface—if everything went according to plan.

In the final days before the attack, the midget sub crews prepared themselves for the likelihood of death. Despite Yamamoto's insistence on a recovery strategy, the odds of survival were more like Russian roulette. Consider the mission: the subs were to invade the harbor undetected, fire their torpedoes at a well-armed 90-ship fleet, then sneak out to rendezvous more than 20 miles away in an area bound to be teeming with destroyers, all this before expending the charge in their batteries. Add to that the navigational difficulties: the approach would be made at night, the channel and harbor entrance were narrow, and there were few landmarks to help the pilots navigate. It was impossible to escape the obvious conclusion: this was a doomed mission, no matter the precautions.

The midget sub crew members knew it was a long shot and accepted their fate. They wrote letters home to be delivered after the mother subs returned. Their letters told relatives how honored they were to make such a sacrifice. Sakamaki clipped a fingernail and strands of his hair to send to his parents and thanked them for the opportunity to give his life "for peace and justice." He even included the postage. Another wrote: "Should anything happen to me, do not grieve or mourn, for I have dedicated my life in service to His Imperial Majesty . . . ." Falling cherry blossoms were a recurrent theme. One midget sub crew member wrote: "As the cherry blossoms fall at the height of their glory, so, too, must I fall . . . ." Sakamaki would douse himself in perfume before embarking on his mission so he would "smell like fallen cherry blossoms." Their superiors admired their spirit; as one captain noted: "The firm de-

termination not to return alive on the part of these young lieu-
tenants and ensigns who smilingly embarked on their ships cannot
be praised too much."

The midget subs were launched in two waves. *I-16* and *1-20* positioned themselves 7 miles out and just east and west of the harbor
entrance; *I-18*, *I-22*, and *I-24* fell back in a semicircle at 10–12
miles out. The subs were launched over a period of several hours,
with *I-16-A* leaving first at about 1:00 A.M., *I-20-A* detaching at
about 3:00 A.M., and *I-24-A*, which had continuing equipment
problems, picking up the rear.

It was a good night to sneak into Pearl Harbor. The waning
moon had risen at 10:05 P.M., and the seas stayed fairly calm. The
sub crews drew close enough to hear music drifting out from the
clubs and bars of Waikiki and to see the neon lights. A few U.S.
ships seemed to be patrolling the channel entrance, but clearly the
Americans were not on high alert. The chances of the subs entering the harbor looked excellent.

It helped that the anti-submarine nets at the harbor entrance
had been left wide open. At 4:58 A.M., the gate vessel pulled back
the nets for two returning minesweepers. With a tug scheduled to
go out at around 6:00 A.M. to meet the *Antares* and the 500-ton
barge it had in tow, the nets weren't closed, and in fact wouldn't be
shut until after the first air attack was almost over. With the entrance open, the midget subs had a clear path. Originally, all the
midget subs were to stay submerged on the muddy seabed outside
Pearl Harbor, then between the first and second waves of the air attack, make their move, but that plan was scrapped before December 7. No one was sure the subs could stay submerged that long at
that depth. It was decided that it would be more effective if the
subs made their move as soon as the attack began.

At least one of the subs, *I-22-A*, made it into Pearl Harbor, just
as the Japanese strategists had hoped. Spotted at about 8:15 A.M.,
the midget sub was about 200 yards from the USS *Medusa*, just off
Pearl City in the harbor's northwest area, more than four miles

inside the harbor entrance. By then the first wave of 183 Japanese aircraft was strafing ships, dropping bombs, and unleashing torpedoes in the harbor itself, while American gun batteries blazed back. Ships started signaling each other that an enemy sub had been spotted. Even Kimmel's signal tower could see the sub and sent the message, "Japanese submarine in harbor." What followed was pure chaos. The seaplane tender *Curtiss* opened fire with its big guns and a bevy of three .50 caliber machine guns. Two other ships joined in. That day's ready-duty destroyer, *Monaghan*, would carry the attack to the enemy, though the skipper's first reaction to all the ricocheting gunfire was that his fellow commanders "must be crazy." But he quickly joined the swirl of battle.

The midget sub fired a torpedo at the *Curtiss*, but the shot missed its target and blew up a nearby dock. The loss of the torpedo's weight had an unintended effect on the little craft—it caused the boat to bob up. The *Curtiss* kept pounding with its 5-inch guns and .50 caliber rounds that tore into the sub's conning tower, much like the shot from the *Ward* earlier that morning. Meanwhile, the *Monaghan*, guns firing, headed toward the sub. The destroyer's aim was off, however: one shell struck a shoreline derrick, set it on fire, and scattered the stunned civilian workers. Cornered, the midget sub launched its last torpedo at the pursuing *Monaghan*—and missed again. This torpedo exploded on the muddy bank at Ford Island and sent a waterspout harmlessly into the air. The *Monaghan* continued its charge at the now helpless sub, rammed it, and dropped depth charges. The explosions blew the midget sub to the surface, far enough to reveal its punctured conning tower and smashed bow. The direct hits sank the little sub 200 yards off Ford Island. The victorious *Monaghan* had scant time to celebrate, however. The ship's hard ramming charge sent it on a runaway course straight into the burning derrick, which was ready to explode. The captain ordered, "All engines back—emergency full speed!" He was too late. The ship ran aground in the mud and crashed into the burning derrick. As sailors scrambled to spray water on the bow to keep the fire from spreading, the captain frantically reversed the engines and tried to rock the destroyer out of the mud. The *Monaghan* popped loose and proudly entered the channel on its way to the open sea. Men cheered from nearby ships; it was the only successful retaliation anyone had seen so far. The harbor signal tower sent a message: "Witnessed *Monaghan* sink enemy sub by ramming and depth charges. Excellent piece of work!"

As the air strikes continued, the first big ship to make it out that morning was the cruiser *St. Louis*; its race for the channel and escape from torpedoes most likely fired by a midget sub became something of a legend and helped it earn the nickname "Lucky Lou." As the first bombs fell, Captain George A. Rood ordered his crew to fire up the boilers for "full power, emergency." A steel cable between Dry Dock No. 1 and a dredge blocked the ship on the way out to the open sea; the *St. Louis* snapped through the cable and charged ahead. The posted speed in Pearl Harbor where the *St. Louis* set out was 8 knots. The cruiser hit about 23 knots as it churned past the piers at Ford Island. Boatswain's Mate Howard French watched and thought the cruiser was moving faster in the channel than any ship he'd ever seen. Two patrolling minesweepers did their best to clear out of the way as the *St. Louis* shot through the anti-submarine gate (which was still open). Rood, a former submarine commander, figured that the most dangerous area would be the harbor entrance because enemy subs would try to sink a big ship there to bottle up the channel. He was right. He and another officer, Commander Carl K. Fink, saw two torpedoes fired at them from between 1,000 and 2,000 yards away. Rood said to Fink, "If you want to see a ship get torpedoed, come take a look." Both men were amazed when the first torpedo hit a coral shoal 200 yards from their ship. The explosion threw off the second torpedo, and it missed as well. Lucky Lou's streak had just started. The officers did not actually spot the little sub, but after hearing about the attack in the harbor, they figured it had to be another midget. Only minutes later the *St. Louis* fired on what appeared to be a periscope poking out from the water's surface. Both officers said the gunners hit the target. Certainly they hit something. The minesweeper *Crossbill* had a mine probe (called a paravane) out that might have been mistaken for a periscope, and the minesweeper noted in its December 7 action report how it had been fired on by the *St. Louis*. On a day often described as the blackest in U.S. naval history, a little harmless friendly fire didn't raise much concern.

The torpedoes intended for the *St. Louis* came squarely from the area where the little subs could have been lurking. That incident, however, is the last hard evidence that the midget subs attacked American targets. The rest is conjecture, some of which seems logical. Of the midget subs recovered or located, three still carried torpedoes in their tubes. The sub that fired both torpedoes in its encounter with the *Monaghan* was recovered exactly where it sank, so that leaves only one other sub that could have fired that day, and it has yet to be found—the mystery sub that likely fired at the *St. Louis* or, as has been speculated, may have entered the harbor and torpedoed the battleship *West Virginia*, definitely a long-shot theory. Much of what's known about the midget subs has been pieced together through archeological evidence and eyewitness reports. Some records are simply incomplete: while the *I*-boats and the midget subs they carried are a matter of record, none of the midget subs had a marking that designated it *I-20-A* or *I-16-A* or *I-24-A*. Without knowing the crews' identities, there's no way of knowing which midget sub is which.

Only one sub could reliably report its entire mission: *I-24-A*, piloted by the lone midget sub survivor, Kazuo Sakamaki. He literally wrote the book on the midget sub attack. Published in Japan in 1948 and in the U.S. in 1949, *I Attacked Pearl Harbor* became a best seller. However, his war memoir was the antithesis of the *Kaigun* serial: it did not inspire one's warrior spirit. Sakamaki would receive letters from his countrymen suggesting he commit suicide.

Kazuo, which means "boy of peace," came from a family of modest means in a small village on Shikoku Island; he seemed an even more unlikely candidate for the Naval Academy than Yamamoto.

Like Japan's top naval leader, however, Sakamaki excelled at his entrance exam and became an outstanding cadet. He braved, as did Yamamoto, the same kind of hardships the military imposed to harden the bodies and win the minds of young men. Besides a regimented academic routine, the cadets underwent physical ordeals, such as rowing for miles in rough seas. Sakamaki endured the rowing challenge even though the friction from the oars and the hard wooden seat was so great that his "hands and underwear were bleeding." The physical ordeals eliminated cadets, who, Sakamaki wrote, "became sick and had to drop out." Sakamaki, on the other hand, graduated in August 1940, and in April 1941 received orders to join a special secret assignment. He was one of twenty-four young men who had been singled out, all with similar backgrounds: they were recent graduates, unmarried, and there were other males in their families. Sakamaki was honored by being asked to be part of this mission. But, as it turned out, he would spend almost all of the war agonizing over his fate, a prisoner in an area known as "Stalag Wisconsin."

Sakamaki in his book openly refers to his unit as a suicide squad. Certainly the goal of the mission and the multiple obstacles the midget subs faced at Pearl Harbor tipped the odds toward death, but other pitfalls also came into play. The crews had been trained for only fourteen weeks to operate their subs, and they'd made night runs for a very short time—just over a month, from October to November. Also, the subs churned out from the Navy's shipyard were the first mass-produced batch. There were bound to be problems the young crews were ill-prepared for—as *I-24-A* would discover.

To navigate a submarine safely, the pilot needs a gyrocompass. Whereas a simple magnetic compass would be affected by the magnetic fields created by the sub's electrical systems and metal framework, the spinning action of the gyroscope keeps the compass calibrated to true north. This highly accurate compass allows the pilot to steer a course without any outside visual aids. And, by knowing his speed and heading, the pilot could calculate his rough location and plot his position on a chart (a process called *dead reckoning*). *I-24-A*'s gyrocompass started malfunctioning on the voyage to Hawaii, and Sakamaki and his crewman, Warrant Officer Kiyoshi Inagaki, worked on it right up until they cast off just after midnight on December 7. The captain of *I-24* warned Sakamaki that without a gyrocompass, he couldn't find his way underwater. Sakamaki reasoned that he could use a simple magnetic compass and his periscope to find the way into the harbor. His mission couldn't be aborted for a faulty piece of equipment. After hearing Sakamaki's explanation, the captain shouted "On to Pearl Harbor!"

Sakamaki and Inagaki shouted back, "On to Pearl Harbor!"

At 12 miles out, *I-24* went through the maneuver to release the midget sub. The big sub surfaced and all the cables but two were released. In the rush of launching *I-24-A*, however, its telephone had not been connected to the mother sub. So when the final release occurred, the crew of the midget sub knew it was free only when they heard the clank of the last two metallic lines striking the sub's hull. When *I-24-A* hit the water it promptly flopped on its side like a sick fish. Scrambling to level the boat, Sakamaki and Inagaki carried lead ballast from the heavy side of the sub to even the weight. That worked; the sub leveled off, and Sakamaki's craft slid underwater. He avoided his worst fear: being spotted and giving away the attack. He extended his periscope and scanned the darkness to try to find Oahu. Nothing. Unable to see, he and Inagaki settled in, opened some sake and sandwiches, and waited for, as Sakamaki wrote, "the fatal morning."

Dawn broke, and Sakamaki could see ships patrolling the entrance to the harbor he so desperately wanted to penetrate. He wondered about the other four midget subs and whether they had managed to enter the harbor—the thought only made him feel more anxious. *I-24-A* crept forward, close enough so that Sakamaki saw through his periscope the white uniforms of American sailors on the deck of a warship. He surveyed the ship and knew that its four stacks meant it was an old destroyer. Not wanting to waste a torpedo on such an insignificant target, he sneered at the old ship, when suddenly his sub shook violently, and he hit his head, knocking him unconscious. He'd been depth charged. What he didn't know was that the "old destroyer" already had one midget sub kill to its credit. Sakamaki had crossed paths with the *Ward*.

The explosion damaged the midget sub's batteries and filled it with acrid smoke. When he regained consciousness, Sakamaki groped through the white haze for the controls and set the sub on a course as far away as he could from the *Ward*. After a few minutes, the midget sub drew close enough to the surface to extend its periscope again, and there Sakamaki saw a glorious sight: columns of black smoke rising from Pearl Harbor. He shouted to Inagaki, "They've done it! Look at it!" Their joy was short-lived. The destroyer, white foam churning behind it, closed in and dropped more depth charges. Trying to slip away, *I-24-A* ran aground on one of the thousands of coral reefs that surround Oahu. Sakamaki hit maximum power and broke loose, but the collision created a new problem. The coral reef crimped the end of one torpedo tube and rendered it useless. The batteries, further damaged, fouled the air, and the gases building inside the sub made the pressure almost unbearable. The destroyer kept prowling the coastal waters like a cat "playing with a little mouse," Sakamaki wrote; he, of course, was the mouse. Nonetheless, he didn't want to waste his last shot on "such a tiny ship." His real quarry from the beginning had been the *Pennsylvania*, the Pacific Fleet's flagship. To conserve energy, Sakamaki maneuvered the midget sub at slow speeds. It was well past noon, and the men had been in the sub for 12 hours. Sakamaki approached the harbor entrance again—and again ran aground on a coral reef. He revved the engine, but the sub held fast. Then he and Inagaki started moving lead ballast aft to tilt the sub backward enough to slide off the reef. The batteries continued leaking, and in the watery slush on the sub's deck there was an electric charge that shocked the men as they crawled back and forth. Sakamaki estimated they were stuck there for several hours. They broke free, but discovered that their last operational torpedo was damaged by the crash. Floating defenseless outside the harbor,

Sakamaki had a hopelessly ambitious plan. "The only thing we can do now is plunge right into the *Pennsylvania*. If we can't blast the enemy battleship, we will climb onto it and kill as many enemies as possible."

Inagaki replied dutifully, "Yes, sir."

When night fell on December 7, Sakamaki could look through his periscope and see his elusive target, Pearl Harbor, now ablaze, evidence of Japan's success, and his failure. Exhausted, Inagaki was in tears over their bad luck. They'd come nowhere near the Pennsylvania.

Sakamaki wept as well. He set the sub on course toward his rendezvous point at Lanai Island and passed out. Around midnight, he awoke. The sub had drifted for hours with the hatch open, so at least the air had cleared. All he could do was wait for daylight. At dawn, he believed their luck had at last changed when he saw land and thought he had safely reached the rendezvous point of Lanai. The *I-24-A* was still out of luck, however. It actually was on the northeast side of Oahu, heading directly toward Bellows Field and Kaneohe Naval Air Station. The midget grounded yet again on a coral reef about 200 yards offshore. The batteries had lost their charge, and any chance of escape with their sub had ended. This left the crew with one alternative: All the midget subs came equipped with explosives so if captured this "secret weapon" would not fall into enemy hands. Sakamaki lit the fuse, and he and Inagaki abandoned ship, jumping into the Pacific. With waves crashing around them, the men started to swim toward shore. Sakamaki wrote that he saw his crewmate go under the waves. His own strength sapped, he let the breakers carry him where they would, his mission for the "special underwater unit" now at an end. One of his last conscious thoughts was the realization that the scuttle charge had not exploded.

Sakamaki felt sand as the waves washed over him, and he crawled onto the beach, but this was no *From Here to Eternity* moment. He looked up to see Army Lieutenant Paul Plybon holding a .45 caliber pistol. Plybon was shocked as he looked down on a soaking wet Japanese man wearing a military undershirt and what looked to Plybon like a G-string. Sakamaki had dressed in traditional warrior garb consisting mostly of the samurai wrap-around belt, similar to the kind sumo wrestlers wear. Plybon simply told Sakamaki, "You're under arrest."

The next concern was that there might be more Japanese storming the beach, despite the decidedly unthreatening, drowned-rat appearance of the 5-foot-3 1/2-inch, 131-pound Sakamaki. Second Lieutenant Steve Weiner, armed with a .45 and a shovel, had already started digging a foxhole to prepare for the next "wave" of attackers when he spotted Sakamaki with two men guarding him. "Where in the hell did you get him?" Weiner asked the guards. One man replied, "He walked right out of the water." Weiner could see that Sakamaki had been in the water a long time. The prisoner's skin, he said, "looked like a prune."

The body of Sakamaki's crewmate, Inagaki, would be found two days later floating near Bellows Field. When it was recovered, the body had been damaged, but the extent of the injuries has remained a mystery because the autopsy report was classified by the Navy in 1941. Even in 2004 the Navy won't explain exactly why the report is classified, except to say it is still "secret." Bodies of Japanese airmen were recovered around Oahu (one headless), and these corpses and their condition were a matter of record. What was unusual about Inagaki's body? Speculation is that he was killed by a self-inflicted grenade explosion or fatally wounded in some other way. There were in fact explosions nearby that came after the sub was grounded. It seems the midget sub drew the attention of an eager air patrol, which immediately started dropping bombs. The planes were ordered to stop, but that was only after several bombs hit near the sub.

The men who would interrogate the little Japanese man in a G-string were as befuddled as their prisoner. He was the first POW, and no one knew exactly what to do. They took him to a small tin shack to question him, and though he understood English, he wouldn't talk. Weiner pressed the .45 against Sakamaki's head, but it didn't unnerve the prisoner at all. In fact, Weiner noticed that it was he and his colleagues who were nervous, not the Japanese captive. Weiner figured Sakamaki wanted them to shoot him. They finally gave Sakamaki a shot of booze and a hard-boiled egg. After more failed interrogations with different translators, Sakamaki asked in English for a pencil and paper. He wrote: "I am a Japanese Naval officer. My name Ensign Sakamaki. . . . My ship catch on coral. I jump in water. Swim to this airplane land. No tell about ships. Kill me an honorable way."

That message they understood. They put Sakamaki in a big laundry bag with his head sticking out and pulled the drawstrings to hold him. He was carried away like a parcel to Fort Shaffer on Sand Island near Honolulu. One of the guards there was a strapping 18-year-old high school football player named Thomas Unger. He'd rushed out of his house on the morning of December 7 to help during the chaos of the attack and rescued a wounded soldier. By the evening of December 7 he was carrying bodies to a temporary morgue at Fort Shaffer. He was quickly recruited to guard an area with high fences and a roll of barbed wire strung across the top. There, Sakamaki was locked inside. To Unger, Sakamaki "looked like someone who could fit right into the population downtown. He seemed like a nice guy." Sakamaki's journey as POW No. 1 was now underway.

His sub's future as another kind of POW (Prize of War) had started as well. The air patrol bombs hit close enough to break *I-24-A* away from the coral reef. A crew of Navy men on beach patrol received orders to bring in the sub. They dragged it toward shore until it hit bottom, found a long piece of rope, and tied the little sub, like a stray horse, to a tree. That the sub might be dangerous finally dawned on someone in command, and on Tuesday December 9 experts in torpedoes and radio equipment went aboard, where they discovered the explosive scuttling charge with a partially burned fuse. After disarming the charge, their next priority was the radio, which could give the Navy much-needed intelligence about Japanese communications. Radioman Charles Jackson pulled out the radio, rammed it up the narrow conning tower, put it on a life jacket and floated it ashore on a wave.

The sub itself was searched thoroughly. Items found included a detailed map of Pearl Harbor (most likely courtesy of the two spies who visited on the ocean liner), navigation charts, an apple, two crudely drawn flags (one American, one Japanese), a sword, and sake bottles. After the little sub was considered safe, it didn't take long for a crew to figure out that it could be unbolted and taken apart. Experts started examining the boat. The periscope was a copy of an American model; the torpedoes were better than anything the U.S. had; the strong construction of the sub made it a "superior" craft for its mission; the gyrocompass was patterned after a German model. After a few taps, the compass seemed to work perfectly, apparently correcting the mechanical failure that doomed Sakamaki's mission. The sub was taken apart, put back together, and repaired well enough to look seaworthy. Like a model from a kit, it was put on a pedestal for viewing at Pearl Harbor's Submarine Base; then, not long afterward, some creative genius at the Treasury Department came up with the idea that the little sub could join the likes of Lana Turner and Frank Sinatra in attracting crowds to buy war bonds. By late August, *I-24-A* had been shipped out to the U.S. to make a forty-one-state tour. Someone stenciled on the long, tube-shaped craft: "Tojo Cigars Inc. The Bonds You Buy Will Liquidate This Corporation."

The first days after his capture would forever remain a blur to Sakamaki, but they were not good ones. The first internee camp to hold him grew crowded as "suspicious people" of Japanese origin (now considered a threat to U.S. security and presenting a special problem on Hawaii, where 40 percent of the population was of Japanese descent) filled the makeshift prison. Sakamaki was moved to a hotel, where he was further interrogated by Lieutenant Commander Eddie Layton, the Navy's chief of intelligence at Pearl Harbor. Here directly in front of Layton was proof of the Navy's abject intelligence failure, but Layton couldn't take the prisoner seriously. Sakamaki seemed mentally unhinged. Layton concluded his report: "In accordance with the samurai code, the prisoner requested that he only be allowed to commit suicide."

Mug shots of Sakamaki seemed to reflect his mental state. He was allowed one cigarette a day; but apparently upon learning his picture was to be taken, he used the cigarette to burn triangles on each cheek just below his eyes. In the frontal mug shot, he is grinning like a madman. How deranged he might be concerned his guards. They concluded they would still let Sakamaki smoke, but only while they were watching.

His "Interned Alien Enemy" record notes the burned areas, plus his refusal to identify someone to contact in case of emergency. The person who typed up the form simply put "Refused to disclose. Notify Navy Department Tokyo Japan." The form also included his height and weight, his color ("yellow"), and the color of his hair ("black") and eyes ("brown"). Authorities shipped Sakamaki back to the States, first to San Francisco, then by train through the Rockies, into Minnesota. He arrived on March 9, 1942, at Camp McCoy, Wisconsin. German prisoners of war were also being sent there, so when he entered the camp, there were already about fifty POWs in residence. Sakamaki met some Germans; one he noted in particular who seemed to have a knack for being captured: he had been a POW also in World War I. Like Sakamaki, he was a submarine commander.

Not long afterward, the Japanese and German prisoners were loosely segregated, but the Germans continued to be friendly toward Sakamaki and brought him hot water for his bath. He begged them to stop because he knew his military comrades were suffering in battlefield conditions. From then on, he took cold showers and would not light the coal stove in his room. Though there was snow on the ground he refused to wear clothes heavier than a light cotton shirt and pants. He was told he was being foolish, but he wanted to keep the faith with his fellow sailors and soldiers. This was one way to do it.

Prisoners were allowed to read newspapers, and on April 9,

1942, headlines told of the fall of Bataan, a Japanese victory that caused grave concern in the States. Sakamaki was surprised at the open criticism leveled at the U.S. government and the Allies in the American newspapers. While the victory in the Philippines boosted his spirits, news on April 18 that Doolittle's raiders had bombed Tokyo "was like a stab in my chest." As the days wore on he counted the victories and defeats: Corregidor was his; Coral Sea went to the Americans. A U.S. colonel started to bring a newspaper every day, slipping it through the fence. Sakamaki saluted him and said "Good morning, Colonel." For many weeks, these were the only words he said to anyone. He knew his keepers considered him insane.

As the war in Europe escalated, the Wisconsin camp filled with German prisoners. Some Japanese prisoners, Sakamaki among them, were transferred to Tennessee and Louisiana. Sakamaki would eventually return to Camp McCoy, but by 1944 it had grown dramatically, especially in the number of German soldiers. Across Wisconsin there were more than thirty-five "branch" POW camps, housing more than 22,000 prisoners—19,000 German and about 3,500 Japanese. The area even had a nickname: Stalag Wisconsin.

(The German prisoners were shipped to America for a specific reason. The Allies thought holding them in England might present a threat. There were intelligence reports that Hitler wanted to airdrop weapons into the POW camps with German prisoners; Wisconsin was far enough away to thwart the German plan.)

There was virtually no publicity about this huge prisoner influx, mainly because the U.S. didn't want to alarm people. Actually, few if any people in Wisconsin were concerned; about one-third of the population was of German descent. It was easy for the locals to see a young 20-year-old from Berlin and think he could be the kid from next door. Another reason Wisconsin became a POW stronghold was because of the labor shortage; prisoners were put to work harvesting crops and working in canneries. They picked and processed peas, sweet corn, beets, and tomatoes. Language wasn't a problem because there were always German-speaking Americans in the fields or canning factories. POW workers were paid between ten and twenty cents an hour, which came to about $19 a month. At the start of the war, a private in the U.S. Army earned about $21.

Not all the prisoners cooperated. Some of the hardcore Nazis tried to stir insurrections and bully the other prisoners. They were weeded out and in some cases executed for crimes, but overall the general prison population seemed to adapt well. "Everybody was happy," said former German POW Kurt Pechmann, who was imprisoned in Camp Lodi in Wisconsin. "We were happy to be out of the war, a roof over our head, and all the beer we could drink. There were no problems." In fact, Pechmann and some other prisoners liked it so much they immigrated to Wisconsin after the war. Some used their wages from working in the canneries to finance the trip.

When Sakamaki returned to Camp McCoy, he found the few thousand Japanese more segregated and closely guarded than before he left. Betty Cowley, author of *Stalag Wisconsin*, noted that if a German escaped, it was to beat a path to the nearest town to meet girls and drink beer; if a Japanese prisoner escaped, he felt obligated to find his way to Mexico in order to return to Japan or to commit suicide.

In fact, the entire Japanese portion of the camp seemed on permanent suicide watch. Over the years, the suicidal and depressed Sakamaki met other Japanese war prisoners who also felt ashamed for surviving. Sakamaki found himself counseling the new Japanese POWs and trying to help them cope with their shame. One hard case was Commander Nakamune, chief engineer on an aircraft carrier. His ship was sunk at the Battle of Midway, and he drifted in a lifeboat for more than two weeks before being picked up by an American ship. When he arrived at the camp, he explained to Sakamaki that there was no telling what was in store, but he was prepared to die. "[H]e was always attempting suicide and failing at it," Sakamaki wrote. "He once cut his belly with a razor blade. He jumped from a beam. One day he brought a baseball bat to me and said: 'Ensign Sakamaki, will you hit me with all your might?' He bent down and patted the back of his bald head." Sakamaki refused, but he sympathized. He remembered that in his early days as a prisoner, he had felt the same way.

In trying to help other prisoners, Sakamaki reflected on his own mental state and found, as he wrote, "I was becoming a human being." The flowers, birds, and other animals he had not even noticed on his previous stay at Camp McCoy now became a joy to observe. The brainwashing of the naval academy at last faded. When news came that his midget sub would be on display in Milwaukee, less than a hundred miles away, he didn't feel anxiety. He realized that he and his sub were prisoners, the war was lost, and he and his colleagues had a duty to rebuild their homeland, if they were destined to return home at all.

Sakamaki's little sub fascinated Americans. The sub received a face-lift before it went on tour. It had a new torpedo guard, salvaged from the sub the *Monaghan* rammed, as well as a different propeller, also from the *Mongahan*'s kill; one of *I-24-A*'s original propellers had been bent, either from reef collisions or from being dragged ashore. To make the sub more accessible to the thousands who would see it, portholes were cut in the side so people could look in at the equipment crammed in the small space. Two mannequins, dressed like samurai, stood at the controls. People who bought a war bond or stamp were allowed to peer into the sub that attacked Pearl Harbor. The midget sub was tangible proof of Japan's clear intent to kill Americans.

War bond drives were enormously successful; the promotional campaigns were everywhere, and 60 percent of all Americans bought at least one bond or stamp. The nation's media—from radio and billboards to magazines and newspapers—donated the space or air time to drive home messages like "You Buy 'Em, We'll Fly 'Em." The *I-24-A* was an ad man's dream, the kind of curiosity sure to draw a crowd. The little sub made a grand appearance at Times Square in New York City, but more typical was a trip to

Rochester, New York. On June 8, 1943, the sub arrived to a jam-packed downtown area. The *Rochester Democrat and Chronicle* reported: "Spectators got a big kick out of seeing the sub." Some reactions, according to the newspaper, were: "It's bigger than I thought it would be" or "it looks like a fish." The crowds passed by at about 2,500 people per hour.

The midget sub did its job by attracting 25,000 contributors who bought bonds or stamps. The goal was to raise $500,000, the amount it would take to build a Navy sub chaser, just the type of vessel needed to track down a midget sub. The money-raising drive topped $700,000 in Rochester alone. It seems *I-24-A* performed better for the American fund-raisers than it ever did for the Japanese Navy.

Sakamaki's stay in American POW camps changed him. After the war he was sent back to Japan in a cramped ship; he was one of 12,000 men to be returned from the U.S. to a devastated country. He arrived on January 4, 1946, a little more than four years after being captured. The repatriation staff told Sakamaki that the POWs from the United States "are the best in appearance" and were less likely to be crazy; "others are emotionally rather unstable. Some cry, some sing, others jump around like little children. But they are mostly incoherent."

Sakamaki's parents had survived the war, and he joined them on their farm. The return of POW No. 1 attracted attention, and newspapers reported he was home, the only one of the ten midget sub crew members to survive. People felt compelled to write him, some several times, and many letters were harsh: "No wonder we lost the war, Mr. P.O.W. No. 1. Although I am a mere merchant, I know how to commit hara-kiri . . . . I will gladly come and show you how it is done." Job offers and career suggestions poured in, too. A newspaper tried to persuade him to write for it since, as the recruiter explained, "you lived in the United States and understand democracy. Is it not your duty to interpret it as a newspaper writer?" The U.S. troops occupying Japan found democratizing a land that had been dominated for centuries by feudalism a slow process. However, Sakamaki, whose observations of democracy came from behind a prison fence, respectfully declined the offer to write for the newspaper. One correspondent recommended that Sakamaki find a job in the religious arena and give guidance to a people who seemed lost. He wrote: "You have had a most unique career as a suicide skipper of a submarine. You must have developed an appropriate philosophy of life."

His country, largely ruined, was in chaos. He noted in particular the resentment against the Japanese military who had misled the nation and driven it into such misery. The American forces were gradually accepted, he wrote, and General Douglas MacArthur, Supreme Commander of the Allied Forces in Japan, became "supreme in name and fact." A new noun came into use; if a woman dominated her husband, people used the phrase, "She is a MacArthur."

Sakamaki received an offer from Toyota (spelled Toyoda in those days) to work in its personnel office, a job that enabled him to talk to a wide range of people. He became a keen observer of Japanese attitudes and politics. It was during those first few months on the job that the war-crimes trials of Tojo and twenty-seven other Japanese defendants had gotten underway. It was a wrenching affair for the Japanese nation, Sakamaki wrote, for the Japanese people also felt on trial for their beliefs and actions. The trials took two and a half years (two defendants died during the proceedings). Tojo and six of his colleagues were sentenced to death and executed by hanging. With those deaths, the shaken nation seemed at last to begin to recover, the presence of Japanese uniforms no longer loomed, the past finally started to fade.

There were remnants, however. Sakamaki received a letter from a friend: "I was walking in a street in Kyoto not long ago. I saw a familiar figure. He was bald-headed and was mumbling something unintelligible. People paid no more than passing attention to him. I recognized him as Commander Nakamune."

Sakamaki would adapt to a new world much better than other

prisoners did. He met a young woman whose family was from Hiroshima; her father and brother had died from the bomb dropped there on August 6, 1945; Sakamaki married her on August 15, 1946, the first anniversary of V-J Day. They had a baby, and he and his family transferred to Brazil, where Sakamaki would eventually become the chief executive of Toyota for all of South America.

As with so many veterans, he was not quite done with the war. The fiftieth anniversary of Pearl Harbor in 1991 would revive memories long buried and reunite him with *I-24-A*. After its tour as a war bond attraction ended, Sakamaki's sub landed in Key West at the Truman Annex. It sat there for several years and then was moved to the Key West Naval Museum across the street from Ernest Hemingway's house. In 1980, the USS *Arizona* Memorial at Pearl Harbor, managed by the National Park Service, made an effort to obtain the sub to put it on display. Controversy soon arose over whether a Japanese assault weapon—inept though it had been—should be next to the sunken American ships and the watery graves of those who'd lost their lives during the attack. In the meantime, the *I-24-A* found a new home at the National Museum of the Pacific War and the Admiral Nimitz Foundation in the Chester Nimitz's hometown of Fredericksburg, Texas. The sub was refurbished to look as it had in 1941.

In 1991, Sakamaki was invited to attend a conference in Texas marking the Pearl Harbor anniversary. After many years of trying to remain anonymous, he stepped into the spotlight at last for a reunion with his old craft. A picture shows him looking like an executive, walking with a briefcase around *I-24-A* and inspecting the sub. His reaction is hard to surmise from the picture. A news report noted that upon seeing his boat, Sakamaki wept.

During the conference, Sakamaki reacquainted himself with Americans he'd once briefly met. Steve Weiner, one of the captors who'd put a .45 to Sakamaki's head, attended and described their encounter at Bellows Field fifty years earlier. Other American military veterans praised Sakamaki for his bravery, asked numerous questions, and listened intently to his answers. According to news reports, Sakamaki seemed surprised at the warm reception.

Actually, Sakamaki had made a journey back to his wartime past at least once before. He returned anonymously to Hawaii in the 1950s for a specific reason: he wanted to ensure that his crewmate, Inagaki, had received a proper burial and marker. Showing such respect for his crewmate is easy to understand. However, there also was an unofficial report that remains unresolved to this day. One of the men who found Inagaki floating in the water said that the Japanese submariner had a bullet wound in the back of his head. If that is true, it's likely only one person could have put it there. It was not uncommon in a ritual suicide for the superior officer to execute a crew member before killing himself. Also, while Sakamaki's sword was recovered from *I-24-A*, his pistol was not. With no autopsy report available, what really happened to Inagaki may never be known, but the possibility that Sakamaki shot his crewmate sheds a different light on the utter madness he experienced for so many months after his capture. Perhaps it was caused by a terrible, terrible guilt. No one will ever know for certain. Sakamaki died in 1999.

5

Deadly Distractions and the Battle of Midway

ONE OF THE BEST military questions ever posed about the midget subs came from Commander Mitsuo Fuchida, the pilot who helped plan the air attack on Pearl Harbor. When told how the submarines would be used, he asked, "What possible good could [they] do?" He noted the obvious: if the air attacks succeeded as planned, the subs would be useless; further, he speculated (correctly) that they could accidentally alert the enemy to a surprise attack. Nonetheless, by May 1942, glory continued to fall like a cascade of cherry blossoms on the subs. Crew members, posthumously promoted two ranks (but not the disgraced Sakamaki, of course), were referred to as Hero-Gods. In the Japanese public eye, they had a perfect record; like little arks of the covenant, the subs used their special prowess to vanquish the nation's enemies. At least that is what people seemed to believe. As the legend of the midget subs reached mythical heights, the boats were again slated for a mission.

The next action for the midget submarines would come in Australia and Madagascar, with a cameo role at the Battle of Midway. Japan's battle plan unfolded in a months-long debate among war strategists. The speed of Japan's early military success surprised even its own leaders; as the naval historian Paul Dull wrote, "the victories outpaced the planning." The Japanese Army and Navy spent the late winter and early spring of 1942 arguing over tactics. Japan needed to counter enemy efforts to establish strongholds in the southern and western Pacific, particularly islands in the South Pacific. Like stepping stones, the islands in the South Pacific could provide the Allies with bases leading straight to Japan's sacred home islands. (A U.S. admiral called the island chain Japan's "cojones.") Stopping this buildup would also protect Japan's flank in southern Asia.

Isoroku Yamamoto had a radically different idea in mind. Lieutenant Colonel James Doolittle's air raid on Tokyo in April 1942 unnerved the commander in chief of the Combined Fleet. He wrote that "he had been caught napping just when one was feeling confident and in charge of things." While the raid did almost no damage to the nation's war machine, Yamamoto realized that a smattering of bombs from sixteen B-25s was just a prelude. The air strike was, he wrote in a letter, "just enough of a taste of the real thing" to hint of much more and much worse. Its ingenuity wasn't lost on Yamamoto, either. One of his biographers wrote: "The idea of putting army men and large army bombers on an aircraft carrier . . . [had] never even occurred to anyone . . . at least in Japan." Lumbering off the carrier USS *Hornet* like overfed geese, the B-25s were the only aircraft the Americans had with the range to reach Tokyo. (Even then, the planes couldn't make a round trip; the landings had to take place in China, and of the sixteen planes, fifteen were ditched.) No one realized better than Yamamoto how vulnerable Japan would be once America unleashed its industrial and scientific power, though he couldn't foresee the fire bombs delivered by General Curtis LeMay or the atomic bombs created by J. Robert Oppenheimer. Yamamoto had to press his bet, win or lose, to bring America to its knees. Now. The midget subs would play a role, previously unknown, in Yamamoto's rococo battle plan. Again, it's hard to overemphasize the early success Japan had on land and sea, and the Japanese public perception of invincibility. Allied ships smoldered and sank; General Douglas MacArthur fled the Philippines; Japanese soldiers—as ruthless a conquering army as any in history—captured islands and secured critical natural resources. Even Doolittle's raid became a favorite pun in Tokyo: it was referred to as "do-nothing rather than do-little." Consider that the first wave of midget sub pilots had been required to memorize the layouts of five harbors. After Japan smashed Pearl Harbor, it then conquered "invincible" Singapore and Hong Kong; by March 1942 that left only two on the original list of five: Sydney, Australia, and San Francisco, California. Morale and confidence in the Japanese Navy were so high, its officers came to believe they could do as they pleased—they could deploy forces in the South Pacific and fight on other fronts with little difficulty.

Bordered on the west by Australia's Great Barrier Reef, the Coral Sea became the theater where America changed the thrust of the Pacific War. What would be known as the Battle of the Coral Sea unfolded over two days in May 1942, and on the surface seemed the kind of conflict so typical in war: neither side could claim an outright victory, though Japan seemed to suffer less critical damage. In reality, the battle played an extraordinary role in the outcome of World War II.

Three American ships were lost: an oiler, *Nesho*; a destroyer, *Sims*, and the big loss, the carrier USS *Lexington*. The Japanese showed superb aerial skill in the *Lexington* attack, their planes performing a scissors maneuver (diving in from opposite sides), leaving the carrier vulnerable to torpedoes no matter which way it turned; at least three tore into "Lady Lex." The other carrier at the battle, *Yorktown*, evaded torpedo strikes, but after about a dozen near misses from dive bombers, one bomb dropped through the flight and hangar decks and exploded. Two more bombs soon pounded the *Lexington*. When Japanese pilots flew away that day, they left two ships listing and in flames, thereby seeming to eliminate 50 percent of America's carrier force in the Pacific. Well, not quite. The *Yorktown*'s skilled crew righted the ship and then helped rescue the crew of the *Lexington*. Leaving a wide trail of oil, *Yorktown* limped home to Pearl Harbor for repairs.

Naturally, the Japanese press portrayed all this as a whopping victory for the Imperial Navy. The Emperor extended congratulations, and the Navy's PR machine claimed two carriers *and* two battleships destroyed. But America had the real success. The U.S. Navy could say it had at last sunk a Japanese carrier, even though it was a light carrier, the *Shosho*. The Navy also damaged the heavy carrier *Shokaku* and wiped out dozens of planes and pilots from the carrier *Zuikaku*.

Some positive results of the battle were not immediately apparent. Officers in the Japanese military started having second thoughts. A top admiral at fleet headquarters seemed stunned by the Coral Sea outcome, perplexed that the Japanese Navy "cannot progress as [it] wishes" and "shaken that a dream of great success has been shattered."

One thoroughly triumphant aspect of the Coral Sea battle couldn't be trumpeted at all; far removed from the blue waters of the South Pacific, it took place in a basement called Station Hypo, the top-secret intelligence operation on Oahu.

After missing the warning signs for the Pearl Harbor attack, American intelligence quickly rebounded. Eddie Layton, who'd served as Admiral Kimmel's chief intelligence officer, now worked for Kimmel's replacement, Admiral Chester Nimitz. As it turned out, Layton—the man who before Pearl Harbor was mistaken when he said that the attacking carriers were anchored in homeland waters—would have as clear a preview of the Pacific operation in the spring of 1942 as anyone in history. He not only was privy to the strategies employed by the U.S., but he also read the messages being sent by the Japanese.

American code-breakers could decipher roughly 10 percent of the messages sent by the Japanese Navy in its operational secret code, called JN-25. (There were progressions in the code, too, known as JN-25(a), JN-25(b), and so on.) Cracking the code came at a slow pace—a few phrases at a time. The Japanese Navy used numeric designations for words and then subtracted a set of numbers to encipher the word; at the receiving end, an additive was used; for example, the number for the word "submarine" might be 84978; depending on the day, a code book would designate another five numbers to be subtracted from 84978. For May 3 it might be 43121; the difference between the numbers (no numbers were carried)—41857—would be sent; when the message was received, the additive for May 3—43121—was used and the message would read 84978, or submarine. Typical would be a message (which is actually one sent by the Japanese and decoded at Hypo): *Depart RXZ at 11:00?———arrive 12:30?———Each force commander———.* There were often as many blanks as there were words, and even then guesses were made for dates and times (which were often super-encoded, meaning another additive was used with the original additive); also, destinations, such as RXZ, were often unknown as well.

As Layton pointed out in his book, station Hypo in Hawaii—led by Commander Joseph Rochefort and manned by talented Japanese language experts such as Lieutenant Forrest "Tex" Biard—churned out reams of decoded messages. (The top people at Hypo all had spent time in Japan and learned the language there. Biard noted they were taught "radio" Japanese, meaning a dialect almost all Japanese could understand. This was also the dialect used for military radio transmissions. It is an interesting contrast with the failure of the United States in 2001 to have a large group of Middle East language experts in its intelligence forces when it really needed them.)

While only about 10 percent of the messages could be read, there were 1,000 messages a day, and buried somewhere within them were Japan's war plans. These dozen or so people living in a Hawaiian bunker came to rival in importance those at Los Alamos working on the Manhattan Project. Biard, the last survivor of the group, described his colleagues like teammates on an all-star squad: Layton was a "hot shot . . . fantastic person"; Biard had a desk next to Rochefort, an eccentric genius who could be found wearing a smoking jacket or his pajamas, and was "highly intelligent . . . so often right"; Joe Finnegan, an all-Irish guy and language genius, was considered so important that Biard even wondered if the war would have been lost if Finnegan had been killed when he was on the battleship *Tennessee* on December 7; their boss, Nimitz (they called him "the man with the blue eyes" because of his penetrating stare), was not only smart but courageous enough to tell his superiors in Washington "to go to hell." Some men received more critical assessments: of *Yorktown*'s Admiral Frank Jack Fletcher, Biard said "whatever you heard is not bad enough . . . [he] should have been prosecuted criminally." (Biard believed Fletcher needlessly put British forces in harm's way.) Certain Washington officers, especially the Redman brothers who ruled Navy intelligence there, were prattling bureaucrats.

The negative view of Washington personnel reflected the feud that had evolved between Hypo and the intelligence officials in D.C. It was a classic battle between "field operatives versus power-hungry desk jockeys." Usually the smartest guy in the room, Joe Rochefort dismissed what he considered ill-informed opinions of the Washington code-breakers. He said the analysis coming out of Hypo shouldn't put "any particular stress on their brain"—a roundabout way of saying he thought the Washington intelligence corps was stupid. His colleague, Tom Dyer, told Layton that "If we listen to Washington, we will all end up as Japanese POWs."

Fortunately, the man in charge of the Pacific fleet, Admiral Nimitz, brought an incisive mind to the task and an instinctive understanding about what was important. Layton considered his former boss, Kimmel, a fine commander unfairly blamed for Pearl Harbor, but Nimitz was simply extraordinary in every respect, according to both Biard and Layton. Nimitz also had the savvy to keep Eddie Layton on as his intelligence man despite the lapse at Pearl Harbor. He told Layton that he expected his chief intelligence officer to play the role of "the admiral commanding the Japanese forces and tell us what you're going to do."

Layton did just that. The Battle of the Coral Sea proved so significant for U.S. intelligence because it established Station Hypo's accuracy in predicting enemy ship movements and made radio intelligence a key part of the U.S. Navy's battle plans. Hypo estimated what Japanese ship movements would be with incredible accuracy. In the naval battles of World War II, radio intelligence would make a crucial difference, a fact readily apparent in the Coral Sea: it was the first major naval engagement in history during which the primary ships fighting never saw each other. For Layton and the intelligence crew, Coral Sea was a huge success. They'd solidified Nimitz's confidence, and that would serve them all well for the next battle against Yamamoto.

It's been said that the war plans drawn by Admiral Isoroku Yamamoto reflected the strategies he used in games. He was especially fond of the Japanese board game *shogi*; each player has twenty pieces and tries to capture the opponent's king. While similar to chess, there are differences: pieces that make it across the board gain power (like a king in checkers); captured pieces can be put back on the board by the player who seized them. One particular aspect must have appealed to Yamamoto: with so many ways to attack, there were few tie games.

Yamamoto's *shogi* strategy (at which he was considered an expert) was explained by a young diplomat who played him in Washington in the late 1920s. Yamamoto attacked and immediately "wiped the floor" with the young man, named Hoketsu, who recollected his encounter in a memoir. Observant, Hoketsu noticed that Yamamoto "depended rather too heavily on rush tactics." After a few games, he was beating Yamamoto consistently, and as a result Yamamoto (apparently a sore loser) never again asked him to play.

By mid-May 1942, Yamamoto's American military opponents had experience, too. Even then, Washington still didn't quite buy that there was a massive attack in the works. It seemed more logical for Japan to continue to expand to the south, as its forces had for months. Admiral Ernest J. King, the Navy's commander-in-chief, was "still being wrongly advised by his own intelligence staff that the enemy was going south instead of east," Layton wrote.

Finally Rochefort came up with the proof of what he had suspected all along. (He had help in this from the intelligence unit in Melbourne called Station Belconnen.) There was a buildup of the Japanese Navy, all aimed to attack somewhere in the middle of the Pacific. Nothing was more in the middle than the two islands located almost exactly in that ocean's geographic center—Midway. Rochefort had two direct intercepts indicating that a big operation, called K, was headed toward a target called AF. Rochefort knew AH was Oahu in the Japanese code and AK was a place called French (Frigate) Shoals, which also would become an important site as the days passed. There's a famous story of Rochefort sending a "plain language" message that Midway was having problems with its water distillery; it was supposed to be easily intercepted by the Japanese, and if they passed the info along using AF to designate Midway, it would prove Rochefort's case. More importantly, however, it would convince Washington and shut down the intelligence bureaucrats there who were variously predicting attacks at Fiji, Samoa, the Aleutians, San Francisco, and the Panama Canal. In truth, there was a pretty good reason for Washington's reluctance to accept AF as Midway: in one of the strangest coincidences in intelligence history, the United States also used the designation AF for Midway. Officials in Washington, especially the chief of intelligence, Joseph Redman, simply couldn't believe that the Japanese and the U.S. had chosen the same two letters. When the Japanese, taking the bait, relayed that AF's water supply was limited, Washington dropped its opposition. Layton and Biard both said that Nimitz was convinced weeks before (May 14, to be exact) that Midway was Yamamoto's target. (Nonetheless, Rochefort wisely played politics and had the AF "discovery" sent through the Australian Belconnen station so that Hypo wouldn't be flaunting itself in front of Washington.)

It also helped that one other "A" designation (AK) proved Hypo right again; in hindsight this discovery proved critical in the battle to come. The Japanese wanted to know what ships were at Pearl Harbor and planned to send a reconnaissance flight over the island.

(In March, they'd already sent two planes on a similar mission, and while they were scouting Oahu, they dropped a few bombs for good measure. At least one exploded in the jungle about a mile from cryptologist Tommy Dyer's house.) Through decoding messages, Hypo figured out that AK—French (Frigate) Shoals, an atoll about 550 miles west of Oahu—was where the Japanese reconnaissance plane would meet in May with a submarine to refuel. Nimitz sent two seaplane tenders there to intercept them, and the scheduled flyover of Pearl Harbor never took place. It was the kind of luck the Americans needed.

By late May, Layton had no doubt that Midway was the target. He met with Hollywood movie director John Ford, who was making war films for the Department of Defense and looking to go where the action would be. Layton said he could pretty much guarantee a location that would provide loads of footage. Ford and his crew didn't know where they were headed when they boarded two PBYs and flew west. Ford would be wounded, and the remarkable film his crew shot would become the basis for his Academy Award–winning documentary, *Battle of Midway*. Layton would later be rewarded when he landed a bit part in the Ford movie *Big Jim McLain* (1952), starring John Wayne. Layton also noted that without several breaks going the Americans' way, John Ford could easily have been a POW of the Japanese.

Part of Yamamoto's complex Pacific battle plan would involve deception. Japanese strategists apparently wanted to convince the allies an attack was initially coming in the western Pacific. At last, it seems, someone had come up with the answer to Commander Fuchida's question of what the midget subs were good for: they made a superb diversion.

The little subs' second act debuted in late May 1942. Five big Japanese *I*-boats rendezvoused about 11 miles off the entrance to Australia's Sydney Harbor. A reconnaissance float plane, carried along in an water-tight deck hangar, was launched by *I-29* to survey the harbor and confirm potential targets; it says something about the state of defense around Sydney that people waved at the pilot. On May 30 a plane left at 3:45 A.M. to reconfirm that there indeed were a heavy U.S. cruiser (USS *Chicago*), a destroyer (USS *Perkins*), an Australian cruiser (HMAS *Canberra*), plus half a dozen other ships still there. The reconnaissance plane was again spotted, this time by harbor watchmen; unalarmed, the tower at the local airfield turned on the runway lights. When no one landed, it was written off as a plane from a U.S. ship cruising outside the bay—that is, until somebody pointed out there wasn't a U.S. ship in the area.

Among the five *I*-boats, two as mother subs had previously carried midget craft—*I-22* and *I-24* at Pearl Harbor; they were now joined by *I-27* and its little sub. Sydney Harbor made a perfect strategic target: it was viewed as a safe haven from the Japanese forces, so the attack would strike terror; a bold assault would also send a message the American Navy couldn't ignore: the Japanese Imperial Navy was entering the western Pacific theater, and that was *exactly* what the Japanese wanted the Allies to think.

On the night of May 31, three midget subs set out on their stealth attack. From a navigation standpoint, Sydney presented considerably less of a challenge than Pearl Harbor. The entrance was wide and the bay itself deep—130 feet in places, compared to Pearl's average of about 40 feet. But the midget sub launched from *I-27* soon fell into the kind of bumbling misfortune that seemed to dog the little subs wherever they went. *I-27-A* became entangled in an anti-torpedo net (an obstacle the midget subs didn't have to contend with at Pearl Harbor). A watchman spotted "a suspicious object" and rowed a skiff over to check it out. He surmised that *something* was going on, so he reported it to the patrol boat *Yarroma*. Its skipper thought it might be a mine and sent another skiff over. The man aboard yelled out "submarine," and the *Yarroma* asked headquarters for permission to open fire. Though the midget subs were equipped with extremely sharp net-cutters both fore and aft, they apparently didn't work. With people yelling and boats closing in, the sub crew presumably were aware that they had been detected; from the experience of Sakamaki and his crewmate, it's easy to imagine the degree of panic and frustration the two men aboard *I-27-A* must have felt. They'd been struggling in the net for at least an hour. Then, at about 10:00 P.M., the midget sub set off its scuttling charge and blew itself up. While it didn't damage the enemy, the suicidal explosion at least served another purpose. It drew attention and allowed the two other subs to slip into the harbor to attack.

The midget sub from *I-24* surfaced about 500 yards from the USS *Chicago*. As soon as it was spotted, the little sub provoked a response much like the ones from the *Curtiss* and *Monaghan* off Pearl City—shells started flying and, since it was night, the pom-pom tracer fire from the *Chicago* lit up the harbor. A few minutes later HMAS *Geelong* joined in, shooting, and missing. The sub slipped away without being hit, then 20 minutes later fired at the *Chicago*. The first torpedo veered off course and stuck in a mud bank without exploding. The second missed the *Chicago*, too, but did do damage. It hit the wall where HMAS *Kuttabul* was docked and blew off its stern. The ship (a converted ferry boat) quickly sank, and twenty-one sailors were killed. Midget sub *I-24-A* managed to escape, at least temporarily.

So much is known about the movements of the little subs because of eight electronic cables (called loops) buried in the bed of Sydney Harbor. When a ship passed over a cable, it made a "signature," which was recorded on a sheet of paper; the blips of the ships coming and going look like jags made on a lie detector test. It's believed that *I-24-A* escaped the harbor (there's a blip indicating a ship passed at 1:58 A.M.), but it never made it back to its mother sub. No further trace has ever been found.

With a history of being detected and destroyed, it's no surprise what happened to the third sub (*I-22-A*), which had a special crew member on board. The spy, Lieutenant Keiu Matsuo, listed as a doctor on the manifest of the *Taiyo Maru*, which visited Hawaii a month before the Pearl Harbor attack, finally landed the mission he desired. He'd been on *I-22* on December 7, but his expertise in deploying the midget subs was considered so valuable he wasn't allowed to join the battle. Now he had his chance, undoubtedly because the number of trained midget sub crews was dwindling at a pretty rapid rate—so far, no one had ever returned from a mission. Matsuo's sub was detected in the harbor before midnight, depth charged, and disappeared from sight. Then early in the morning, around 5:00 A.M., spotlights caught the sub and round after round of depth charges were dropped from three ships. Oil smeared the water. On the following day, a diver found the sub on the bottom, its propeller still slowly turning. As seemed to be the midget sub's fate, it soon attracted press attention.

A CBS radio reporter stationed in Sydney broadcast the story of the sub as it was being salvaged. The aft end had been damaged by depth charges, and the torpedoes in the bow had been crushed by the explosions. Two scuttling charges were still intact, and the sub had to be carefully lifted out of the water. The reporter, William J. Dunn, told his audience, "The question of whether the probable two-man crew is still aboard is not yet answered. Naval officers who inspected the craft briefly through the open hatches reported the first object they were able to identify through the mud was a neatly folded umbrella!" It actually was a samurai sword. The bodies of Matsuo and Petty Officer Masao Tsuzuku also were found on board. They had committed ritual suicide. Each had a gunshot wound to the head.

At almost the same time in the western Indian Ocean, more action for the midget subs was underway, this time on the northern tip of the island of Madagascar. Though it's not known for certain whether the Madagascar attack and the Australian one were coordinated, they both registered as part of the same tactical plan with Allied intelligence keeping tabs on Japanese movement. The harbor of Diégo Suarez, a key shipping location, had been controlled by the French. Under the Vichy government, some French foreign posts sided with Berlin and some didn't. Diégo Suarez, manned mainly by natives, fell in with the Vichy puppets. The British had no intention of letting either Germany or Japan control a key port in the empire's strategic shipping lane south of the Suez Canal. Thus began a kind of Gilbert and Sullivan drama, complete with midget subs. Unlike an operetta, there would be real casualties.

The British sent forces into northern Madagascar on May 5. Commandos from the No. 5 commando unit landed that morning, seized two artillery batteries, and captured 300 prisoners with virtually no resistance. Then the commandos and the Royal Welsh Fusiliers marched across the island and ran into a French officer driving his car. He was sent back to headquarters with the British demand for surrender. That gentlemanly offer backfired. With the element of surprise removed, the French forces dug in; what looked like a quick campaign turned into a siege that would last for several days. On the far side of the harbor, advancing British troops captured the town and freed British prisoners, including a very lucky British spy named Myers who was scheduled to be executed the next morning. Near the mouth of the harbor, a battery with 12-inch guns refused to surrender—that is, until a commander of the Welsh Fusiliers drove up to the battery, taking along a man with a bugle, a white flag, and two bottles of gin. He came back with the French battery's commanding officer and the siege was over.

All the while, the Japanese subs lay waiting in the wings, about 10 miles off Diégo Suarez. On the evening of May 29, *I-10* catapulted a float plane into the sky to survey the harbor; ten ships were anchored there. A harbor so rich with targets prompted the obvious order: send in the midget submarines. *I-16, I-18,* and *I-20* prepared to launch their papooses. If the midget subs were ever to have a real success, this could be their night. Ships enter Diégo Suarez through a narrow channel less than a mile wide. Inside, however, the harbor, shaped like a clover leaf, is deep and wide. Subs could sneak in and maneuver without being discovered. Then, at the right moment, they could fire away with at least some chance of escape. The night of May 30 the midget subs carried by *I-16* and *I-20* headed out without a hitch on their mission.

The little sub strapped on *I-18* suffered engine trouble and never left the staging area.

By 8:25 P.M., *I-20-A* had pierced the harbor entrance and fired a torpedo. According to one British account, it was "sometime after dinner" that the battleship HMS *Ramillies* took the hit and started listing badly before making it to shore. This old 30,000-ton vessel, which had served in World War I, had been dispatched to "guard" the Indian Ocean, ample evidence of how depleted the British fleet had become after more than two and a half years of war. The torpedo attack alerted the three British corvettes, also at anchor; they began dropping depth charges, but in a big harbor at night, they had no luck. *I-20-A* had fired and escaped. An hour later the little sub fired again. It hit the *British Loyalty*, a 7,000-ton tanker, and sank it on the spot. From that point on, *I-20-A* was never seen again. It didn't return to rendezvous with its mother ship.

Whether *I-16-A* ever entered the harbor remains unknown. Based on very sketchy reports, it either developed mechanical problems or ran aground on a reef, both believable scenarios since previous midget sub missions had suffered the same fate. All that's known for certain is that it, too, did not return to its mother ship.

However, there were reports that a few days after May 30, two Japanese men came ashore armed with swords and pistols and attacked a British shore garrison equipped with a machine gun. Two men assaulting what amounted to a fort sounds insane, but perhaps it's not such an exaggeration in light of Kazuo Sakamaki's desperate plan to jump onto the deck of the USS *Pennsylvania* and fight it out with the U.S. Navy. Reports that have survived indicate that the two Japanese men were told to surrender. This they would not do. They were shot dead and buried on a hill in Madagascar.

Out at sea, *I-18* still had its midget sub, but after more than a week, it apparently could not be repaired, and it was dumped in the Indian Ocean. To this point, the summary of midget sub action couldn't be considered very positive. Of the group of twenty-two men sent on midget sub missions, only the two *I-18-A* crewmen (who never left their ship) and Sakamaki had survived. With *I-18-A* discarded, what might be called the first wave of midget sub attacks ended. *I-18* moved on to harass ships at the mouth of the Suez Canal.

By the time reports came in from Australia and the western Indian Ocean of the midget sub attacks, no one was buying that some massive Japanese operation was in the works there. As Layton wrote, the Hypo team wasn't "fooled by their elaborate efforts to divert our attention . . . [to persuade us] that Japan might be preparing to invade Australia." At this point, Hypo "knew too much about Yamamoto's operation to be taken in . . . ."

From May 31 on, almost everything went wrong for the Japanese. In retrospect, it's difficult to understand why Yamamoto laid out such an elaborate plan and, as events would unfold, divided his forces, breaking the basic rule navy commanders everywhere knew: concentrate your fire power for a major battle. While Yamamoto often showed he was an analytical and clear thinker, the battle plan for Midway has so much flourish, it amounts to the military equivalent of grandstanding. (Biard, who lived in Japan for two years just before the war, believed an officer on Yamamoto's staff was the impetus behind the overly complicated strategy.) Yamamoto had at first faked west with the midget subs; the next deception came by launching a substantial force far, far north aimed at the Aleutian Islands; at the same time the bulk of his navy steamed toward Midway. Of course, if he had won, the Americans would have been unnerved even further by his genius, which presumably is exactly what he wished.

The Battle of Midway has been called the most important event of World War II, even more important than D-Day, according to some. There's a big "if" factor at play in that estimate. *If* the United States had lost its three carriers at Midway, there would have been nothing much to stop the Japanese from heading east with their carriers and troops and launching an attack on Hawaii, which they viewed as rightfully theirs in the first place. Would Yamamoto, inspired by his fabulous victory in Hawaii, have gone on to attack America's West Coast? There were some early signs this could have happened. The midget subs' pilots knew their way around San Francisco Bay. Washington intelligence at one point believed the West Coast was the primary target for the coming Japanese assault, and there were scattered instances of Japanese shots fired on the West Coast. (Rochefort and his colleagues laughed at the notion of a full-scale assault; they knew Yamamoto didn't have the tactical support to make such a leap.)

No one will know whether California would have fallen to Japan, largely because Eddie Layton might as well have been on board the Japanese ships attacking Midway, with a force that included at least six midget subs. American intelligence knew precisely what the Japanese were planning; they were coming in from two angles. Their occupation force transporting 5,000 Japanese Army and Navy personnel to assault the island was moving in from the southwest; in this force were two seaplane tenders, one carrying midget submarines. A four-carrier armada was attacking from the northwest. Yamamoto himself stayed on the western edge of the theater in his battleship *Yamato*, escorted by ships and a carrier ready to come in and mop up after the American defense crumbled, as it seemed it must. Midway consists of two small atolls, one (Eastern Island) only 328 acres; the other (Sand Island) 850 acres. The American force there numbered only a few hundred troops and a few dozen airplanes. The Imperial Navy seemed to have overwhelming superiority.

Unknown to the Japanese, however, three American carriers had rendezvoused at a longitude-latitude position they'd designated as Point Luck. Japan's Navy was clueless about these carriers, not only about their location but also about their number. Shored up by timbers, *Yorktown* had been repaired in a time that seemed impossible; the welding crews at Pearl Harbor had worked nonstop and used so much electricity the drain caused a brownout on Oahu. For the *Yorktown* to go to war, three months' work was done in three days.

On the morning of June 4, the Japanese carrier force had closed to within about 200 miles of Midway. American PBY scout planes were on the lookout for Japan's striking force. At 5:45 A.M., Lieutenant Howard Ady spotted the Japanese ships and sent a two-word message: "ENEMY CARRIERS." He quickly ducked into some clouds to avoid two pursuing Japanese fighter planes and then finished the message: "PLANE REPORTS TWO CARRIERS, TWO BATTLESHIPS, BEARING 320 DEGREES, DISTANT 180 MILES. COURSE 135 DEGREES, SPEED 25 KNOTS." When the message was received both by the American carrier fleet and at Pearl Harbor, Nimitz reminded Layton of his estimate of where the carriers would be; in an ocean that covers about half the earth, Layton was off by 5 miles.

The American carriers, closing in on their targets, remained undiscovered by the Japanese until about 8:00 A.M. Rochefort's crew picked up a message from a Japanese scout plane reporting that it had seen ten surface ships, but it did not signal that a carrier was among the group. Then a few minutes later, "Enemy is accompanied by what appears to be a carrier bringing up the rear"—the resurrected *Yorktown*.

Leading Japan's four-carrier force was Vice Admiral Chuichi Nagumo himself, the initial victor of the Pearl Harbor attack. For the first time, he found himself in a serious pinch. He'd already sent most of his planes to bomb Midway. Now if he wanted to attack the *Yorktown*, he had either to wait for his planes to return from their run, then arm them with torpedoes and bombs for a carrier attack, or send out the remaining planes he had, which was far less than the full force needed. Either choice was a loser.

Worse awaited. Nagumo couldn't anticipate an attack from two other American carriers, which had now drawn close to his position because he believed the *Hornet* and the *Enterprise* were 1,000 miles away in the South Pacific; in fact, they were 175 miles to his east and on the verge of launching 155 planes. As the U.S. carrier aircraft took off, planes from Midway arrived to unleash their bombs on the Japanese carriers. The unskilled attack scored no hits, but it still caused confusion, further aided by the submarine USS *Nautilus*, which fired torpedoes and also missed.

The seemingly futile air attack launched from Midway was followed by another courageous but ineffective wave from the *Hornet*'s torpedo bombers, the *Enterprise*'s Devastators, and more torpedo bombers from the *Yorktown*. Total hits on the Japanese force: zero. Most of the pilots didn't make it back. The planes destroyed and airmen lost were a sacrifice of immeasurable importance—the attacks distracted and flustered the Japanese, leaving them unprepared when the *Enterprise*'s Dauntless dive bombers at long last took the Pacific War full bore to the Imperial Japanese Navy. Onboard the *Akagi*, Commander Fuchida, the man who led his fellow pilots in the attack on Pearl Harbor (and who asked the pertinent question about the worth of the midget submarines), ran for cover from what he called "hell divers." Bombs tore holes in the *Akagi*'s flight deck and soon the Japanese bombs and torpedoes set to be loaded on planes started a chain reaction of explosions. The *Kaga* fell next to the American air assault, then the *Yorktown*'s bombers zeroed in on the *Soryu*, which quickly was engulfed in flames. The *Nautilus* finished the job with two torpedoes to the carrier.

Nagumo, the hero of Pearl Harbor, took his flag to a cruiser and ordered his forces to retreat. Like everyone else in the Japanese Navy, Yamamoto was shocked at Nagumo's fleeing the battle scene and leaving three carriers burning in the middle of Japan's ocean. Now the last carrier in the area, the *Hiryu*, stood alone. Yamamoto's fleet could provide no help; it was more than 700 miles away.

The Japanese did inflict some damage. Their pilots managed to locate the *Yorktown*, set the ship on fire and thus prevented the carrier's Dauntless planes from returning. The planes found a new home on the *Enterprise*; after landing on the carrier's deck, they quickly rearmed and refueled; then, with the taste of one carrier kill still fresh, the *Yorktown*'s planes tracked down the carrier *Hiryu* and soon made it into a pyre. *Hiryu*'s captain, Yamaguchi, refused to be rescued and went down with the ship. The ships that could have ensured a Japanese victory at Midway were scattered all over the Pacific. The Japanese had 145 warships on the attack that day versus a U.S. surface fleet of 35. Many were far, far away on Yamamoto's strange strategic errand. The force attacking the Aleutian Islands was meant as a distraction from Midway, but if all went according to plan, that force would later close in on American ships when they recklessly sailed out to avenge the Midway attack. The Aleutian fleet would join forces with Nagumo, and together they would overwhelm the American Pacific Navy. By this point, however, the fleet under Nagumo's command was either at the bottom of the Pacific or on fire.

The Japanese Aleutian attack force comprised a considerable armada of 20 warships. Even today it remains unclear how well American intelligence had assessed the possibility of an Aleutian assault. Layton wrote that Hypo did not know from radio intercepts the details of the mission. "We didn't have any intelligence," he reported. At one point, however, Washington's continually changing analysis predicted that the full thrust of the Japanese Navy would be on the Aleutians, the string of islands once part of the land bridge connecting Asia and North America.

Even as a distraction, the Aleutian attack remains something of a mystery. First, the military value of the Aleutians seemed questionable. Yes, the location made it a *possible* point from which to launch an attack on Japan, but it was a secondary strategic spot at best. (One further aspect of the Japanese plan was that after the projected success at Midway, the Aleutian base would give Japan mid-Pacific and North Pacific strongholds to fend off attacks from the east, though the two points are 1,000 miles apart.) The second unusual part of the attack was that it seemed to ignore the single most amazing aspect about the islands: the Aleutians probably have the worst weather in the world. In spring and summer, it is cold, foggy, and subject to squalls. In winter, it's worse.

Dutch Harbor, on the Aleutian chain's Unalaska Island, was slated for the first Japanese strike. The "hot" targets there were the local airfield, an oil tank farm, and a radio station. Near Fort Mears, a simple army barracks, a few ships were anchored, including a beached hospital ship, a destroyer, a submarine, a Coast Guard cutter, and two army transports. Two waves of Japanese planes were sent to attack on June 4. The first from the carrier *Junyo* ran into dense fog and couldn't find the target. Nine attack planes from the carrier *Ryujo* suddenly broke through the fog and by luck found the harbor. They'd been detected by radar and faced anti-aircraft fire, but the general quarters alert wasn't early enough for the ships to escape from the harbor. The air attack set the tank farm on fire and damaged the hospital ship and Fort Mears. The Japanese planes also spotted two subs and five destroyers at nearby Makusin Bay and radioed back the information. A new strike force of forty-five planes was sent to attack, but since the fog in the Aleutians never really lifts, they had to return to their carriers without ever seeing an American vessel.

On June 5 Yamamoto ordered another run, this time at Adak Island, west of Dutch Harbor. Bad weather aborted that mission, so planes were sent over Dutch Harbor again. They re-bombed their old targets, and altogether thirty-two American lives were lost. As part of the campaign the Japanese actually landed forces on two islands more than 1,000 miles west of Dutch Harbor. For their trouble they disturbed numerous seals and some polar bears and captured an abandoned U.S. Navy weather station.

As the Aleutian operation wound down, Yamamoto knew his Midway strategy had failed. He made one more try as he steamed east and looked for a fight. With his forces headed toward Midway, Yamamoto wanted to sucker the American ships into a night engagement if he could lure them into "chasing the stern" of the retreating Japanese fleet. Admiral Spruance didn't budge. At last Yamamoto sent the signal that afternoon "Midway Operation Cancelled." He'd heeded his own advice: "In battle as in *shogi*, it is the fool who lets himself be led into a reckless move through desperation."

The Japanese would have the small satisfaction of delivering the last blow, though it would not change the outcome of the battle. A submarine hit the already smoldering *Yorktown*, and the ship, without any power to run its pumps, slowly sank in 17,000 feet of water. The importance of its presence at Midway could hardly be overstated: it came out of nowhere to surprise the Japanese, and its planes helped sink two carriers.

The *Yorktown* would be found in 2001 by Bob Ballard. Ballard discovered the ship, listing to starboard, settled in mud on the ocean floor. No evidence showed whether there had been any crew members trapped on board. Ballard's ATV (advanced tethered vehicle) camera peeked around inside the ship and entered the below-decks room that served as an auditorium. On the wall in that room, Ballard and crew could see the amazingly well-preserved mural on the wall that, as he wrote, "depicted all of the voyages of the *Yorktown*"—except, of course, its last one.

The news of the *Yorktown*'s sinking saddened the Navy men who loved her, including Layton. On that Sunday morning of June 7, he also learned that the Japanese had landed on American territory in the Aleutians and captured two islands. The "victory" there hardly equaled the loss of four carriers, one cruiser, 2,500 men, and 322 aircraft. The U.S. loss: 347 lives, *Yorktown*, a destroyer, and 147 aircraft. Admiral King would put the American victory in perspective: "The Battle of Midway was the first decisive defeat suffered by the Japanese Navy in 350 years."

How the battle was played by the Japanese press at home was predictable. Headlines screamed about the assault on the Aleutians and how these American bases were now in Japanese hands. The press also reported false results at Midway: two U.S. carriers sunk, one Japanese carrier sunk and one damaged. The men who survived Midway were sent to bases away from populated areas and confined there. Others were shipped off to the South Pacific without even being given the chance to see their families for fear they would report the truth.

Yamamoto especially hated the misleading reports and the propaganda that rang so hollow. His plan had failed and his nation now had only defensive options. The war had turned, and so had the role of the little subs, which never saw action at Midway; the force they were part of never reached the islands.

It actually was worse than Yamamoto had guessed; the Aleutian feint was a mistake with lasting and devastating consequences and undermined one of Yamamoto's own outstanding achievements. Yamamoto had been a key proponent of the Japanese Zero, the premier airplane. One was hit in the oil feeder line and couldn't return to its carrier. The pilot, a 19-year-old, guided the Zero (No. 4593) toward Akutan Island, where a submarine was supposed to be waiting if Japanese airmen needed rescuing. When the plane landed on the island, it flipped over, and the pilot was trapped. The wingman escaped, and like all Zero crew members, he knew he was supposed to scuttle and destroy the plane to keep the technology secret; he fled without destroying his Zero because he feared the pilot was still alive. The 19-year-old pilot died, however, and the plane—still very much intact—was discovered by American forces in July 1942. It was sent directly to the Grumman aircraft factory in San Diego. Kept under guard, the plane was fully repaired and taken for numerous test flights. It became a key source of information for engineers trying to design an American plane that would outperform the Zero, considered at that point one of the elite fighter planes in the world. It had been manufactured by Mitsubishi and Nakajima; the final Grumman design produced the Hellcat, which became the deadliest airplane in the American arsenal. Of the roughly 6,500 carrier-based enemy aircraft shot down during the war, an amazing 4,947 were Hellcat victims.

When the midget sub special attack force was first formed, it was designated a suicide squad. Yamamoto refused to accept this waste of life and equipment. From Midway on, however, the lives of midget sub crews and other submersible pilots became far less precious. The manufacture of the subs continued at a fast pace— hundreds were being produced—and their desperate role would come to reflect the defensive posture of the Japanese and the increasing anxiety of a nation facing an enemy that, as Yamamoto had feared, was rising to the challenge. In the United States, the initial reaction to the Pearl Harbor attack veered between displays of resolve that eventually would carry the nation to victory and outright panic over Japan's military prowess. A good indicator of the determination of the United States, as historian Stephen Ambrose noted, came the day after Pearl Harbor. The American military had more enlistments on December 8, 1941, than on any day in its history.

6

The Assassination

THE LOSS AT MIDWAY shocked the Japanese Navy and eliminated any sort of "quick strike" strategy it might have employed to bring the United States to its knees. Yamamoto would not be anchoring his flagship off Oahu or presiding over a stockade full of American Navy officers or (as he once wrote) marching down Pennsylvania Avenue to the White House. The battles to come would all be fought in Japan's backyard. Still, despite the losses at Midway in June 1942, Yamamoto's Navy—a massive fleet especially skilled at night fighting—ruled its side of the Pacific. The Japanese Army, which had easily overrun Southeast Asia and the islands of the Pacific, stood poised for battle against an American army it believed would literally start crying at the first sight of blood; Japanese commanders felt so confident they showed their troops Laurel and Hardy movies rather than prepare for island combat that lied ahead. Fully expecting to win, the Japanese suffered a shattering defeat on the island of Guadalcanal; it reverberated through the military chain of command. With the loss, Japan's leaders belatedly learned they were in for a fight—exactly as Yamamoto had predicted before December 7, 1941. He repeatedly told top government officials he could hold off the Allies for twelve months, perhaps eighteen. After that, not even the emperor, the Son of Heaven, was safe from the wrath of an angry America.

The long, hard-fought Japanese retreat from Guadalcanal was completed fourteen months after the Pearl Harbor attack; the loss of that one island carried significance beyond its strategic location. Vice Admiral Robert L. Ghormley, who was the U.S. Navy's South Pacific Area commander in mid-1942, wrote that Guadalcanal was ". . . not only a base of major value of the nation holding it, [it's the] first foot of ground taken from an enemy who has had some cause to consider his armies invincible. . . ."

Stunned, Japan's war council fell back to a tactic dating back centuries in the country's military playbook and far removed from any "sudden victory" Yamamoto had in mind. In an about-face, military officials told the world they would now march ahead with "a One Hundred Years' War," or basically a war of attrition; they almost sounded excited about it. The ever-expanding Greater East Asian Co-Prosperity Sphere, in which Japan crushed and ruled countries, had popped.

Guadalcanal was the first significant American land action in World War II. Here U.S. military men proved they were the toughest fighters in the world, a shock to the Japanese, who believed that the weak-kneed American troops would start "bawling" and run away. In addition to men on the ground, American aces like Captain Joe Foss came to own the skies, with upgraded aircraft and well-trained pilots out-gunning the dwindling Japanese air force; the sea battles were slugfests, as America began to flex its shipbuilding muscle and the Japanese tried gamely to respond (including an expanded role for their revered midget subs).

The conflict unfolded over the front pages at home, and news reports left no doubt about, as the *New York Herald-Tribune* thundered, "the magnitude of the stakes." This was a fanatical foreign enemy already guilty of slaughtering Chinese, torturing prisoners, and launching a sneak attack on unsuspecting Americans. Any positive news early in the Pacific War boosted the spirits of a nervous nation. Richard Tregaskis's *Guadalcanal Diary* was a Book-of-the-Month Club selection in November 1942 (a remarkable pick in light of the decisive Guadalcanal battles still to come during December and January). Novelist James Jones, who fought at Guadalcanal as a mud-slogging soldier, wrote that on this island, a generation proved itself. Pilot Foss's "Flying Circus" became a legend: nine Marine pilots earned the Congressional Medal of Honor at Guadalcanal; overall, eighteen men were awarded this top medal of the nation for their bravery on this single battleground. (Only one other U.S. Pacific battle topped that number; Iwo Jima had twenty-seven winners, almost half of them awarded posthumously.) To those who fought, the public glory was always tempered by the memory of the thousands of comrades who died—as every veteran acknowledges, "the real heroes"—and, of course, the fear. Foss admitted that at times he shook uncontrollably when the Japanese shelled the island. Jones, who wrote *The Thin Red Line* about his combat experience there, later said, "I was scared shitless just about all the time."

One other outcome was not so immediately apparent, but it had a profound effect on the war. If Guadalcanal had not been lost by the Japanese, the Americans likely could not have pulled off the complicated and intricately timed assassination of Yamamoto. The airfield on Guadalcanal became the launching pad for the men sent on this special op; considering the distance they had to cover, the planes available, and the alterations the aircraft needed for the mission, Guadalcanal's airstrip was the one feasible place from which to start. The events from there—amazingly—went according to script and ended with Yamamoto's death on April 18, 1943.

It's probably a stretch to say that with Yamamoto dead, Japan was destined to lose the war. However, Commander Eddie Layton, a key man in pulling the trigger on the assassination plot, put Yamamoto on a very high pedestal: He was irreplaceable. A Japanese military strategist, upon learning of Yamamoto's death, conceded it was "all up for Japan." The Hundred Years' War would last another twenty-eight months.

The largest of the Solomon Islands, Guadalcanal sits about 600 miles south of the Equator on the eastern edge of the Coral Sea. From a distance it looks like a poster for a South Pacific vacation:

"Blue-green mountains, towering into a brilliant tropical sky or crowned with cloud masses, dominate the island. The dark green of jungle growth blends into the softer greens and browns of coconut groves and grassy plains and ridges." So wrote one Marine before actually landing. The island's highest peaks loom like sentinels as part of the Pacific Ring of Fire, an unpredictable chain of volcanoes that spew boiling lava and hot gas. Guadalcanal has two seasons: rainy and rainier. The impenetrable jungle harbors malaria-carrying mosquitoes and waist-deep quagmires of mud. Draped in liana vines, mahogany and banyan trees form a canopy that blocks out sunlight. Even the softer-looking grassy plains and ridges on closer inspection are covered in tall kunai grass that cuts like a knife blade. In three words: Hot. Muddy. Miserable.

The first Western explorer to discover the archipelago, the Spaniard Don Alvaro de Mendaña, found surface gold on Guadalcanal in 1568 and claimed he'd uncovered the mines of King Solomon. He christened the Solomon Islands accordingly, and the name stuck. The islands run roughly parallel to each other for about 600 miles and form an elongated O—like a necklace. In the middle is a channel known as The Slot. It starts in the northwest at Bougainville (named for the French navigator who "rediscovered" the islands in 1767), runs southeast past Santa Isabel, and trails off into a three-island triangle of Savo, Florida, and Guadalcanal. (The small island of Tulagi also falls within the triangle; it would become known as the base where Lieutenant [jg] John F. Kennedy took command of *PT-109*.)

Named for a port in Valencia, Guadalcanal has two major rivers that empty on the north side at a spot called Lunga Point. Among the inhabitants of the island are mynah birds and cockatoos, and native Melanesians. The Melanesians, whose ancestors arrived 5,000 years ago, live in scattered villages. These natives became well-known among soldiers for their frizzy hair, but neighboring tribes had already become legendary for the peculiar practice of chopping up people and eating them. They were headhunters.

Palm tree plantations etched out one of the few marks of civilization. Many were owned by the U.S. corporation Colgate-Palmolive-Peet. (The Peet name was dropped in 1953.) Palm oil—especially when mixed with other oils, such as olive—helps harden soap and keeps it from melting. U.S. Marines would discover that the palm groves had another handy use: the way they were planted, the trees made perfect "pegs" to tie down four corners of a tent.

In 1942, these island names were unfamiliar to most Americans, but the Allied leaders were acutely aware of their military significance. In July of that year, masses of troops and ships proceeded to their Solomon destinations, the eventual targets kept top secret. But even after sailors were told where they were headed, many didn't have a clue where the location might be. As one Navy man said, "[we] naval officers were just plain geographically ignorant . . . ."

To defend Guadalcanal's more than 2,000 square miles, the Japanese deployed thousands of troops and tons of weaponry—including a full complement of midget subs, whose normal surprise role was somewhat changed against the Allied counteroffensive. Imperial Navy commanders saw these islands as the perfect place for the little subs to do their best work. One plan was to use the subs to sneak close to enemy ships and distract them (or even sink them) while the Japanese unloaded men and supplies onto Guadalcanal; the stealthy subs could also ferry goods close to the island, in shallow water if necessary; it seemed a perfect way for the subs to utilize their small size.

The first report to the Allies of the little subs came as ships left New Zealand for the Solomons. In response to a force estimate offered by Vice Admiral Kelly Turner, a rear admiral noted that "we have had persistent reports of growing numbers of submarines in the Rabaul area as well as reports of large and small . . . submarines in the Solomons. I regard the former as a menace at sea and the latter as a great menace after we have arrived, for their small size makes them very difficult to detect . . . . I hope that I shall prove wrong."

As the Allies approached, Yamamoto remained in Kure, Japan— next door to Hiroshima and a long way from Guadalcanal— ensconced on *Yamato*, a ship so luxurious and elaborate it was re-ferred to as "Hotel Yamato." He longed for his single showdown in the Solomons —the "decisive battle" at sea— but what he got in-stead was a drawn-out, six-month fight. During that time a whop-ping fifty Japanese and Allied ships sank around the Solomons, many in a graveyard that became so littered with ships (and dead sailors) it became known as Iron Bottom Sound. Military reality dictated that Japan make a defensive stand on the islands of the South Pacific, for these stepping-stone islands—Japan's now-exposed cojones—led straight to Tokyo. Each Japanese setback made the enemy more of a threat, for the islands served as unsink-able land "carriers" from which to provide air cover and launch air strikes. That offensive power worried Yamamoto—he never quite stopped hearing the echoes of Doolittle's Raiders, and he was pre-scient again. The final blows to Japan would come from two air-craft leaving Tinian Island in the Marianas. They needed to be near Japan to deliver their cargo. One carried an atomic bomb nick-named Fat Man, the other carried one called Little Boy.

The key to Guadalcanal would be a flat stretch of land Japanese engineering crews started work on in July 1942. They'd been build-ing a 2,000-foot runway for almost three weeks but ran for cover when the U.S. Marine 1st Raiders marched in virtually unopposed on August 7, 1942. American engineers found abandoned Japanese construction equipment ready for use: six road rollers, four genera-tors, six trucks, handcarts for moving dirt (plus shovels), and two miniature train engines used to pull dirt-hauling hopper cars. The American crews immediately tackled the task at hand of filling in a 180-foot gap in the center of the runway. By August 12, they had a working airstrip. Using the captured equipment and U.S. trucks that had made the amphibious landing, the men soon extended the strip to 2,600 feet, an they lengthened it again, to 3,778 feet, by

August 18. From a pilot's standpoint it looked a little bumpy. The good spots contained gravel held with wire mats; the rest was matted dirt. The field ran east and west, and crews (using explosives the Japanese also left behind) started blowing away tall trees that blocked the approaches. The first American craft to land was a Catalina, the personal plane of Admiral John S. McCain, flown by his aide, Lieutenant W. S. Simpson. After inspecting the field, the admiral declared it open for business. The island's first medical airlift was underway when Admiral McCain's plane carried out two injured Marines. They called the airstrip Henderson Field (it still is), named for a Marine squadron commander, Major Lofton Henderson, a much-admired pilot who had died at Midway. The surprised Japanese also left behind other odd loot: canned foods, rice paper for writing home, Japanese cigarettes (pretty bad, even by war standards), plus records and a Victrola, even a refrigeration system. The Marines settled in fast. Another satellite runway, Fighter One, soon followed about a mile east of Henderson; it was extended to 4,600 feet of rolled grass.

Around Guadalcanal over the following months, sea battles often occurred in the same vicinity, so they had to be numbered. The First Battle of the Solomon Sea was near the tiny island of Savo and came on the heels of the Japanese retreat from Henderson Field. The Imperial Navy rushed to overcome the ground loss and immediately made the U.S. Navy look inept. The first battle featured poor command decisions by American officers and thoroughly exposed a Navy weakness: when it came to night battles, the Japanese clearly had the edge. One reason is that they had trained for night fighting. Japanese sailors drilled for night battles, check-listing specific duties ("remove all deck flammables"), using flashless powder, and scanning the darkness with refined optical equipment. Also, the fundamental Japanese strategy for night battles called for torpedoes. Next to impossible to see at night, the virtually wakeless Long Lances were far superior to the Mark XVs employed by the American Navy. The Japanese torpedoes carried a

1,000-pound-plus warhead and had a range of more than 12 miles. By the morning of August 8, the American fleet had scattered. Admiral Turner wrote, "We took one hell of a beating. The Japs sank four cruisers, but missed their greatest opportunity during the war to sink a large number of our transports . . . . This was at a time when it would have really hurt because we didn't have 50 big transports in our whole Navy." Inexplicably, Vice Admiral Gunichi Mikawa of the Imperial Navy's task force turned around and headed north to Rabaul. Historians have compared the move to the failure of Vice Admiral Chuichi Nagumo to continue bombing Pearl Harbor. Mikawa's early exit allowed the U.S. naval forces to regroup and transports to keep running. Thus, the Japanese lost their best chance to turn back the Allies.

For round two—the Second Battle of the Solomon Sea—Japan laid out two "modest" goals: recapture Guadalcanal and wipe out the Allies' South Pacific Fleet. The clash came less than two weeks after the first naval encounter, and the Imperial Navy felt confident. The Japanese threw 58 ships and 177 carrier-based airplanes into the effort. The Americans had an equal number of planes but far fewer ships—only 30. Historian Paul Dull described the outcome: "It was a peculiar sort of battle, resembling a match between two overly cautious chess players: one player lost a knight and a pawn, but endangered the other's queen (read carrier); then both players quit the game." There were consequences: by August 25 when the smoke cleared, the Japanese had lost 60 airplanes, and their carrier air force now numbered just 100 aircraft fit for combat.

Meanwhile, Japanese soldiers were starving on the island's southeast end. The Japanese couldn't win the land battle unless they landed more troops and supplies. They'd tested a variety of ways to send in goods and soldiers in anticipation of American blockade maneuvers. One large sub went through supply exercises by fashioning torpedo-shaped plywood boxes loaded with rice and firing them out of its tubes. It didn't work because the pressure needed to discharge the plywood torpedo destroyed the boxes and scattered what was becoming precious foodstuffs on the bottom of Tokyo Bay. The Japanese even disarmed parts of the subs, removing torpedo tubes and guns so more supplies could be loaded aboard. Eventually they turned to smaller, faster craft delivering less but with a better chance of avoiding detection. The night convoys shooting down The Slot became such a regular run they were called the Tokyo Express. Among those making the deliveries were the midget subs.

Imperial Navy reports show that the subs were part of the group in October trying to make a night delivery of troops, howitzers, tractors, ammo, and medical supplies to Guadalcanal. The only known result of the foray was that the howitzers made it ashore. The continuing Japanese efforts to build up their strength on the island set the stage for the Battle at Cape Esperance, which was fought over October 11 and 12, a rare night win for the U.S. Navy. The admiral aboard the Japanese heavy cruiser *Aoba*, which was leading the convoy, was mortally wounded in the first minutes of the conflict. The nine-ship U.S. task force pounded the Japanese ships, sinking a heavy cruiser and a destroyer and damaging three others. Naval historian Samuel Eliot Morison called it "a heartening victory" that delivered "a sound spanking." Dull noted that it was more a missed opportunity to really punish the Japanese. "The battle could be called an American victory," he wrote, but last-minute goofs by the Navy kept it from being "a disastrous defeat for the Japanese." It was, in a way, like the first Solomon battle, when the Japanese sailed away early rather than crushing the Americans; this time the Americans missed their shot.

Yamamoto sensed his chances slipping away and wanted to go much more on the offensive. His ships and aircraft joined the battles throughout the Solomon Sea, but the net gains on Guadalcanal were next to zero because the Japanese Army couldn't stop dithering. Yamamoto had reduced American air power so much that, by mid-October, all but a few of the airplanes at Henderson Field had been destroyed by shelling from the Imperial Navy. A lieutenant colonel addressing the 67th Fighter Squadron at Henderson said, "I want you to pass the word along that the situation is desperate. We don't know whether we'll be able to hold the field or not. There's a Japanese task force of destroyers, cruisers, and troop transports headed this way. We have enough gasoline left for one mission against them. . . . Good luck and goodbye."

On October 16, Yamamoto declared: "I now have confidence that we cannot lose this battle." It was a rare beam of optimism from the man who dismissed sunny predictions. But whatever chance the Japanese had for victory, they blew. It took until October 24 for the Imperial Army to mount a counteroffensive. Soldiers slogged across the island in mud up to their waists, their polished bayonets now rusting. By the time they reached the American defensive perimeter, many were too tired to fight. Poor reconnaissance also hurt them; they thought they were much closer to Henderson Field than they were. Still, in the very early morning of October 25, Yamamoto received the message he'd been hoping for: ". . . captured the airfield . . ." But the news was premature. In a bloody battle, the Japanese had indeed broken through the Marines' line, but they were cut off, and the rest of the American forces held. When the nightmare of a night ended, American planes were still landing and taking off. The Marines counted 1,000 Japanese dead; the stragglers were hunted down and either killed or captured; there was worse to come.

Japanese soldiers made another frontal assault the next night, and again were repelled. Marine Sergeant Mitchell Paige found himself facing waves of Japanese by himself. All in his platoon were killed or wounded, and he moved single-handedly from one machine gun to another to hold his position. When help came, he led the bayonet charge that drove the enemy back from the break in the American line, as his Medal of Honor citation says. Sergeant John Basilone found himself in a similar fix. His position came under heavy fire, and there were only three men left. He repaired one machine gun and kept firing. Then, when they ran low on ammo, he retrieved more through a rain of fire he shouldn't have survived. The line held and the Japanese regiment was annihilated by a handful of brave men; his Medal of Honor citation noted the extraordinary courage. Basilone would later die from mortar fire on the West Coast of Iwo Jima.

By the 26th, the body count showed 90 Americans dead, while the Japanese lost 2,200 men and at least another 500 wounded, though the actual Japanese casualties probably were much higher. With the defeat, the Japanese Army was pinned down in a malaria-infested rain forest, desperately short of supplies, reinforcements, or hope. Those stranded on the island called it "ga-to" or "starvation island." Most of the soldiers were now walking with canes.

Midget subs might have gone on the offensive on November 7 when a torpedo hit the 1,800-ton Navy cargo ship *Majaba*, and destroyers were sent out specifically to find the little attacker. It seems more likely, however, that the sub *I-20*, not a midget sub, fired the torpedo that damaged the ship—which was beached and repaired.

It is certain, however, that one determined little sub attacked on the morning of November 28. The cargo ship *Alchiba* had pulled close to Lunga Point to unload supplies for the troops, whose number was steadily increasing. Five destroyers screened for the ship, a 14,000-ton vessel built in the late 1930s as a civilian freighter and purchased by the Navy in 1941. The little sub eluded the screen, and suddenly a torpedo ripped into the forward section of the *Alchiba*, fire broke out, and the ship listed badly. The *Alchiba* had been hit by midget sub *HA 10*, launched by *I-16*, the mother sub that had also launched small subs at Pearl Harbor and Diégo Suarez. The *Alchiba*'s skipper decided to beach the ship to prevent it from sinking or exploding—its stores of airplane fuel, ammunition, and bombs could have blown at any second. Smoke poured from the ship, and bullets from exploding machine gun ammo zinged around the sailors. Nonetheless, they successfully fought the fires and repair work began. Then, about a week a later, *I-24* set loose another midget sub (*HA 238*), and it torpedoed the beached *Alchiba*. U.S. crewmen actually spotted the sub; after firing, the sub had the usual hiccup that exposed it on the surface. However, the little sub escaped.

Alchiba seemed a total loss, as the Navy announced, but the crew never gave up and the *Alchiba* was sufficiently repaired and later played a role in the invasion of Bougainville.

History records the string of resounding naval clashes: the Solomon Sea battles, the battles at Cape Esperance and Lunga Point. But in between the historic battles, there were small conflicts that added up to massive losses for Japan. The Japanese desperately attempted to supply Guadalcanal, and though partially successful, they consistently missed their quotas. Meanwhile, their soldiers wasted away. Consider what happened over a 20-day period: On December 7, 1942, the first anniversary of the Pearl Harbor attack, the Japanese sent 11 destroyers to the task; they were attacked by 14 bombers and 40 fighters. Two of the destroyers were severely damaged and forced to turn back. The *I*-boats had a better series of runs, but on December 9, *I-3* came to the surface only to find itself sandwiched between two PT boats. *PT-59* fired a torpedo, sinking the sub on the spot. On December 12, destroyers made it to the island, but another PT boat crippled one ship so badly it couldn't be salvaged. Of the 1,200 cases of rations marked for delivery, only 200 made it to shore. By January 1, 1943, the Japanese had lost six destroyers, a sub, and a cruiser in a three-week period. Yamamoto's floating inventory was running low.

Guadalcanal by then had three runways, and that meant more planes poised to strike. Air battles started to even up, and the daytime belonged to the Allies. Joe Foss's Flying Circus bedeviled the Japanese in a way they hadn't previously experienced. One Japanese officer fretted about the waves of airplanes, grousing that "... they just send in more," as though they were Mongol hordes. By early 1943, Foss alone had shot down twenty-six Japanese aircraft (tying Eddie Rickenbacker's World War I record), gaining him hero status even among his peers. As one squadron member described him, "All the balls of any man who ever walked the earth." The Grumman

Wildcats he flew (predecessors of the deadly Hellcats) were still not as maneuverable as the Zero, but they were better armored to protect the pilots, who also were now much better trained. As for the Japanese, their pilot corps had stood like elite samurai at the start of the war, each man hardened by tough training and years of disciplined instruction. But because the process to produce this deadly squad was so selective, their number was limited. As more and more pilots fell victim in battles such as Midway, there weren't enough pilots to send in as replacements. American pilots began to notice. On Guadalcanal, Lieutenant Marion E. Carl of Oregon said simply, "[D]unno why, but we got shot up a lot more [at Midway] than we do here. Maybe the pilots were better than these." It was an understatement. Lieutenant Carl was one of only two pilots from his squadron at Midway to survive the attack of Japanese Zeros. One of the top American aces, this survivor would live to punish Japanese fliers—he become known as "The Zero Man." He nailed more than eighteen Japanese planes during his combat days in the Pacific. Admired widely for his skill—he was described as "a natural pilot"—Carl didn't always come out a winner; he and his colleagues—Foss included—had endless narrow escapes. Carl was once forced to bail out of his Wildcat and found himself heading out to sea on a receding tide. Out of nowhere came some island natives who picked him up in a canoe. Fortunately, they weren't hungry headhunters. He returned to the base five days later and resumed out-gunning Japanese pilots and harrying Japanese supply vessels. (Carl later would set an air-speed record, only to be eclipsed by Chuck Yeager.)

Now on the defensive, the Japanese were reduced to attempting delivery missions only during the darkness of the new moon. The great attacking *shogi* player, Yamamoto, had waited too long, hindered by ineffective Army leadership, inexperienced pilots thrown into battle, and a remarkably resilient enemy. By January the outcome at Guadalcanal was clear, and the Japanese created a clever ruse to evacuate their troops. They pretended to build up forces at Rabaul, located on the northeastern end of New Britain, as though preparing for another big assault. Anticipating the next wave, the Navy paid less attention to the Japanese on Guadalcanal and the transport ships that slipped in. The last Japanese soldier left Guadalcanal in January 1943, but the Marines didn't discover that the enemy had fled until February 7.

After fierce campaigns like Guadalcanal, there are fragments of war scattered everywhere, spent pieces, evidence that tries to tell a story. Sometimes it does. There's a classic photograph of two discarded Japanese craft left behind at Guadalcanal. An abandoned midget sub lies helplessly on its side, beached where it had been pulled ashore by U.S. Navy Seabees; near it is the wrecked Japanese cargo ship *Yamazuki Maru*, shot to pieces, run aground, left behind. They sit, posed like lifeless models, on a Guadalcanal beach. Japan was in retreat.

In 1937, Imperial Navy Vice Minister Isoroku Yamamoto invited a group of American and British naval officers on a duck-hunting weekend on one of the emperor's estates near Tokyo. The Westernized Yamamoto enjoyed socializing with his opposite numbers, and they in turn liked him. Though relaxing, the outing was invested with a military precision. Western officers remembered later that Yamamoto was extremely conscientious about punctuality and ran a split-second schedule of events. Among those in attendance that weekend was Edwin Layton. That recollection would be important in plotting Yamamoto's death.

By 1943, things had changed for the Japanese Navy's brightest light. Unusual pressure came from Tokyo for Yamamoto to become more actively involved with the troops on the front lines. Despite the luxurious accommodations on his flagship, Yamamoto's health started to fail. People noted his pallor and lack of appetite; it's suspected he had beriberi. On April 4, he celebrated his 59th birthday; his closely cropped hair had turned gray during the time he monitored the defeat at Guadalcanal. Nonetheless, he remained extremely well-regarded among his naval colleagues, who constantly turned to him for guidance. Even after Midway and Guadalcanal, there seemed no lack of faith in his leadership in Japanese public opinion. American naval officers also believed Yamamoto a singular figure; Nimitz and Layton agreed there was no one in Japan equal to him; they shared that opinion before Nimitz ordered Yamamoto assassinated.

The mission—called Operation Vengeance—required perfect timing. The first hint that Yamamoto might become a potential target came from an intercept made on the Aleutian Islands by the Dutch Harbor code-breakers. The coded message received immediate attention simply because it was copied to several different Japanese commanders. The code-breakers reasoned that only a message about someone important would be sent to numerous officers. Then they discovered that its code sign was Yamamoto's ship. Interest increased: this was some sort of travel schedule. The IBM punch cards used to decipher messages poured out of printers. The Hypo crew in Hawaii slaved over pinpointing locations, days, and times.

In Washington, Navy translators also worked to unravel the numeric puzzles. It has been reported that the message intercept came to the attention of Secretary of the Navy Frank Knox. This is probably true, but from then on, the accuracy of the subsequent events has been long debated. This is one version: Knox took a look at the decoded message and went to lunch. While he was eating, someone mentioned that individual duels used to be the preferred method of settling a fight—mano a mano. If the United States wanted an individual payback for Pearl Harbor, Yamamoto was a pretty good candidate. The idea brewed in Knox's mind: if Yamamoto was traveling, he could be vulnerable to an attack. Knox supposedly called in two Army aviators for help, plus a pilot with a lot of experience in flying over open water, Charles A. Lindbergh, who measured distances and gauged the amount of fuel necessary to intercept Yamamoto. The Washington involvement in the mission has been disputed on several fronts, including the key point of whether President Roosevelt gave his approval. The president was out of town rallying Americans in the Southwest during those days in April, but no one can prove he didn't receive a message outlining what was up. It is a little easier to believe that Washington officials worked in parallel with officers in the Pacific. Another factor to consider is that Roosevelt demanded that he be kept informed about almost everything. Someone in Washington wouldn't have missed the chance to fill him in on the plot.

But the final decision lay with Nimitz. He had been fighting this Japanese naval genius for more than a year. He knew the order would risk the lives of U.S. aviators and could reveal that the Allies had broken Japan's top-secret code. The question came down to whether the death of Yamamoto would deliver a severe enough blow to make the mission worth it; that answer was easy, and Nimitz sent the execution order to Admiral William F. "Bull" Halsey.

While the Japanese regrouped following Guadalcanal, the Allied forces had grown exponentially stronger. Supplying Japanese-occupied islands to the north of Guadalcanal, using Rabaul as the base, became increasingly difficult; in contrast, Henderson Field now had hundreds of airplanes, and Japanese convoys faced heavy bombing even at night. The ten dark nights surrounding the new moon became an even narrower slot through which to slip.

Often overlooked in the death of Yamamoto are his last concerted efforts to bomb Henderson Field into oblivion. One try came on April 1, 1943. Yamamoto ordered five carriers into the area and unleashed 60 planes to do the job. This seemed like sufficient firepower, but when the dogfights were over that day, the Japanese had lost 18 planes and the Americans six. Henderson Field remained open for business. Afterward, Yamamoto yet again resolved to regain Guadalcanal, but this attempt produced the same kind of poor results. None of Yamamoto's field officers wanted to deliver the bad news to him. Only one U.S. destroyer and four auxiliary ships were sunk during the one-week assault that, besides Guadalcanal, also included Oro Bay, Port Moresby, and Milne Bay. In reality, little had changed, and the aircraft at Henderson were fully operational. The Japanese failure would make this Yamamoto's last command. Had they succeeded in shutting down the airfield, the assassination plot against Yamamoto would have been impossible.

On April 13, Station Hypo decoded the following message:

ON 18 APRIL CINC COMBINED FLEET WILL VISIT RYZ, R——— AND RXP IN ACCORDANCE WITH THE FOLLOWING SCHEDULE:
    DEPART RR AT 0600 IN A MEDIUM ATTACK PLANE ESCORTED BY SIX FIGHTERS. ARRIVE AT RYZ AT 0800. PROCEED BY MINESWEEPRER TO R——- ARRIVING 0840 (——HAVE MINESWEEPER READY AT #1 BASE.) DEPART R AT 0945 IN ABOVE MINESWEEPER AND ARRIVE RXZ AT 1030 . . . .

The first decoders added their note that "this is probably a schedule of inspection by [the commander in chief of the] combined fleet." The unofficial reaction was a whoop from the codebreakers and the declaration by analyst Red Lasswell: "We've hit the jackpot!"

There was only one type of aircraft available to do the hit on Yamamoto. The P-38 had the range to make the flight to RYZ, which was Bougainville, but even it needed a special addition. The planes had to carry 310-gallon supplemental gas tanks, which had to be delivered from New Guinea, then attached at Henderson Field, where the planes were stationed. That tank, along with the regular 165-gallon tank on the fuselage, would supply a round trip of about 970 miles. The cruising speed of the P-38 was around 220 mph, so with the extra time needed to climb, the flight up would take about 2 hours and 30 minutes.

There was some debate whether to ambush Yamamoto's plane out of the air or wait for him to board his launch and then have the planes try to sink it. With so little time to mull over the plan, it quickly became apparent the sea-assault idea had huge flaws. Even if the pilots spotted the right boat, sinking it was always iffy; also, every effort would be made by the Japanese to rescue their combined fleet commander. Shooting down the bomber in mid-air dramatically increased the chances of a successful kill.

There were other wrinkles: The first sight of American planes would likely unleash a bevy of Zeros to protect Yamamoto. It was thought these planes might even be in the air already to greet and escort the admiral. (The Americans had extended their air cover for Navy Secretary Knox's visit just a few weeks earlier.) With this in mind, some of the P-38s would need to gain an altitude of more than 6,000 feet, ready from there to pounce on the Zeros that surely would come to rescue the Yamamoto squadron. That would leave the other P-38s free to do their job.

The group chosen for the Yamamoto special op all had outstanding combat records. The leader, Major John W. Mitchell, thought that even if they missed Yamamoto, the P-38s could inflict major damage on the Zeros drawn into the battle. As for the chances of actually intercepting the right plane, at the right time, from a distance of almost 500 miles, he considered the odds 1,000 to 1. Years later, he said he had reconsidered that estimate; it should have been 1,000,000 to 1.

Altogether there were eighteen planes sent out on the mission. Seventeen took off that day; one plane hit a rock on Fighter Two runway and punctured a tire. As the planes gathered for the below-radar flight, they tested their fuel tanks. The larger tank would be used for the flight up and then would be jettisoned as they neared the target. One plane's tank malfunctioned, so that left sixteen.

The low-altitude flying presented a unique problem. It was easy to lose perspective when out of sight of land and over what seemed an endless sheet of water. Mitchell warned his pilots to stay alert. Still, one dropped close enough to the surface to have his propeller tips hit the water and spray his windshield, a mistake he quickly corrected but which scared him enough to keep him awake for several nights afterward. It was also "hot as hell in the cockpits," recalled Mitchell. "I dozed off a couple of times but I got a light tap on my shoulder from the Man upstairs and caught myself."

Mitchell divided the mission into five "legs," each with its own bearing. The flight path took them west of New Georgia, well outside The Slot. After 55 minutes the squadron turned 25 degrees to a heading of 290; 27 minutes later they moved to 305 for 38 minutes and then turned to a heading of 20 degrees for 40 miles; the last turn was 90 degrees. At that point, Mitchell wagged his wings and the planes joined their attack formation. They were 4 minutes from intercept.

Plenty of people tried to persuade Yamamoto not to take the flight. A fellow officer had followed a similar route in February and run into thirty American fighter planes, but the Japanese pilot flew into the clouds and managed to escape. The incident was passed along to Yamamoto, who simply congratulated the officer for his good fortune in avoiding danger. The most serious (and well-founded) warning came from a rear admiral who fumed about how stupid it was to bandy about a detailed message about the travel plans for the Combined Fleet commander so near enemy positions, where the message could be intercepted. He went to see Yamamoto, who brushed aside the threat. He invited the rear admiral for dinner the night he expected to return.

On April 18, Yamamoto did not wear his usual dress whites. He came out to the airfield in a simplified uniform of new dark dress greens; there's no record that anyone thought the greens might make him less of a target in a combat zone, and on the morning he arrived at the airfield, two other officers were wearing their whites. Yamamoto was a little miffed that the orders about the color of the uniform of the day had not been passed along. It was the sort of inattention to detail he disliked.

He boarded the plane, a Betty bomber in Allied terms, a Type-1 land-based attack plane to the Japanese. Yamamoto's group—two bombers (he was in the lead plane) and six Zero escorts—took off from the east airfield at Rabaul right on time. They reached an altitude of 6,500 feet and after 90 minutes approached Bougainville. A note came back from the captain that they would land on time at 0745. At that moment, one of the Zeros moved ahead, and the pilot pointed down. Below them about a dozen P-38s flew in formation at about 5,000 feet. Their tanks dropped, and the planes broke into two groups.

The Japanese pilot in the second bomber soon saw a red tracer shot go by. He reacted not unlike the young soldier who first saw on radar the Japanese aircraft attacking Pearl Harbor on the morning of December 7, 1941: it couldn't be true, yet something was wrong. He hesitated as he tried to comprehend what was happening, but by then the P-38s were in hot pursuit. The chief officer on board ordered the pilot to stay close to Yamamoto's plane ahead of them.

Two pilots pursued Yamamoto in their P-38s: Tom Lanphier and Rex Barber. As the Zeros attacked, Lanphier drew their fire. Barber, who was Lanphier's wingman, then pursued Yamamoto's plane, which quickly dropped to 1,000 feet. The Betty descended even lower and started to skim the jungle treetops when Barber opened fire from 50 yards. He knocked pieces off the right engine cowling, then ripped through the rudder. With smoke pouring from the engine, the plane banked and crashed. One down, but the Americans weren't sure which plane Yamamoto was on, so they took off after the second Betty. The P-38s caught it over the water and riddled the plane with bullets from 50-caliber machine guns and 20-mm cannons. It crashed in the water. With both bombers down, the American pilots felt exhilaration and a sense of certainty: Yamamoto was dead.

The cable sent at 2:30 P.M. from the Japanese commander-in-chief of the Southeast Fleet reported that Imperial Navy planes "encountered and engaged in combat more than a dozen enemy fighters . . . The No. 1 . . . plane [carrying Yamamoto] was seen to dive at a shallow angle into the jungle. . . ."

Those officers who received the message in Rabaul were all said to be grim-faced and solemn. The search didn't really begin until the next day, when Yamamoto's devoted staff officer, Yasuji Watanabe, flew in a seaplane over the site. He had cut open rubber balls and inserted the message: "This Watanabe. Please wave your handkerchiefs." The balls were dropped, but there was no movement on the ground.

Watanabe formed a search party and headed into the dense forest. Other search parties had entered from a different direction, and a group of soldiers stationed nearby were also ordered out. They pushed into the deepest jungle and started to return to camp at sunset when one of the men smelled gasoline. They rushed toward the clearing ripped open by the plane, spotted the tail, and then saw that the wings and propellers were still intact. The fuselage was burned and dead bodies were scattered around the wreckage. A seat had been thrown clear, and in it was a man sitting as though he were waiting, his head leaning forward.

The squad searching knew only that there were high-ranking officers aboard, not their names. They saw that one man had medals and ribbons on his chest and wore white gloves. His left-hand glove had two of the fingers sewn together, for the person had only three fingers. His hand was still gripping his sword.

Not all the P-38s made it back to Henderson Field. Some of the planes used more fuel than others during the attack, and Major Mitchell received a call on the radio as the squadron returned. "Mitch, I don't think I can make it." Besby Holmes knew he had no chance to return to Guadalcanal. He'd been in the group fighting off Zeros (they believed they'd gotten three) and after attacking the second bomber, he'd double-checked his fuel gauge. He radioed back: "I definitely can't make it back to Henderson. It'll have to be the Russells or ditch." Ditch seemed more likely. The Russell Islands were 1 hour and 40 minutes away, and he had enough fuel for 1 hour and 10 minutes of flight. He lowered his air speed to 170 and headed down The Slot, praying no angry Japanese planes intent on revenge were out on patrol. At last, with his fuel gauge on empty, he saw the Russells. He asked his running mate to buzz the field so they'd clear the runway of equipment. The strip was only 1,700 feet long. (Fighter One runway at Henderson was about

3,000 feet longer.) Holmes landed safely. He would refuel and head back to rejoin his squad.

The American assassination mission suffered one loss; Lieutenant Ray K. Hine's plane had been hit by Zeros and crashed into the sea.

Back on Guadalcanal, the word spread fast about Yamamoto's death. To the outside world, however, the American military said nothing. Leaders didn't want to alert the Japanese that the Allies had broken the JN-25 code. The official word sent to Bull Halsey was marked top secret. It read:

POP GOES THE WEASEL. P38S LED BY MAJOR WILLAM J. MITCHELL USAAF VISTED KAHILI AREA ABOUT 0930L SHOT DOWN TWO BOMBERS ESCORTED BY 6 ZEROS IN CLOSE FORMATION . . . . APRIL 18 SEEMS TO BE OUR DAY , , , ,

The mention of April 18 referred to the mission launched exactly one year earlier, when Jimmy Doolittle bombed Tokyo. Halsey had commanded the task force that accompanied the carrier *Hornet*, which carried the Raider's B-25s.

The sword Yamamoto had in his death grip had been a gift from his oldest brother; crafted by a swordsmith named Shibata Amada (the same given name as Yamamoto's father), the weapon was special because it reminded him of both his father and brother. With the sword set aside, Yamamoto's body, along with the other corpses, was covered with banyan leaves. Laid in coffins, he and ten others were cremated. Yamamoto's pyre was separate from the rest. His ashes were gathered by Watanabe and put in a box. From there his remains went to Rabaul and then by ship back to Japan.

The Japanese brass considered the intercept of Yamamoto and the fatal attack a lucky coincidence for the Americans. As one of Yamamoto's fellow officers had declared the day before they left: "How could they possibly break the Japanese code?" The Americans played the deception up by sending planes back the next day to the Bougainville area on no specific mission, pretending they were searching for some more "lucky" targets after the success of the day before.

Gossip and rumors fill the days of servicemen who often have endless hours of waiting or traveling. It passes the time. The stories about Yamamoto spread as soon as the word inevitably came out that he was dead. On the Japanese side, one tale had it that he wasn't dead at all. This probably stemmed from the report that he looked so alive when his body was discovered. Other stories had him crippled but still living, possibly in a coma.

On the American side, the top officers emphasized that the less said the better. That didn't stop reporters from piecing the story together and having it ready to run for publication in May. Halsey was furious, and since the P-38 pilots had to be the source of the report, he balked at giving Air Medals of Honor to the men who'd done the shooting; they eventually received Navy Crosses. Halsey felt that leaks in wartime were unconscionable.

Nevertheless, the leaks continued until there were stories circulating in newspapers. *Time* had a correspondent on Guadalcanal, and the magazine, a long-time chronicler of Yamamoto's career, gave him his last story on May 31, 1943, complete with caricature. It laid out the basic facts, but left out the names of the airmen. In the article, an anonymous serviceman predicted that when the name of the man who shot Yamamoto became known, he'd be a national hero. "The only better news would be a bullet through Hitler."

There was an interesting disinformation attempt, too. The Associated Press reported on June 16, 1943, that the Chinese were speculating that Yamamoto had been killed by members of the Japanese military, reflecting a long-standing feud between the Army and the Navy. This harkens back to the plots to kill Yamamoto when he was a Navy minister. A Chinese military spokesman said there was fresh evidence that Yamamoto had been killed in May and that it could not have been part of an air raid because there was "no [A]llied attack on Manila around that time." Nothing of substance in the Chinese account was even close to correct, so it seems to have been a not-so-clever plant.

Yamamoto's ashes were secretly brought back to the battleship *Musashi* and placed on board. The crew knew something was up. The smell of incense seeped from the cabin where the commander would normally have stayed. A *shogi* board sat by the box lined with leaves meant to cushion the ashes of the beloved admiral. The Japanese nation officially learned of Yamamoto's death on May 21, 1943. The announcement told how he had encountered the enemy on the front lines and died bravely. He had "met a gallant death," according to the report. His ashes were placed on a train bound for Tokyo station. People heard about the special train and lined the tracks. A motorcade carried the ashes to the Navy Club in Shiba; there his box rested on a Buddhist altar. People came to pay their respects, and some brought gifts.

Yamamoto's friends were left to console his family—and his mistress. The family accepted the loss stoically, but the mistress nearly fainted when told the news. Some friends were concerned about the many letters Yamamoto had written not only to his last mistress but to others from years before. There seems to have been an effort to collect the letters to destroy them, but it was half-hearted. One mistress said she was urged to kill herself. The woman blew off that advice, and some of Yamamoto's geishas crashed the memorials held in his honor.

The state funeral came exactly three weeks after the announcement of his death. Chopin's "Funeral March" was played as his ashes were buried next to those of Admiral Togo, the Navy commander who had cited Yamamoto for bravery when he lost his fingers in the Russo-Japanese War. Actually, those were only half his ashes. The rest were taken to his hometown of Nagaoka, in Niigata province, and placed in a grave in the Yamamoto family plot on the grounds of a Zen temple. A small gravestone marks the site. A separate memorial honoring the place where Yamamoto was born contains "half" a statue of him. In December 1943, a full statue of Yamamoto was erected at the air school where he served. It was torn down after Japan's surrender, during MacArthur's reign. The general ordered all military statues toppled, and Yamamoto's had been cut in half and thrown in a lake. The top half of the statue was recovered some years later and taken to Nagaoka. There it sits, resurrected in a small park frequented by kids and parents.

The death of Yamamoto led to the appointment of Admiral Mineichi Koga to the post of commander-in-chief. A conservative, by-the-book strategist, he was chosen over Yamamoto disciples who might have carried on his bolder and more innovative tactics. Though more fiercely fought naval battles awaited, there was definitely a sense of resignation among the Japanese. On hearing of Yamamoto's death, one veteran officer remarked that it was "the beginning of the end." Others even thought beyond defeat. They lamented Yamamoto's death because he—familiar with Western ways—could have been a key figure in Japan's reconstruction after the war.

Isoroku Yamamoto would not, as he had once said, dictate the terms for peace by walking down Pennsylvania Avenue and strolling into the White House to make his demands. That boldness died with him. There was no offensive plan now for Japan. As the war turned, the Japanese retreated to the familiar, the customary. That, of course, was suicide.

The Suicide Squads

THE AMERICAN SPORTS columnist Jim Murray once penned a telling line about the Indianapolis 500 motor race. He wrote that before dropping the flag, the starter should have said over the loudspeaker, "Gentlemen, start your coffins!" In 1944, as Allied forces evicted Japanese troops from one South Pacific stronghold after another, the same could well have been said by Japan's leaders. To the Japanese, suicide missions were an easy sell. Land troops had already been making *bonzai* (hurrah) charges; every soldier knew that the Japanese Code for Fighting Men recommended death for the defeated: "Rather than live and bear the shame of imprisonment, he should die and avoid leaving behind a dishonorable name." The ultimate self-sacrifice was seared into Japanese mentality, as white-hot and fundamental as the belief in the emperor's heavenly heritage. To die in an honorable cause meant a happy time in "Great Japan . . . the land of the Gods," wrote one future suicide. "The land of the [G]ods is eternal and cannot be destroyed . . . we now offer our lives as a sacrifice for our country. Let us get away from the petty affairs of this earthly and mundane life to the land where righteousness reigns supreme and eternal." Onward and upward.

Of course, the midget sub crews initially had their tickets stamped for "the land of the Gods" as part of a Special Underwater Unit—the euphemism for suicide squad—until Yamamoto demanded that a retrieval plan be implemented and the mother subs at least try to rescue the submariners. He wanted his men back to fight another day, though that rarely happened. But even the revered Yamamoto couldn't stop some early voluntary suicides—Japanese pilots whose bombs missed would crash their planes into the targets. (Yamamoto thought this was stupid, especially with the shortage of pilots.)

These sacrifices were named after a historical event all military men knew by heart. In 1274, samurai warriors joined together to fight Kublai Khan, the grandson of Genghis Khan. Khan's 600 ships and 23,000 troops sailed into battle, only to have a typhoon strike the Mongol Fleet and wipe it out. Khan attacked again in 1281, and after weeks of fighting, was hit again by another typhoon. Shinto priests credited the victories to the Gods watching over Japan; they called it the Divine Wind or *kamikaze*.

By 1944, the Japanese needed a new Divine Wind to stop the Allies and decided to fan Fate with something besides prayer—in this case, suicide submersibles and aircraft. The Kaiten (or "heaven shaker," also translated as "the turn toward heaven") became the submerged mini-weapon of choice, and it went to the head of the manufacturer's list. For air attacks, two planes rolled off the lines: the Nakajima Ki-115 (basically a bomb with a plane attached) and its sister, Yokosuka Ohka, also nicknamed the *baka*, or "idiot," plane, an aircraft made specifically to explode on impact.

The initial Kaiten designs began in 1943, and prototype tests, some of which proved fatal, carried over into 1944. The brainchild of Imperial Navy Lieutenant Hiroshi Kuroke and Sub-Lieutenant Sekio Nishina, the Kaiten sprang in part from their frustration. Even with Yamamoto dead, the Imperial Navy still longed for the decisive "dream" battle in which submarines, large and small, would target fleets of American ships before they could rain their shells on Tokyo. Meanwhile, Allied forces gobbled up island after island. The submariners looked desperately for ways to take the battle to the enemy. Certainly the Kaiten seemed suited to do just that. They started with a torpedo, added a cockpit with a little periscope, then juiced the fueling system and motor so it could hit

30 knots and run for 25,000 yards (14 miles). The result: an 8-ton guided, submersible missile with a 3,400-pound warhead (three times the power of a normal torpedo). Its entire mission was to blow the enemy to smithereens; the downside was that the one-man crew was also headed to oblivion, not unlike in the film *Dr. Strangelove,* in which the character played by Slim Pickens straddles his atomic bomb like a bronco and rides to glory from his plane's bomb bay doors.

More than 300 of these weapons were produced. Kaitens mainly were deployed by mother subs, though at least one cruiser was converted to carry them. A big sub could tote six Kaitens; they were strapped on, just like the midget subs. Pilots entered the Kaitens through flexible tubes and had telephones on board to receive the final "go" order. One of the pluses for the Kaiten was that the pilot at the controls could guide the craft and if it missed its target, the torpedo could make a U-turn and take another shot.

The first Kaiten mission was aimed at the U.S. Navy anchorage at Ulithi Atoll in Micronesia, which offered a target-rich environment for the human torpedoes—the Allies had hundreds of ships anchored there. For the initial attack in 1944 the Japanese mustered only two subs and nine Kaitens. The big subs had to sneak fairly close to the harbor entrance to release the Kaitens—they had nowhere near the range of the midget subs. Crudely constructed and prone to leaks and oil fires, the Kaitens fell well short of the high quality of the sturdier midget subs, whose crews could (at least theoretically) make round trips.

On board the big sub, the Kaiten pilots were toasted every night—they might not be around for the next meal. They seemed to accept their doom. Before departing, one of the Kaiten pilots shook the hand of the sub's captain and politely told him, "Thank you for all your help. Give my regards to the boats that follow me." When a Kaiten pilot said *sayonara,* he meant it.

At around 4:30 A.M. on November 20, 1944, five Kaitens were launched, one from submarine *I-36* and four from *I-47*. At 5:45 an explosion hit the USS *Mississinewa,* an oiler. The blast knocked

Seaman John Mair to the floor. He'd moved from the regular crew quarters to sleep near the engine room where there was a better breeze. The move saved his life—most of the men who died were in their usual bunks. Mair threw on his shoes and pants, then climbed to the ship's fantail. He saw that from the bridge forward, the ship was "engulfed in smoke and flame," and oil leaking into the water spread the fire so it surrounded the ship. He looked down at the only open spot—a 20-foot drop to a 15-foot-wide area. He and his buddies jumped in and swam to a boat that was loading men as fast as it could. Fifty men died; more than 80 were wounded.

The USS *Rall* had been patrolling the Ulithi harbor entrance for a few days, and its crew was antsy. They'd been out in convoys before arriving, and the sailors wanted to go ashore on Mog Mog Island. Hardly Honolulu, it was at least solid ground. Relieved of duty on November 19, they never got their break. On the morning of the 20th they saw the *Mississinewa* explode in flames. Dick Graves, a deck officer, thought it might have been the work of a Japanese bomber that had sneaked in; then the word spread that midget subs had launched the attack. Soon afterward the ship had a Kaiten alongside it, and the captain took a chance by dropping a depth charge set to explode in shallow water. It could have damaged the ship, but he couldn't risk being torpedoed. The Kaiten dropped deeper, and the *Rall* unloaded more depth charges. The crew saw the Kaiten split open. The entire action took seven minutes.

The Allies reported destroying three "midget subs" that day— they were in fact Kaitens; the American military had no idea this type of suicide sub even existed. A subsequent attack on island anchorages at Kossol Passage near Palau Island ended with the sinking of another big sub (*I-48*) and 19 Kaitens missing their mark. The total damage inflicted by all the missions: one U.S. ship, the *Mississinewa*, sunk. The Japanese lost *I-37* and its crew of 106, plus nine Kaitens; it then lost *I-48* and its crew of 128, plus 19 Kaitens.

Even with those thoroughly miserable results, more big subs were armed with Kaitens and sent to sea; desperate measures had become the order of the day. As the end of December 1944 approached, the submarine *I-58*, specially equipped to carry the Kaitens, headed for the top-secret sub base at Kure. Here the big sub loaded up its Kaiten cargo and pilots, all ready to go, their heads wrapped in white towels, their swords at their sides. *I-58*'s insignia now reflected its new mission, called Konga—the line that would stop the Allied onslaught. As the big sub slowly motored out to sea, sailors cheered. The sub unfurled a flag with the inscription, "The unpredictable Kaiten." It could not be more prophetic.

The *I-58* set out for the waters between Ulithi and Guam; along the way the officers and crew celebrated New Year's Day, 1945, breaking out the booze and toasting the emperor, even though drinking alcohol on board was prohibited. It would be a single bright day in what became the bleakest year in Japanese history. As for the Kaiten pilots, they sat on their version of death row—they had no duties on board the sub except to inspect their craft, test the periscopes, and contemplate the next life. One pilot had been scheduled to participate in a previous attack at Ulithi, but his torpedo malfunctioned, so he'd already had a stay. He made the best of it. He fell into a routine of playing chess, and became quite skilled. Another pilot, overweight and stoic, mounted his torpedo with his sword in hand. They waited.

Sending these young men to slaughter troubled the captain of the *I-58*, whose boat would become famous and who himself would gain a kind of celebrity as a holy man after the war. Captain Mochitsura Hashimoto, who lived into his 90s, had among the most remarkable war careers of any Navy man ever. He'd been the torpedo officer on the *I-24* on the morning of December 7, 1941, and helped oversee the launch of Kazuo Sakamaki in *I-24-A*. Now he would watch a new sacrificial wave and play an integral part in Japan's suicidal rear guard naval action. He remembered training the chess-playing pilot for submariner duty as a youngster in 1943. Now this boy, as the officer wrote, was "billed for certain death in this attempt to turn the tide of war." Japan was killing its youth. These suicide volunteers, for both air and sea demolitions, were for the most part well-educated and fully aware that the best they might achieve with their deaths was a long-shot chance at a truce that would stop the Allies. Despite this, the captain noted that the suicide squads were gaining popularity "apace." The spirit of human sacrifice seemed on the rise.

I-58 worked its way toward the first showdown on a trail that would lead the sub through major South Pacific theaters—Guam, Iwo Jima, Okinawa. Each time *I-58* surfaced, the captain prayed the sub wouldn't be spotted. Its radar proved unreliable for detecting aircraft, and *I-58's* radio operators instead listened for Allied pilot chatter to determine when it might be safe. A report came in that an American carrier was anchored at Guam, and the information was relayed to the Kaiten pilots, apparently to inspire them. To destroy a carrier would give them bragging rights in the next world.

I-58's periscope broke the surface at 11:00 P.M. on the night of January 11. The captain scanned the horizon and thought he saw nothing but a cluster of clouds. Good fortune was with them, however—it was Guam, as he had hoped. The navigator had done a good job, and the sub lay only 26 miles out. The final leg of the Kaitens' journey was underway. The sub closed to 11 miles, then crept in at a speed of 7 knots. The captain tried to cheer up the Kaiten crews, but the latest intelligence now reported a dearth of big ships in a harbor filled mainly with transports. The captain recommended floating docks as strategic targets, but that suggestion had to fall flat with the pilots who were soon to depart forever— die for a floating dock? Perhaps a carrier had returned in the last few days, the captain offered as a last-minute encouragement. One pilot left behind this note and in it revealed a trace of bitterness about how his life was being wasted: "I wanted all the details of the photographic reconnaissance. Was it not irresponsible to send us into the attack without giving us some idea of the enemy's defenses or the conditions inside the harbor?"

That pilot's second thoughts probably were shared with his colleagues, but the other notes left behind reiterated their belief in the pure happiness that awaited them. They embraced the sacrifices that must be made for eternal Japan: even a nation protected by Divine Gods required the Kaiten missions because "without effort there is no sincerity." So wrote one pilot. As the Kaitens peeled off to attack, the last words from the human torpedo designated Number 4 were a hearty, "Three cheers for the emperor."

I-58 could only watch the sacrifice from a distance. Puffs of white smoke appeared over Guam, but no official report from either side recorded any losses or damage to Allied ships. The message from I-58 back to Tokyo read, "All torpedoes launched. Results of attacks not confirmed." The Konga line and the highly unpredictable Kaitens were off to a poor start. I-58's adventures would continue as it headed next for the black sands of Iwo Jima, as more Kaitens would be thrown into the mix to stop the grinding assault on Great Japan.

Naval historian Paul Kemp wrote that the Kaitens sailing bravely into battle were like samurai—and just about as helpless in the scheme of twentieth-century warfare. They counted on their courage and willingness to die to achieve victory. With that mindset, the crew of I-58 loaded on new Kaitens, plus pilots, and enjoyed another festive send-off at Kure on February 10. The sub's Kaiten carousel was now restocked with live missiles and doomed men.

Official orders called for attacks only on ships at anchor around Iwo Jima; in the meantime, I-58 would pass by plenty of moving targets, but the directive from Tokyo prevented it from firing; the captain reported that the crew was disgusted at sailing silently by the enemy when they could have inflicted damage, but there apparently was a grander strategy in the works. Toward the end of the first week of March, the first acceptable target—a group of anchored American ships—came into range. At the evening meal, the Kaiten crew dined separately, meditating together over their last supper. Delays occurred when American destroyers showed up on radar; the Kaiten pilots were already loaded, but would have to wait three hours. They were given drinks to soothe them while they sat in their cockpits.

Then an order came, and Captain Hashimoto almost did not obey it. He'd been told to abort and head to Okinawa. He mulled the option of launching the Kaitens anyway, but did as ordered. The pilots stood down, and the Kaitens were dumped at sea on March 9. They'd have to stop at Kure yet again to reload. The order to sail to Okinawa, however, signaled something other than a new whim from the Imperial Navy brass. By March 9, the land battle on Iwo Jima was about half over, and about half of Japan's force of 21,000 was dead. Ensconced in caves and dug in deep to hold their ground, these Japanese soldiers were crack troops, veteran fighters who would be impossible to defeat, or so thought the Japanese military. The Japanese soldiers tested the very best American fighters, the Marines at Iwo Jima, arguably the bravest and toughest men who ever went to war. But the retreat order to *I-58* revealed what the Japanese commanders had come to realize: Iwo Jima was lost. By March 27 all except for 1,083 of 21,000 Japanese would be dead.

A new replenished submarine task force, called the Tatara Unit, left for Okinawa in early April, each sub carrying six Kaitens. *I-58*'s captain wrote that the enemy had "complete control by sea and in the air," and that in turn forced the sub to stay submerged as much as possible until it approached the island. This created problems. For a sub like *I-58*, it took up to six hours on the surface to fully charge its batteries. Air cylinders used to clear the tanks of water required less time to replenish—about half an hour—but the air pressure was especially critical. Captain Hashimoto noted that "careless handling" could leave the sub permanently stranded at the bottom of the sea.

I-58's radar sporadically picked up aircraft, and that heightened the tension on board as the sub fell further behind schedule. The sub at last approached Okinawa from the west and spotted a mast of a ship it presumed to be the enemy. Instructions came to "go in and fight to the death . . . ." That order was being obeyed in full. With the Kaitens below and the specially designed kamikaze airplanes above, Okinawa was a suicide fest—there was a very black, party-like attitude to the theater on land and sea. As *I-58* prepared to attack, more than 3,000 kamikaze aircraft were readied on Okinawa; more than 100,000 troops were stationed there as well. On April 6, 350 suicide planes were sent out to crash into the Allied fleet. Their motto: one plane, one ship. (The Japanese Army's motto on land was similar: kill ten Americans before succumbing or destroy one tank, take your pick.)

The U.S. Navy's 40-mm anti-aircraft Bofors guns pounded away, and the sky filled with flak. The Japanese planes weaved their way through the puffs of black smoke and took dead aim at ships. Allied gunners said afterward they tried to create a curtain of anti-aircraft fire to stop an enemy clearly determined and seemingly insane. Besides being terrifying, it was weird. Vice Admiral C. R. Brown wrote that there was a kind of "hypnotic fascination" in watching an aircraft draw closer and closer, the pilot wearing a white silk scarf around his head and willing "to die in order that he might destroy us in the process." As they threw more and more and more planes at the Allied fleet, the Japanese suicide pilots did real damage. They hit destroyers like the *Mannert L. Aebele* (which went down in five minutes) and crashed into the carriers *Hancock*, *Intrepid*, and *Enterprise*—all were struck over the course of April 7–16. Early in May, the carrier *Bunker Hill* suffered a devastating kamikaze strike that killed 350 of its crew.

Yet another Japanese "suicide" craft was by this time underway, but it was so unlikely a vehicle on such a crazy mission that it still defies a reasonable explanation. The battleship *Yamato*, once the flagship of Isoroku Yamamoto himself, was heading to Okinawa with an escort of eight destroyers and one cruiser. The world's largest battleship was to sacrifice itself by attracting the fire of Allied forces and taking down with it as many of the enemy as possible. This mammoth craft, once described as a folly, carried enough fuel for a one-way trip. (It wasn't because of a fuel shortage—the dwindling Imperial Navy had fewer and fewer ships to refuel; it was intentional.) There also were no life rafts or life jackets aboard for the crew of 3,332, though there was no shortage of sake ("oceans" of it by one account.) *Yamato's* mission, called *Ten'ichigo,* roughly meant "a heaven-sent opportunity to reverse one's fortunes."

Ensign Mitsuru Yoshida served as assistant radar officer on the *Yamato.* His remarkable account, *Requiem for Battleship "Yamato,"* offers an almost poetic play-by-play description of how men die in battle. He watched from *Yamato's* deck and later wrote: "The tracks of the torpedoes are a beautiful white against the water, as if someone were drawing a needle . . ." There was a big debate among the crew—who all knew the battleship was doomed—about the real goals of the mission. The honor of dying for the emperor was a given, but there were rumblings about the futility of sending the most visible symbol of Japan's naval strength to the bottom of the sea. One crew member said, "We die for sovereign and country. I understand that. But isn't there more to it than that? . . . What the devil is the purpose of all this?" That kind of talk raised tempers and generated free-for-alls, with the doubting sailors pummeled to "thrash that rottenness out of you." There also was on-board speculation about how the *Yamato* would succumb: B-29s and recon planes were already tracking the battleship; the huge Allied naval task force loomed near Okinawa; submarines lurked as the ship entered Bungo Channel. Some of the young officers thought airborne attacks would do the most damage, and they were right. The ship's 24 anti-aircraft guns and 120 machine guns could not hold off eight waves of Allied planes that were, as Yoshida wrote, "sweeping in like a sudden rain shower." Each assault comprised hundreds of planes; Allied aircraft with bombs and torpedoes zapped the ship. The *Yamato* exploded April 7, sending up a plume of smoke thousands of feet high that was seen more than a hundred miles away. Ensign Yoshida was one of those left splashing in the water and among the few who managed to survive to tell the tale. The naval historian Samuel Eliot Morison considered the sinking of the world's largest battleship the official end of five centuries of big-gun naval warfare. The historian Paul Dull made a more obvious observation, still worth repeating:

"With the sinking of the great battleship . . . the once-formidable Imperial Japanese Navy had ceased to exist."

No one told that to *I-58*. The determined sub was still 45 miles off Okinawa, where it had expected to rendezvous with the *Yamato* on its glorious mission. As it closed in, bad weather and more enemy aircraft harassed the sub—the captain estimated it had been attacked fifty times. The captain worried that the sub had fallen even further behind schedule, but he didn't know the big battleship was already a goner. Ready at last to attack, the captain received an order. Based on the now-regular retreats of the Japanese, the order could have been predicted—the sub was to head north to the safety of the open Pacific. It was another stay for the Kaiten pilots. While Okinawa had been declared a "great Japanese strategic victory" to the public at home, the losses amounted to outright slaughter. Roughly 110,000 Japanese soldiers were killed; only 10,000 surrendered. In addition, civilian deaths numbered about 100,000, and many of these were suicides. The military had convinced the Okinawa civilians that American Marines were so barbaric they would torture the people, and they'd die horribly. One rumor was that the ruthless Marines had to kill their own mothers before they could join the Corps. The same fear tactic had worked on Saipan, where 22,000 civilians died, many by their own hand. Thousands jumped off cliffs, including the 800-foot high Suicide Cliff, which is just north of another leaping point, called Bonzai Cliff. Among the suicides were mothers carrying their babies on their backs. The "savage" Americans tried to fish out as many survivors as possible from the water below.

I-58 returned to Kure to find it was the only one of the four big subs to have made a round trip. Along with *I-58* there were only three other large submarines left at Kure, including *I-53*, which would see action soon. The losses for the Japanese Navy had become insurmountable, but the military was nowhere near quitting—as long as anyone was left alive.

All of *I-58*'s zigs and zags, retreats, and near misses set it on a course that enabled it to leave a mark on history. The submarine left Kure for the last time on July 18, 1945, packed with Kaitens and pilots. The depleted Japanese Navy now searched for any enemy it could find, relegated to making isolated strikes it hoped would be spectacular enough to stun the Allies and discourage them from attacking Tokyo. The idea of a highly visible strike on a vulnerable target had been in the works for a while. The Japanese had secretly fashioned a torpedo-carrying bomber aircraft that could be loaded into a new class of mammoth sub. Outfitted with aircraft, the *I-400*, with an incredible range of 40,000 miles, prepared to make a long journey across the Pacific. The sub would attack Ulithi in the Caroline Islands on August 25, and then head east to destroy the Panama Canal. The war ended before then, and the captain who had spent years organizing the Panama plan shot himself.

Meanwhile, south of Japan, *I-58* patrolled, eyes peeled for what damage it could do. The captain wrote, "We had the Kaitens and were determined to sink any boat that came our way." The Kaitens were the key to the big-strike strategy. As it turned out, they would actually be bit players in the single worst open-sea loss of life in the history of the U.S. Navy.

I-58 was spotting targets periodically. At sea for ten days on the afternoon of July 28, the sub saw a three-masted tanker, and fired two Kaitens. The last pilot out shouted the familiar, "Three cheers for the emperor!" The sub waited for an explosion, but heard nothing. Fifty minutes later one blast was picked up and 10 minutes later, another. The Kaitens apparently missed their targets, for no damage report or loss of a ship in that area was ever filed. It was thought that if a Kaiten missed, the pilots might have detonated their torpedoes rather than running out of fuel and eventually drowning in the middle of the sea. The *I-58*'s big day was still to come.

The night of July 29, Captain Hashimoto lay down for a while and arose when a petty officer reported all was well. The *I-58*'s skipper stopped by the ship's shrine, then climbed up to the conning tower and used the night periscope to survey the water. Convinced there were no enemies in the vicinity, he ordered the sub to surface. Wonderful fresh air came in, and the sub pumped out water. Hashimoto kept watch with the telescope, and surface radar stayed on alert when suddenly the navigator reported, "Bearing red nine-zero degrees, a possible enemy ship." The captain yelled "Dive!" and ordered "Kaitens stand by." The ship was coming straight at them. Hashimoto worried it might be a destroyer set to depth charge the sub. By coming directly at the sub, the ship presented a narrow target, and as Hashimoto wrote, "it would have been difficult to score a torpedo hit . . . ." As the ship closed within torpedo range of 1,500 yards, Hashimoto first thought it was an Idaho-class battleship. Ready to attack, the Kaiten crew questioned the captain: "What about the enemy?" "Where's the enemy?" The captain thought the bright moon shining from behind the sub, plus the proximity of the enemy, made the mission too risky, even for a suicide squad. The Kaitens could be used to finish off the ship. He fired conventional torpedoes at 2-second intervals. In about 12 seconds, all six were heading toward the target.

On board the USS *Indianapolis*, a heavy cruiser, the ship had just finished what had been described to the crew as a "special mission." The *Indianapolis* had been hit by a kamikaze airplane at Okinawa and had returned to San Francisco for repairs. It was then ordered to Pearl Harbor to pick up a shipment, the contents top secret. A doctor aboard the ship remembers the captain saying that every day they shaved off the trip "was a day off the war." Just how special the cargo was became clearer when the *Indianapolis* arrived at Tinian in the Marianas on July 26. The doctor noticed that the men unloading the crates weren't the usual dock hands but top officers working "like they were a bunch of stevedores." One piece of cargo was sealed in a canister welded onto the deck. It contained the radioactive components (uranium) for the atomic bomb known as Little Boy; the other piece was a large crate that carried the bomb's triggering mechanism.

The *Indianapolis* was then ordered to the Philippines to prepare for the next invasion—the home islands of Japan. Captain Charles B. McVay had asked for an escort; the Navy brass said he didn't need one: no ships passing through the area had reported any trouble, or so the captain was told. The decision was that *Indianapolis* would zigzag during the day to make the ship less vulnerable to torpedo attack; at night it would cruise straight ahead.

No one bothered to mention to the captain the recent, critical deployment of the destroyer escort USS *Underhill*. On July 23 it accompanied a convoy of LSTs and an Army troop transport also heading toward the Philippines, where staging for the invasion of Japan had begun. There were eight escort ships, all alert for submarines. On the hunt in the area was *I-53*, which, like *I-58*, was part of the unit that had left Kure armed with Kaitens. The *Underhill* detected the big sub and dropped a pattern of depth charges; *I-53* apparently had already launched a Kaiten, for the *Underhill* rammed it and triggered the torpedo, which blew off the bow of the ship. When the *Underhill* exploded and sank, 118 crew members were lost; about 55 were rescued from the water by the other ships in the convoy. As one officer wrote, "there's no doubt the *Underhill*'s aggressive action had saved the convoy" and many hundreds of lives. It wasn't until later that Captain McVay of the *Indianapolis* learned about the incident; and it was also revealed in the 1990s that code-breakers knew there were Japanese *I*-subs patrolling the area and had passed the information along to Navy intelligence, which did not, however, pass it along to McVay.

On July 30, just after midnight, with the crew unaware of any approaching danger, the *Indianapolis* suddenly shook and burst into flames as *I-58*'s torpedoes tore into it. The explosions were so loud the sub crew thought they were being depth charged. Hashimoto, who could see the *Indianapolis* burning through his periscope, knew he'd mortally wounded the "battleship." (He didn't know it was a cruiser until after the war.) While the *Indianapolis* was still floating, the Kaiten pilots begged again to get in on the action. "Since the enemy won't sink, send us." The captain waited a few minutes and scanned the ocean again. The ship was gone. He knew it was too severely damaged to have limped away.

It took only 12 minutes for the *Indianapolis* to sink. One of the ship's doctors, Captain Lewis L. Haynes, remembered survivors scattered for a mile behind because the ship had slowly continued forward. Survivors started to huddle together; most of them had swallowed enough fuel oil to make them gag and throw up. The doctor remembered the image that horrible night of black faces, white eyes, red mouths, and men vomiting.

Knots of survivors were so tossed by the wind and waves they ended up miles apart. As the sun rose that day, the water looked incredibly clear—almost good enough to drink. Doing so meant death. As the heat increased, some men drank the salt water. It caused diarrhea and more dehydration and eventually sent the victims into raving fits, foaming at the mouth. Efforts were made at first to save the ailing men, but they eventually were pushed away because no one could afford to expend the energy. There was worse to come—sharks, most of them a species known as white tips.

The groups of men tried to stay close together in the water at night. They could feel their legs being bumped. Suddenly one would be carried off, screaming. "I've seen men taken an arm's length away," reported one survivor. The terror of the attacks drove some men mad. The blood from victims attracted more sharks. As one survivor said, "it was easier to die than to stay alive."

It took five days for rescue crews to show up, and that was more or less an accident. A bomber pilot on submarine patrol radioed back he'd spotted a number of men in the water. He reported they were in a big oil slick, and the rescuers needed to hurry—he could see sharks were attacking the survivors. The *Indianapolis* had tried to send a Mayday message—men risked their lives on the sinking ship to ensure one was sent, but either they failed or no one picked it up. (The captain believed it had been sent.)

Why did the rescue take so long? It seems almost inexplicable. An Army pilot had actually seen flares burning in the darkness either late on the 29th or in the early morning of the 30th. His report was ignored. When the *Indianapolis* didn't show up in the Philippines, apparently no one asked why. This was the ship that had set the sea speed record from San Francisco to Pearl Harbor. Also, it is now known that Hashimoto sent a message back to Imperial Navy headquarters that he had sunk a battleship; the message was intercepted, but no one acted on it, perhaps because the *Indianapolis* was a cruiser. Add to that the lack of an escort and the inadequate briefing on enemy sub action in the area. The conclusion: if it wasn't a tragedy that could have been prevented, at least it was one in which hundreds more lives could have been saved. By the time the crew was rescued, only 316 of the 900 men who'd been in the ocean had survived. Altogether, more than 1,100 men died, the largest number of Navy men lost on a single ship since December 7, 1941.

The Kaitens worked until the end of the war—and even did some overtime. The day after the atomic bombing of Nagasaki, *I-58* sent its suicide submersibles into an Allied convoy and one apparently sank a destroyer; on August 12 the Kaitens were on the hunt again, pursuing a merchant ship. A destroyer interceded, and *I-58* heard depth charges and sighted puffs of smoke, but the Kaiten apparently had failed. Hashimoto reported that "We prayed for the happiness in a future existence of the departed warrior . . . ." The *I-58* was one of only four active big submarines left in the Imperial Navy.

On August 15, *I-58* received a radio communication that the war was over. This didn't sit well with the captain's fighting spirit, and he ordered that the message be thrown away. Hashimoto thought it a mere news report, and he would not hand over his sword unless he received an official order. He "would not dishonor, the spirits . . . of the . . . departed warriors of the Kaitens and midgets . . . ." *I-58* made it back to Kure on August 18. Some men didn't want to quit, and leaflets were even dropped from an airplane encouraging the sailors and soldiers never to surrender. In a final act of obedience, Hashimoto followed the Imperial Order to cease fire.

Hashimoto's dealings with Americans weren't over. He was called as a witness in the court martial in December 1945 of Captain Charles B. McVay, the *Indianapolis* skipper, who had survived. The charge against McVay was that he needlessly exposed his ship to submarine fire because he didn't zigzag at night, when the ship was attacked. Hashimoto testified, but it wasn't what the Navy prosecutors wanted to hear. He said he would have hit the ship, zigzagging or not. Actually, the straight-ahead target was a little tougher for a torpedo shot, but he also could have employed the Kaitens at any point and sunk the *Indianapolis*, no problem. In waters patrolled by enemy subs armed with Kaitens, the *Indianapolis* should have had an escort. McVay was convicted anyway, and he never got over it. He committed suicide a few years later. He was found holding a toy sailor.

In 1999, surviving crew members learned all the facts and wanted their captain's name cleared. By this time Hashimoto was a 91-year-old Shinto priest and a Japanese holy man of some note. On November 24, 1999, he wrote this letter to U.S. Senator John W. Warner, chairman of the Senate Armed Services Committee:

> I hear that your legislature is considering resolutions which would clear the name of the late Charles Butler McVay III, captain of the USS *Indianapolis* which was sunk on July 30, 1945, by torpedoes fired from the submarine which was under my command.
>
> I do not understand why Captain McVay was court-martialed. I do not understand why he was convicted on the charge of hazarding his ship by failing to zigzag because I would have been able to launch a successful torpedo attack against his ship whether it had been zigzagging or not.
>
> I have met many of your brave men who survived the sinking of the *Indianapolis*. I would like to join them in urging that your national legislature clear their captain's name.
>
> Our peoples have forgiven each other for that terrible war and its consequences. Perhaps it is time your peoples forgave Captain McVay for the humiliation of his unjust conviction.
>
> Signed: Mochitsura Hashimoto, former captain of *I-58*

The letter must have helped. In 2000, McVay was exonerated, and he was no longer officially responsible for the loss of his ship.

With the Kaitens leading the way, the original midget sub fleet became a mere coda toward the end of the war. While the suicidal Kaitens exploded across the Pacific, there was still a little scattered action involving the midget subs in the Philippines—they actually had a shot at an American General. Around Cebu, Zamboanga, and Davao in the Philippines they fired torpedoes and harassed different task forces, including the one transporting General Douglas MacArthur, who apparently observed the action, chomping on his corncob pipe. However, the subs mainly were taken out of offensive assaults and used for defensive purposes.

The little subs' role carried on into 1945, but the results are a little hazy. Successful sub action, described by Samuel Eliot Morison in *The Liberation of the Philippines*, could have been the work of the little boats or of big subs. Most of the reliable reports come from the American side, with the outcomes remarkably similar to past midget sub adventures. One was rammed and cut in two; another was torn open and sunk by gunfire. What has been described as a corral of midget subs was destroyed at Okinawa, but they could have been Kaitens. This in effect was the last action seen by the midget subs. But for history, of course, their story continues.

Two other classes of Japanese midget subs never saw action, but if the Allies had invaded Japan, they certainly would have been unleashed. One was the Koryu (Scaly Dragon), an 86-foot-long, 58-ton class of subs that carried two torpedoes and a crew of five. About 115 were made, most of them found sitting in dry dock at Kure. Because supplies of torpedoes were running short, the Koryu had been converted to a submersible bomb to be rammed into the enemy. The other craft, the Kairyu (Sea Dragon), 56 feet and 18 tons, seated two, and while it also could have launched torpedoes, its payload was a 1,300-pound charge set to explode on impact, like a Kaiten. More than 200 of these were built. These little subs never caused harm, but it is remarkable that the Japanese had completed so many of them in preparation for their final defense. It is even more notable that these craft had *multiple* crew members ready to go on suicide runs. One pilot sacrificed per vessel wasn't enough? The desire to die, as *I-58*'s Hashimoto pointed out, had apparently swept the land.

One of the strangest effects of all the publicity about waves of suicidal sacrifices, such as the "strategic victory" at Okinawa (that in fact spelled the end of the Japanese Navy and sent thousands of Japanese to their deaths), was the impact it had on Allied strategy in the final days of the war. No one really wanted to fight the Japanese on their home turf. Intelligence analyst and historian John Prados made a convincing point about the kamikaze attacks and the propaganda built up around the suicide missions. The assaults "tried to instill fear" and "convince the Allies that Japan would fight to the last man." He noted that after "watching the kamikazes day after day," Americans became believers. Another military historian, Ronald Spector, noted that the outcome at Okinawa "had the paradoxical effect of discouraging the Americans while inspiring the Japanese."

So it seems the extreme sacrifices the Japanese proudly proclaimed to the world played a role in the decision to drop the atomic bomb. The xenophobic Japanese military and cold-blooded emperor were determined to kill enough Americans to force a peace negotiation. Women and children sharpened bamboo sticks to stab soldiers landing on the beaches. To defend the home front in the final conflict, the Japanese had more than 7,000 aircraft and enough pilots to fly them. These planes could go either way: conventional fighting or suicide. Nineteen destroyers were still in inventory, and they could carry about 400 submersible suicide Kaitens, including the five-man "super" Kaitens ready to launch. The Japanese even added new kamikaze wrinkles: suicide powerboats, suicide anti-tank personnel (a person straps on an explosive and crawls under a tank), and suicide frogmen, called *fukuryu* ("crouching dragon"): 1,200 men had been trained and 2,800 were being readied—they were to strap on explosives (called lunge mines) to attach to ships. They were to stage the attacks from sunken ships at strategic underwater locations in the seas around Japan. Also, rocket bombs were placed in a network of caves and set to go.

For the planned assault on the Japanese home islands, Nimitz was to lead the Navy forces and MacArthur the Army. There was a fundamental disagreement between strategists on the best tack to take. The Navy planned to establish bases on the South China Coast and from there send bombers to pound the Japanese and ships to set up naval blockades. Compared to the expected casualties from a land invasion, the loss of Allied lives would be reduced dramatically. The Army poked big holes in that plan. It questioned how much bloodshed would be required to secure the China Coast, plus the eventual outcome of the Navy's plan remained cloudy. How long would it take for the Japanese to fold? These fanatically determined people could feed on rice and nationalistic pride for months or years. Eventually the Army's opinion won out and the invasion of Kyushu became the priority. The number of troops scheduled to make the assault: 767,000.

While it's clear that the losses from the atomic blasts ordered by President Harry S. Truman were horrific, the deaths from a series of Allied invasions would have amounted to a holocaust. One estimate the U.S. officials used for their potential casualties came from the experience at Okinawa, where the Japanese lost 100,000 troops, and the Allies suffered 40,000 casualties. The estimate was that Japan still had 2 million people who could fight, or 20 times the troop strength at Okinawa. Using the Okinawa model, Allied losses would be 800,000. Add to that the assumption that all 2 million Japanese would die. (Another study put the available Japanese fighting force at 1 million, but even then the body count was still numbing. The first assault at Kyushu called for 268,000 Allied dead or wounded.)

One last suicide incident should be mentioned. For reasons unknown, midget submarines seemed irresistibly attracted to the USS *Antares*. Toward the end of June 1945—about a month and a half before the war would end—the old supply ship was heading back to Pearl Harbor after making a delivery to Saipan. On patrol in the area, the submarine *I-36* launched a Kaiten at the ship. Sharp-eyed spotters were still on duty on the *Antares* (which had first sighted the midget sub trying to enter Pearl Harbor back in 1941). The men reported a periscope closing in fast—it was less than 100 yards to starboard. The order was given to veer and the Kaiten missed. Its periscope was in the wake on the *Antares's* port side, but the ship was now equipped with 3-inch and 5-inch guns, a giant improvement over December 7, 1941, when its only weapon was a submachine gun. The *Antares* fired at the periscope and the Kaiten vanished, but soon another periscope popped up and came closing in like a shark's fin cutting across the water. More gunfire followed, but by this time, the destroyer USS *Sproston*, which had been signaled, came to the rescue. The ship picked up sonar pings and closed so fast it had a chance to ram *I-36*; then the *Sproston* unloaded its depth charges. They apparently hit something, for an oil slick spread across the surface. The fight continued as another Kaiten attacked; it was hit and exploded. More Allied ships joined in, and in a desperate attempt to escape, *I-36* sent two more Kaiten pilots to their deaths to distract the destroyers. The *I-36* suffered rudder damage and a leak in its torpedo room, but managed to sneak away. The old *Antares*, groaning back across the Pacific, made it to Pearl Harbor and survived to the end of the war. The ship that was involved in the first U.S. action of World War II, which won two battle stars, was sold for scrap in 1947.

The War without End

WHEN THE "DISGRACED" POW No. 1, Kazuo Sakamaki, returned home, he received little sympathy from his countrymen, some of whom urged him to commit suicide. These attitudes would change. By 1946 the Japanese government's information lid had blown completely off, and people grasped the reality of the Great East Asian War, now lost. One man scoffed: "Before, the militarists and government officials looked important, but I don't think much of them now." Another said he hated the military, a public stance that previously would have been dangerous: "It's their fault that we are having a hard time today." Under the supreme commander for the Allied Powers, General Douglas MacArthur, the prosecution of war criminals by an international tribunal began in May 1946. That hit Japan as hard as any bomb. During the trials, the horror stories of Japanese cruelty—especially that inflicted on the Allied POWs and the Chinese civilians and military—became public knowledge, the shame of the nation now for the world to see, or, as Sakamaki wrote, "It is a trial of us all, our ideas, and our traditional culture itself."

The prosecution, similar to that at Nuremburg though not as well publicized in the West, raises another question, never to be answered, but worth posing: Would Yamamoto have been tried, convicted, and hanged?

• • •

Japan's ready acceptance of suicide intertwines with its attitude toward POWs, both enemy prisoners and its own men who were captured. The glory heaped on the dead midget submarine crews extended the centuries-long tradition of honoring those who gladly sacrificed their lives for their country. The Chi dynasty in the sixth century used the Chinese term *gyokusai*, which translates in Japanese as "shattered jewels." Each soldier's or sailor's death would earn him a shining spot in the nation's holiest shrine, and by his example he would inspire the next generation of soldiers to die. Heroic, honorable death basically equaled deification.

From there, it was a pretty short step to view a POW's life as a disgrace and worthless. The Japanese attitude toward prisoners—their own countrymen as well as those enemies they captured—was far removed from that of any other nation in the world (or in modern history, for that matter). It even was at odds with previous Japanese actions. Infamous for their brutality toward prisoners in World War II, the Japanese hadn't always treated their POWs as something less than human beings. By the time of the Russo-Japanese War, the Japanese had signed the Hague Convention of 1899. It called for the humane treatment of prisoners and addressed weapons bans, specifically, (1) "asphyxiating or deleterious gases," (2) hollow-point bullets ("which expand or flatten easily in the human body...") and (3) the "launching of projectiles and explosives from balloons." The prisoner provisions (later spelled out in more detail in the 1910 convention) were adhered to by both the Russians and the Japanese. The countries exchanged POWs during their conflict, and the names of the imprisoned Japanese were published so families were informed about their sons. There was no shame in being captured.

By 1939, an incident in Manchuria helped set a new tone and sent a clear, official message to every Japanese military man. Some soldiers were captured by the Russians in a border conflict, and the Japanese managed to negotiate their return. Back on their home turf, the Japanese POW officers were all given the opportunity to commit suicide, and it was made clear there really wasn't another option. Enlisted men were treated a little better. Deemed "law-breakers," they performed community service; they then faced exile to some forgotten hellhole outside Japan. The moral: better to die on the front than risk coming home as a former POW.

The official position was published and distributed on January 7, 1941. The Field Service Code, or *Senjinkun*, said simply that "it was impermissible for Japanese soldiers to become prisoners of war." In a section on reputation it further advised: "Those who know shame are weak. Always think of [preserving] the honor of your community and be a credit to yourself and your family. . . . By dying you will avoid leaving behind the crime of a stain on your honor." A dishonored soldier's reputation could harm his family. A sister might not be acceptable to marry, a brother might not be promoted, the parents would forever wear the scarlet letters: POW. Since all able-bodied men were required to join the military—and they had been indoctrinated in this culture since boyhood—the taboo against surrender had a profound effect. A sense of guilt must have overwhelmed many men as they found themselves choosing between surrender and death.

With such a severe attitude toward its own soldiers, it's little wonder the Japanese reneged on the POW-sympathetic Geneva Convention, which they signed in 1929. They now viewed the rules of war differently, based on an obvious reason: in the eyes of official Japan, there was no such thing as a Japanese POW. Thus, the Geneva Convention was a one-way street: Japan would have to abide by the rules of humane treatment of prisoners, and its enemy nation wouldn't have to do anything, because theoretically there wouldn't be any Japanese prisoners to care for.

Though a signatory, Japan eventually refused to take the final step of formally ratifying the Geneva Convention. The reasons for this are summarized nicely by U.S. career foreign service officer Ulrich Straus, who lived in Japan before and after the war. To the Japanese, promising not to harm a POW invited enemy air attacks. It might buoy the courage of pilots on long-range bombing missions (Doolittle's raid, for example) that required a plane to be ditched because it ran out of fuel. The Japanese position was that the threat of punishment might discourage these missions in which pilots had to bail out and possibly fall into Japanese hands. Similarly, the government thought the Geneva Convention encouraged spying by the enemy. A foreign spy might think twice if he or she faced the prospects of a torturous Japanese prison. Last, the Geneva Convention required that Japan feed, clothe, and shelter enemy POWs better than it did its own soldiers. Besides giving small rations of food to its own servicemen, the military treated its personnel brutally, smashing soldiers in the face or pummeling those who fell below standards. Why head down the slippery slope of humane treatment for enemy POWs?

News reports still surface of Japanese soldiers who for years held out in some South Pacific jungle rather than face surrender. In 1972 a soldier, Shoichi Yokoi, was found on Guam. An intelligence officer, Hiroo Onoda, stayed hidden in Philippine undergrowth until 1974. Neither man knew the outcome of the war. As late as 2005, two more soldiers, now in their 80s, emerged from hiding, though it's not known whether they were holdouts, waiting for word of a Japanese victory or, as was speculated, they were deserters who'd rather have lived in a secluded wilderness than face the consequences of desertion in Japan. The code of Senjinkun was well-ingrained.

Not surprisingly, those Japanese prisoners who did end up in Allied hands at first feared the worst. They'd seen how the helpless were dealt with in their own ranks—Japanese officers "dispensed" grenades to straggling wounded or simply shot the ones not strong enough to pull the pins. Konoye Makoto, a medical officer weak from hunger who ended up in an American POW prison camp on Leyte Island in the Philippines, was given an examination by a doctor, a chocolate bar, and a cigarette. He couldn't grasp why the soldiers hadn't killed him. Some were so torn about being captured they basically hid and starved themselves. One such man, Yamamoto Tomio, was found passed out. A picture ran in *Life* magazine of the 72-pound man with the headline, "Live Skeleton." As a POW eating Allied food, he recovered.

By contrast, the Japanese atrocities perpetrated throughout the Pacific and Far East covered a range both horrible and wide. At Sandaken on Borneo Allied POWs were sent on death marches, with those who fell behind bayoneted and shot; one group of 500 POWs had dwindled to six in a matter of weeks. On Banka Island Allied nurses were ordered to march into the ocean and machine-gunned in the water, a single wounded nurse the only survivor left to tell her story. Cannibalism was committed by numerous Japanese soldiers on a number of islands and became commonplace enough that Allied prisoners were called "white pigs" and natives "black pigs."

Overall, the Chinese got the worst treatment from the Japanese. Japan hid behind the ruse that the invasion of China was "an incident" rather than a real act of war. It's very doubtful whether the treatment of Chinese prisoners would have been different if a formal declaration of war had been made. Chinese captives were used for bayonet practice, slave labor, rape, and as subjects in horrible biological and germ-warfare experiments performed by Unit 731, which operated in northeast China.

These crimes against China made up a good portion of the evidence used in war crime prosecutions, which came in three categories—A, B, and C. The biggies were in the A group—the first tried. For leaders, such as Prime Minister Hideki Tojo, the charges were based on his leading Japan into aggressive warfare and committing crimes against peace and humanity. The leadership also got tagged with conspiracy to commit atrocities. The court tribunal concluded that the horrific acts of the Japanese were "committed in all theaters, [so] that only one conclusion is possible—the atrocities were either secretly ordered or willfully permitted by the Japanese Government or . . . by the leaders of the armed forces."

Japanese leadership had been warned their day would come. Allied emissaries met with Japanese representatives in Switzerland during the war to explain to them the consequences of atrocities. Further, in 1942 Japan's foreign minister, Shigenori Togo, told the Allies that though his country hadn't really signed on to the Geneva

Convention, it would change its policies to apply the Convention rules. This, of course, never happened.

Right after the Japanese surrender, Allied authorities rounded up what was left of the Pearl Harbor cabinet and top Army men who'd given the orders for such horrors as the Rape of Nanjing, in which Japanese soldiers killed up to 300,000 Chinese and raped thousands of women. Also included were a deputy Navy minister, the vice chief of the Navy General Staff, and Navy Chief of Staff Osami Nagano. Altogether twenty-eight Class-A war criminals were charged. Of the group, twenty-five were convicted; two died during the trials, and one was declared insane.

Seven were sentenced to death. The best known, of course, was Hideki Tojo, who'd served as prime minister until 1944. Besides the crimes against humanity and a long list of other transgressions, he also was cited for authorizing the attack on Pearl Harbor. Five others who were executed had been involved in incidents in China and the South Pacific, while one was a former prime minister who masterminded some of the strategy in China.

Concerning the sneak attack on Pearl Harbor, Tojo, until the end, held to the conviction that all's fair when a soldier's nation is threatened. He kept a diary while imprisoned that explained his reasoning. (He'd previously tried to commit suicide, but was nursed back to health.) Tojo believed the delay in breaking off diplomatic relations with the United States until after the bombing at Pearl Harbor had started on December 7 was—to his mind—a technical glitch that hardly mattered. The official notification was held up mainly because an inept typist couldn't churn out the official documents fast enough to have them delivered by 1:00 P.M. Eastern Standard Time (or 7:30 A.M. in Hawaii, which was still scant minutes before the first bombs began to fall.) Tojo also noted that, according to reports, President Roosevelt had read the decrypted diplomatic dispatches on December 6 and understood their implication. The president was quoted in a congressional hearing as saying, "This means war." That is true, but Forrest "Tex" Biard, the cryptologist, knew the military attaché in the room that night when Roosevelt made the comment, and the full statement by the president was, "This means war . . . in a few months."

Tojo contended that the final decision to wage war by Japan came late in the game on December 1, and that there was hope for a diplomatic breakthrough until the last hours. In his view the Japanese had heaped "concession upon concession" to keep the peace. Also, his nation believed the United States with its fleet in Hawaii would attack sooner or later, and that America's refusal to export oil and metal to Japan was a prelude to this attack.

December 1 may have been the date the Imperial Conference convened and gave its approval for war, but the big *I*-subs with their midget sub cargoes had long since left Kure, and the aircraft carrier armada was on its way as well before December 1. Isoroku Yamamoto, however, made it clear to his men that they had to maintain discipline and keep in mind that their mission could be cancelled while at sea. So it is arguable that Tojo believed peace was possible until December 3, when the order was radioed "climb Mount Niitaka."

Even Douglas MacArthur had some sympathy for Tojo, who'd made his reputation as a maniacal military leader and war minister and who then rose to the post of prime minister. MacArthur wrote that "the principle of holding criminally responsible the political leaders of the vanquished in war was repugnant to me." He added, however, that Pearl Harbor was a special circumstance. He said that since no prior declaration of war was given, those in charge had to bear the responsibility for the murderous sneak attack. Tojo was hanged on December 23, 1948.

Of the twenty-five men convicted in the war crimes trial, only three were Navy men. One deputy minister received life imprisonment for the treatment of Allied POWs on what were called "hellships." Another, Shigetaro Shimada, vice chief of the Navy General Staff, was given life for approving the Pearl Harbor attack. Admiral Nagano—who okayed the Pearl Harbor attack plan, appeared on the cover of *Time* magazine in 1943, and attended Harvard Law School in 1913—was found guilty but died in a U.S. hospital in January

1947 before he served time. There were also dozens of military men and other leaders who were accused of crimes but never tried. Of them, many found themselves punished in other ways. A former admiral's station in life was so reduced he worked as a menial laborer on a railroad.

In 1955, however, Admiral Shimada was released from prison because of poor health. By then the attitude toward the Japanese military had changed again, and the men who had led the Japanese Navy and Army would find new status. In fact, Admiral Shimada's health improved enough that he survived twenty-one years after his parole and helped organize self-defense groups, such as the Maritime Defense Force, the remnant of what once was the most powerful Navy in the world.

Some military men turned to religion or worked on writing projects about the war. A leader in the air attack on Pearl Harbor, Mitsuo Fuchida, became a Christian missionary. Captain Hashimoto of *I-58* emerged as a Shinto religious figure and later a peace proponent when he defended the captain of the USS *Indianapolis*, which *I-58* had torpedoed and sunk. The man who led the search for Yamamoto after his plane was shot down, staff officer Yasuji Watanabe, also became a dedicated religious man, but later transitioned; he went from Buddhism to the corporate boardroom of a Japanese business.

Accounts of the war by Japanese servicemen became a cottage industry. Sakamaki penned his book, *I Attacked Pearl Harbor*, a best seller in Japan and the United States; Captain Hashimoto's *Sunk!*, published in the United States in hardcover and paperback, also sold well. Other writers dedicated themselves to transforming war diaries into narratives, adding to what was becoming a sizable library of firsthand history.

So what would have been Yamamoto's fate? He told a friend that after the war he likely would "be packed off either to the guillotine or to St. Helena (the south Atlantic island where Napoleon spent the last years of his life)." It's extremely doubtful he would have followed the example of so many Japanese officers and committed suicide. It wasn't in his character. He thought the futile sacrifice of pilots and soldiers for some ideal in the afterlife was a waste. After considering his own value as a future leader in Japan, it's likely he'd have taken his chances in front of the tribunal or perhaps even disappeared by escaping to a South Seas island where he'd live with a favorite mistress and wait for better days. He actually proposed this in a letter to one woman, perhaps fantasizing. In short, Yamamoto was not as fatalistic as the Senjinkun code required.

It is also fair to say that despite his role in the attack on Pearl Harbor, he wasn't the one who messed up the timetable on breaking off diplomatic relations or who recruited a clumsy typist to hammer out a document that was delivered too late. He might have orchestrated the sneak attack, but he didn't deceive Washington officials, such as Cordell Hull. (Hull believed the Japanese representatives in Washington had sunk to new diplomatic depths. He was heard calling them "scoundrels and piss-ants" as they left his office on the afternoon of December 7.)

Also, one of the hopes of those Japanese who knew the war was lost—and who wanted to rebuild their country—was that Yamamoto would be around to lead them. By 1944, factions of war-weary Japanese had already formed, and that included cabinet members who secretly hoped the war would end soon but dared not publicly oppose the military. The Allies did their best to inform the public and littered Japan with leaflets detailing the Potsdam declarations and the call to surrender. Yamamoto would have been perfect to deal with the conquering men from the West: he already knew many of the leaders from past arms talks, and he spoke excellent English. Even Sakamaki had been approached to work at a newspaper and report on the occupation because he had spent so much time in the West, albeit cooped up in prison camps.

It's now a significant part of Yamamoto's legacy in Japan and in America that he was reluctant to go to war against the United States. He said that repeatedly to the highest government leaders. Because he was long considered part of the less hysterical faction of the military, he would have had credibility in Washington. If there were still doubters, he could have cited the assassination attempts that were aimed at him before the war because he seemed too close to the West.

Also consider that Emperor Hirohito walked unscathed from the war crimes trials though he was as guilty as any Japanese war criminal. Joseph Keenan, the chief prosecutor, conceded in 1950 that "strictly legally" Hirohito could have been tried and convicted. To remove the emperor, however, would have taken away the last bit of structure left in Japanese society, and so concessions were made.

Widely admired and trusted, Yamamoto would have been a steadying influence on the Japanese public if he had lived during the occupation. The man who would become prime minister in 1956, Tanzan Ishibashi, said in an interview, ". . . [t]o tell the truth, we'd had a vague idea that [Yamamoto] might take things in hand after the war. You see, if a man with such an illustrious war record took over, the public could be persuaded to put up with their dissatisfactions just by the idea that it was 'Admiral Yamamoto' who was responsible. The very fact that he'd been labeled pro-British and pro-American before the war worked in his favor, as we saw it, in trying to integrate public opinion in the postwar period."

There could have been some American public opinion to overcome for Yamamoto to rise again. Pearl Harbor was infamous enough on its own, but Yamamoto also had a quotation hung around his neck that was repeated often in the American press. In a letter to a person in Japan who criticized Yamamoto for being soft on the West, he wrote that the only way the Japanese could win the war was to stroll down Pennsylvania Avenue, walk into the White House, and dictate the peace. His biographers believe it was sarcasm and that he really meant that America, if aroused, would be a very determined enemy. Bad PR aside, Yamamoto at worst would have fared about the same as Admiral Shimada, served some prison time, then reemerged as a public figure. It's easy to imagine the meticulous man, now in his civilian blue suit, calmly explaining how best to rebuild Japan. Though often described as "reluctant," Isoroku Yamamoto left a legacy that seemed more pragmatic than anything else. If it was war, he'd fight it. If it was peace, he'd implement it.

An Associated Press story, datelined Beijing, April 9, 2005, began:

"Chanting Down with Japan!" more than 6,000 Chinese protesters held a noisy but peaceful rally Saturday demanding a boycott of Japanese goods to oppose new textbooks that critics say gloss over Tokyo's wartime atrocities.

Even after more than 60 years, Japan's attitude about the war still sparks outrage. The nation's view of its role in World War II has metamorphosed over the years. The fervent "blame the military" campaign of the late 1940s changed to a more sympathetic attitude toward some former leaders. Later, studies of war-crime trials appeared and made the case that many of the lesser-known figures (the B- and C-class defendants) were railroaded by the foreign tribunals, and the men were unjustly executed or imprisoned. Prison memoirs began to emerge, and films and television dramas aired with the basic message that these soldiers were just following orders.

However, it isn't just the Chinese who question Japan's selective memory. Historian Stephen Ambrose wrote that the present-day view of the war presented by the Japanese ". . . runs something like this: one day, for no reason we ever understood, the Americans started dropping atomic bombs on us." He pointed out that books on the Rape of Nanjing have been banned in Japan. He added: "The atrocities against civilians in Korea, Manchuria, China, the Philippines, the Marianas, New Guinea, Guadalcanal, Indochina, Thailand, and elsewhere are ignored, forgotten. As to the victims, no apologies, no reparations. American servicemen unfortunate enough to have been captured on Bataan worked as slave labor for Japanese corporations for two or three years—and have received nothing. No apology."

Ambrose recalled a visit to Bataan where a group of former prisoners—they called themselves the Battered Bastards of Bataan—had gathered for a reunion. They shared their horror stories, and

Ambrose quoted one as saying that Americans during the war considered the "Japanese as beasts. . . ." They weren't, said the former POW. "A beast is an animal, and animals kill only to eat. The Japs killed for fun."

Still, the Japanese cling to another past. The Yasukuni Jinja shrine harbors many of these sugarcoated memories. Though foreigners (and some Japanese) condemn the historical exclusion of the horrible violence committed by Japan, a woman in an interview at the shrine made a point that helps explain the complicated feelings held by so many of her countrymen: "(These) are people who died for our country and if we do not respect them, who else will?"

The Puzzle

OVER THE YEARS, the midget submarines created an intriguing historical puzzle. On their hulls, the vessels either had no identifying mark or simply the manufacturing number imprinted when the sub came off the assembly line. Since the subs looked alike, the only way to know which one was which was by the identity of the crews. Bob Ballard thought he was searching for *I-16-A*, but he acknowledged that it was impossible to know which sub had been sunk by the first shot. He wrote in his book *Graveyards of the Pacific*: "What if a Navy dredging operation had later covered our *16-A* or *(I)-20-A* with sand and rubble?"

The fates of the salvaged midget subs vary: some have attained places of honor while another serves as landfill under a U.S. Navy-built pier. There's also speculation that another might have been more successful in attacking battleship row on December 7, 1941, than anyone had ever guessed; and of course the *Ward*'s sub has been the target of intense searches by many underwater explorers.

Two midget subs were accounted for in the first few weeks of the war. Kazuo Sakamaki's sub washed ashore and after being fitted with portholes for viewing and equipped with samurai mannequins for theatrical flare, it gained fame on war bond tours. Rather than being scrapped, however, *I-24-A* became a trophy the Navy couldn't quite bring itself to discard. The little sub finished its war bond duty in Chicago and was stored there until January,

1947, when it was transferred to the Navy's Submarine Base at Key West, Florida. It sat outside and suffered some salt-air corrosion, but inspections showed the well-built craft held up in its new home. In 1964 the sub was moved about half a mile to the Key West Lighthouse Museum, a tourist stop. By 1987, the sub's novelty must have worn off, and the little craft was set for another transfer. The National Park Service, which runs the USS *Arizona* Memorial at Pearl Harbor, considered taking the sub and placing it on exhibit, an addition the Park Service hoped would bring another perspective to the memorial; a Park Service historian even worked to have the sub declared a National Historic Landmark. One idea kicked around was that the sub would be tied above the sunken *Arizona*. Always a magnet for attention, *I-24-A* soon became the target of criticism from veterans' groups, which apparently didn't want a Japanese weapon anywhere near the *Arizona*. The sub's presence would be a "Vulgar disregard of the feelings of the veterans . . . ," according to one organization.

Shunned by the *Arizona* memorial, Sakamaki's sub drew interest from other museums, including two on Oahu. However, the sub found a home at the Nimitz Center Museum in Fredericksburg, Texas (Fleet Admiral Nimitz's hometown). One early photo from that site shows that the sub must have been hastily reassembled after transit because the bow and stern sections had been swapped and looked like a shoe on the wrong foot. Properly assembled, the little sub—launched from *I-24* on December 7, 1941— now sits next to the section honoring the World War II exploits of a very lucky pilot, former President George H. W. Bush. Apparently the president, something of a Texan, held some sway and helped the Nimitz Museum land the sub prize.

The little sub captained by Lieutenant Naoji Iwasa was launched from *I-22* at 1:16 A.M. on December 7. Iwasa had been an early proponent and test pilot of the midget subs. Like many of the officers in the Japanese Navy, he came from the kind of rugged family life that seemed to help them withstand the rigors of the Naval Academy and the training that followed. In early 1941, Iwasa returned to his middle school to address his class reunion. One person asked, "What would you do if a superior officer were to ask you for your life?" Iwasa looked straight at the questioner and replied, "Just die." Then he walked away.

Iwasa's crewmate, Naokichi Sasaki, was another poor country boy determined to have a naval career. He flunked his first entrance exam, which only increased his resolve to pass, which he did on his second try after a marathon of study. That sort of drive and will seemed commonplace among the midget sub crews.

I-22-A was severely damaged by the *Monaghan*. It was raised a few weeks after it sank and placed for viewing at Pearl Harbor. A Marine lieutenant went by to check it out:

> Today we went over to the sub base to take a look at one of the midget submarines. . . . She's out of the water, resting on chocks. And doesn't look like much because she's so small. . . . The conning tower is tiny, with room enough for one man to steer the craft. He's still in there. One of our ships rammed him broadside and he's caught, dead, with his legs still hanging out . . .

The sub drew other curious observers and the area was roped off. One viewer commented that "the stench was terrible."

The physical condition of the sub confirmed the *Monaghan*'s depth-charge accuracy. Pictures show the "washboarding" caused by the underwater explosions; the force rippled and dimpled the sides of the sub. The aft section, between the engine and battery sections, received some sort of direct hit, and the fore section looks as if it exploded from the inside. Sub experts say the crew may have set off the scuttling charge at about the same time the little sub was rammed, the purpose apparently being to blow up the *Monaghan*.

The U.S. Navy had a short funeral service for the two men—their bodies were still in the sub—then rolled it into a ditch, where it lay covered for a decade. In 1952, a dragline working on a dock improvement project was digging in the area when it hit something it couldn't move. The teeth of the dragline bucket had penetrated the long-forgotten sub, which emitted a powerful odor. The nauseous gas came from the batteries, which the dredge had torn into. The workmen, who were gagging on the smell, put on gas masks and helped move the sub into another trench, where it was buried yet again. Navy Lieutenant Earl Bronson, who supervised the work, confirmed that "the crew [was] still inside."

Sometime after the little sub sank, a piece of clothing from one of the Japanese crew members had been recovered. After the war, that item—an insignia on a sleeve—was rumored to have been sent back to the family of the dead sailor. The sleeve allegedly belonged to the pilot, Iwasa, likely the man with his legs dangling from his vessel. The sleeve today is in the War Memorial Museum that honors the Japanese who died in World War II. The museum is part of the Yasukuni Jinja shrine, a memorial to those who "offered up their lives in battle" in what the Japanese refer to as the Great East Asian War. The shrine contains a restructured view of Japan's military history, including a positive characterization of men tried and executed as war criminals; they are referred to as martyrs. The museum and shrine advertise themselves as a way to inform "a generation that does not know war." The museum downplays such horrors as the 1937 Rape of Nanjing—referred to as the Nanjing Incident—with this explanation: "Chinese troops were soundly defeated, suffering heavy casualties. Inside the city, residents were once again able to live their lives in peace." Iwasa's sleeve (he was the only midget submariner with a full lieutenant's rank) is, according to a museum official in 2004, in the "Yushukan," or the "elite" section, his failed mission honored still.

I-18-A had been launched at 2:15 A.M. and most likely never made it into Pearl Harbor. There was such a frenzy of depth charging outside the harbor on December 7, the little sub was extremely vulnerable to the blanket of explosions. The facts about *I-18-A*'s fate first came to light in 1960 in a very unlikely place: 76 feet of water. A diving instructor had taken his students out to Keehi Lagoon at Pearl

Harbor. The water there usually stayed murky from the silt stirred up in the harbor. This day it wasn't. A lone diver came to the surface and told his instructor he thought he'd seen a submarine. The instructor dived back down with the student, and there sat the little sub, nestled upright on the seabed. It was raised by a Navy salvage ship crew, who inspected the inside: pipes were mangled, the engine overturned, and instruments broken—all evidence that depth charges had fatally damaged the craft. The two-man crew had vanished without a trace. The lack of forensic evidence reinforced the rumor that had circulated for years: "They were either drowned and their bodies swept out to sea—or they swam ashore," wrote one submarine historian in Hawaii. "It is remotely possible one or both lived here for years, undetected. Possibly one or both are still alive today." His theory was never substantiated.

Salvaging the sub proved a delicate task. Despite the beating the midget sub had taken, the scuttling charge still sat ready, as did the two torpedoes, packing a total of more than 1,500 pounds of explosives. The deadly force of such a blast wasn't lost on the salvage crews. The decision was made to unbolt the dangerous section of the sub and dump it overboard. The task was relatively simple; even after twenty years underwater, the bolts unscrewed with ease. Two-thirds of a sub came back to Oahu. It then received a cursory inspection as arrangements were made to notify the Japanese.

For some years after the war, the rights of the Japanese nation received little attention from the United States. By 1960, that had changed, and Japan's consul in Hawaii was invited to inspect the sub. As a casualty of war, it still belonged to his country—it was Japanese territory. It was shipped to Eta Jima, near Hiroshima, where the Japanese Naval Academy had been before the atomic bomb blast leveled it and everything else. While there the little sub received a new front end. It was during this restoration that a discovery was made. The Japanese workers found a number of items: a damaged uniform, a boot, a glove, a rubber sandal, and a bottle of sake; all apparently had been overlooked by the

Americans searching the craft in Hawaii. The shoe was identified as belonging to the skipper of *I-18-A*, Sub Lieutenant Shigemi Furuno. Another Naval Academy graduate, Furuno had the right attitude for midget sub duty. His favorite song contained the line, "I'll come back surely in a small casket." His shipmate was Petty Officer First Class Shigenori Yokoyama.

Thus the fate of three subs (*I-24-A*, *I-22-A*, and *I-18-A*) became known. Today Furuno's refurbished sub sits on a pedestal in front of the Self-Defense Academy, the replacement school for the tough, "cold water" naval academy. The little sub has become a shrine of sorts that attracts those curious about Japan's warrior past.

Into the 1970s, '80s, and '90s—especially as the fiftieth anniversary of the Pearl Harbor attack approached—speculation again arose over the fate of the little subs that remained unaccounted for and also whether the *Ward* had actually shot a sub—and if so, which one. Ten years before Bob Ballard's search, *National Geographic* had sent out a camera crew, with National Park Service staff members; they filmed as they searched outside the harbor and picked through the military junk scattered over the ocean floor, but that search ended unsuccessfully. The footage became the basis for a *National Geographic Explorer* television series episode titled "Secret Subs of Pearl Harbor."

When Bob Ballard began his exploration, he brought along *I-16* radioman Dewa, who revealed a critical piece of information. He said he had contact with *I-16-A* about 12 hours after the attack on Pearl Harbor. The three men had agreed before launching that *I-16-A* would send a coded telegraphic message saying *"tora-tora-tora"* (tiger-tiger-tiger) if its mission were successful. Dewa did receive a signal from the little sub, but because of what he believed was a radio malfunction, the message was *"kira-kira-kira,"* (which means glittering) not "tora-tora-tora." After that, nothing.

If *I-16-A* were still capable of sending messages on the night of December 7, it couldn't have been the sub shot by the *Ward* that morning. The crewmen on this sub, yet to be recovered, were

Masaji Yokoyama and Sadamu Ueda. Yokoyama, the skipper of *I-16-A*, had spent countless hours meditating at the graveside of the great naval war hero, Admiral Togo, the victorious leader in the Russo-Japanese war in the early 1900s. Petty Officer Ueda had the typical midget sub crew background: He grew up poor in a mountainous area and through hard work finished high school and joined the Navy; he became a submariner and was later named to the midget sub squad. Like the other crew members, he seemed to know he was never coming back. He packed all his belongings in a couple of suitcases and left them in a flower shop.

But *I-16-A* might have been the most successful midget sub of all. In Japan the first flurry of publicity about the midget subs credited them with torpedoing the battleship *Arizona*. This caused a stir among the Japanese pilots, who knew it was their bombs that blew the ship's powder magazine, which is why it sank so rapidly. Around 1990, another theory was posed: a little sub had indeed made it into the harbor and fired its torpedoes, not at the *Arizona*, but at the battleship *West Virginia*. Autometric Inc., a Boeing company specializing in photo imagery and analysis, examined a famous photograph taken by a Japanese aircraft as it pulled away from its run. It's easy to see the semi-circular shock waves and follow the torpedoes' trails as they streamed toward battleship row. In the background, clouds of smoke—the classic funeral pyre photos of Pearl Harbor—already drift up in the sky. The time was about 8:00 A.M., meaning the worst was yet to come. In the middle left of the photo, just off Ford Island, a skiff is floating; it's not possible to tell if someone is in the boat or whether it is simply adrift. In the same area there seems to be something just in front of the skiff. With photo enhancement, it looks as if a conning tower might be popping out of the water. Also, there seem to be torpedo trails heading straight for the battleships. It has been speculated that this might be *I-16-A* after it fired. The subs were notorious, of course, for bobbing to the surface after launching a torpedo. The skiff's size and the size of the image also provide some sense of scale; in terms of height and length, this could be *I-16-A*. Factor in

Dewa's late-night message, and it is at least possible that the midget sub accomplished what few thought possible.

This theory intrigued history buffs and engineers enough to try an experiment. To prove the point, a crew from the Discovery Channel actually did a mock test in 2003 to see if it were possible that the image was accurate. Marine engineers designed, and a movie prop company built, a fiberglass and Styrofoam model sub, about one-third the size of the real midget sub. They then went to a lake north of Los Angeles to recreate the scene. It's not Oahu's Pearl Harbor, but there are some reasonable similarities. They were able to match the lighting and take a picture from atop a hill that has a similar angle to the original aerial photo. The little sub in the lake has a resemblance to the object in the photo taken on December 7, 1941. It's at least plausible that *1-16-A* made it into the harbor.

The historians and engineers even started matching up the torpedo trails in the photo with splashes made when the torpedoes were dropped from the Japanese aircraft. There are four clear splashes, and the torpedo trails lead back to them. There also are two trails that don't seem to have splashes, but instead are traced back to rooster-tail plumes of water. The theory is that the sub's propeller churned up the water, sort of the way an electric mixer shoots up a column of liquid if the blades get too near the surface. Burl Burlingame, an author who lives in Hawaii and has probably spent more time than anyone else studying the Japanese midget submarine attack, said that it's very likely the photo shows a midget sub in the harbor. He notes that he has studied the torpedo damage to the *West Virginia*, and he believes it received unusually hard hits. The two midget sub torpedoes would help explain the extra destruction.

The Discovery show, "Unsolved History: Myths of Pearl Harbor," couldn't have done much more to explore every angle of the incident. They even included a mock game, played to see what would have happened if the warning of the attack had come at about 4:00 A.M., based on the *Condor*'s contact with what may have been *I-20-A* or *I-22-A*. There was significant disagreement about what would have occurred if the sub's sighting had alerted command at Pearl Harbor. One theory was that the U.S. ships would have left the harbor to search for the Japanese and in the process suffered losses from an open-sea aerial attack about equal to those at Pearl Harbor. Either way, the day would have ended in a Japanese victory. But that assessment probably underestimates the effects of sending up American aircraft and preparing anti-aircraft guns. The first wave of Japanese planes to attack Pearl Harbor suffered only nine losses. The second wave lost 20 planes. Also, if crews had been above deck, they wouldn't have been trapped in sinking ships.

A problem with the theory that *I-16-A* penetrated the harbor is the report from the cruiser *St. Louis*. Its veteran captain and his junior officer both watched from the bridge as two torpedoes missed their ship. No big *I*-boats were in the vicinity; they'd been ordered to stay miles away from the harbor entrance. (One big sub stationed 17 miles out closed to 8 miles at sunset that day.) If *I-16-A* entered the harbor and fired at the battleship at about 8:00, then it wasn't the midget sub that fired at the *St. Louis*.

There's another possibility, though on first consideration it seems far-fetched. Since the photo was taken around 8:00, the little sub crew could have entered the harbor, decided not to fire its torpedoes, and retreated in time to attack the *St. Louis*. This seems extremely illogical when the main mission was to enter the harbor and torpedo the American ships docked there. However, if the idea was to block the entrance to Pearl Harbor to bottle up the fleet, the shot at the *St. Louis* is at least plausible. That a young sub pilot in the heat of his first battle made a crazy choice is not unimaginable. It also helps answer two questions: What was that object in the water? *I-16-A* in the harbor. Which sub fired at the *St. Louis*? The retreating *I-16-A*.

Where *I-16-A* finally came to rest remains a mystery as well. If the little sub headed as instructed to Lanai for a rendezvous, then it's anyone's guess what happened. Did the crew ditch the sub and receive help from a friendly sampan? Did the crew perish when the sub's batteries quit? As Ballard began his search in November 2000, no one knew. Neither *I-16-A* nor *I-20-A* had ever been found.

The Second Attack Flotilla didn't cause quite the stir of the first midget sub attacks, but they had their time in the spotlight. The two midget subs blasted in Sydney Harbor were recovered and hauled ashore. The four bodies of the crewmen were given a military funeral complete with gun salute, and later the ashes of the crew were shipped to Japan for burial. As at Pearl Harbor, the Australian crews took two subs and reconstructed one whole one. (The Pearl Harbor reconstruction didn't require many parts to be replaced because Sakamaki's sub had washed ashore only slightly damaged.) The subs from Sydney required some work to produce a complete craft. The sub emerged and went on the road, just like its counterpart in the United States. Carried on a trailer, the sub toured various cities to raise money for the Australian Naval Relief Fund. Crowds flocked, brass bands played, and fund drives hauled in money—500,000 people came to see it and £28,000 was raised. People even scratched their names and hometowns onto the sub. The sub was transported to the Australian War Memorial in 1943. Decades later, vandals painted the sub yellow, inspired by the Beatles' song, "Yellow Submarine." It was repainted black.

Two midget sub crew members of the attack on Madagascar are buried in a grave overlooking the harbor they penetrated. They had received full praise at home for searching high and low throughout the harbor at Diégo Suarez and destroying all the ships there (one was actually hit), but these submariners didn't make it back, either; the captain of *I-16* had to send his regrets about the losses to the emperor. A marker was erected in the 1960s, and the gravesite still attracts the curious, who leave flowers and other tokens for the crewmen—Akieda and Takemoto. They almost certainly were the two men who charged the machine gun position with swords and were cut down when they would not surrender. The British, however, offered a different story about the midget sub crew. They say the midget sub ran aground on a reef, and the two crew members were hunted down and killed. Either way, they were buried together on the hill.

The Wreck Bob Ballard Couldn't Find

IN MID-NOVEMBER 2000, searching for the last time, Bob Ballard thought he had at last honed in on his target. At sea for almost two weeks with his talented crew, top-notch equipment, and anxious World War II veterans, he came across an algae-covered clump that looked like a group of batteries. They could have been used by a midget sub for power. Next came a torpedo and more debris. This was it. A closer examination, however, showed that the clump wasn't batteries but old ammunition clips, and the torpedo couldn't have been a midget sub's—it had been disarmed and dumped there. Ballard told the crew, "We found a bunch of junk." Then he did something he rarely, if ever, had done. He quit.

The Japanese radioman Dewa poured a green bottle of sake into the sea and clasped ceremonial prayer beads to honor the spirit of his fallen colleagues, still lost at sea. The three surviving sailors looked out across the ocean that had been their battleground. *Ward* veterans Lehner and Reetz told Dewa how glad they were to have met him. They were old men happy simply to have survived such a terrible war. But the ending to their chapter still wasn't written.

The little sub that eluded so many searches remained hidden

from the world's best underwater explorer—a very difficult thing to do. As for the fate of the sub—either *I-16-A* or *I-20-A*—Ballard believed it probably had imploded in 1,000 feet of water, the sub's identity to remain a mystery forever. No one would ever find it. Historian Stephen Ambrose, for his part, wrote that one of Ballard's submersibles had spotted two torpedoes side by side. "They almost certainly were the torpedoes carried by the midget sub," he surmised. Even Ambrose and Ballard could occasionally miss the mark, however. They were looking in the wrong place.

• • •

Terry Kerby looks like a guy who'd be cast in the role of submersible pilot. A trim 5-feet-11, he had the deep tan and blond hair—occasionally tied back with a red bandana—that gave him a look somewhere between a beach boy and a pirate. "Terry's an adventurer," said one of his colleagues at the undersea lab. Hardly the son of a sailor, he had grown up far from salt water, on the edge of Yosemite National Park in Lake Bass, California. To attend elementary school, he had had to endure daily 100-mile round-trip bus rides. He remembered from the time he was a kid in the isolated mountain country, "I always loved submersibles." When he was old enough, he left the scenic Sierras for the sun and surf of Southern California. After a short stint in college (he later returned to earn his degree), Kerby joined the Coast Guard. Serving as a navigator, he traveled to Alaska, Puerto Rico, and the Bahamas, and along the way became an expert diver. He earned a Coast Guard commendation medal for helping save the lives of two people trapped underneath a capsized boat.

Kerby ended up in Hawaii looking for a job. One day he wandered down to the Makai Pier. There he saw it: *Star 2*, a yellow submersible 5 feet in diameter, capable of achieving depths up to 1,200 feet. It was owned by a company called Deep Water Exploration, which harvested the deep-water pink and gold coral used for making jewelry. He landed a job crewing on the submersible; then the company was hired to harvest red coral in the South China Sea between Taiwan and the Philippines. The job was supposed to last one month, but ran to more than three. During that time, Kerby became a pilot. The original pilot, Kerby said, "kind of freaked out." It was grueling, non-stop duty: his weight dropped from 173 pounds to 148.

His job led him to cross paths with Al Giddings, the legendary undersea movie producer, whose credits included *The Deep* and a movie Kerby worked on, *For Your Eyes Only*, a James Bond thriller starring Roger Moore. Kerby was the dive master for the Bond film and helped construct an undersea set complete with Roman columns. His other chores included working as a stunt double and a shark wrangler. Captured tiger sharks brought in by a crew from the University of Miami were let loose and filmed on the set, but it was Kerby's job to recapture the notorious predators after they had left the frame of the camera shot. His instructions were, he said with a laugh, "not to harm the sharks."

After his Bond film experience, Kerby landed back in Hawaii and worked for HURL. He'd actually been thinking about the *Ward*'s midget sub for years. In the 1970s, when he was in the Coast Guard, his crew had been taken to see the movie *Tora! Tora! Tora!* in Seattle because it was supposed to be a realistic portrayal of the attack on Pearl Harbor. Much of the film is forgettable, but in one scene a midget sub periscope trails a supply ship into Pearl Harbor. The image stuck with Kerby. He couldn't know then that the search for that mysterious sub would be an episode replayed in his life for years to come.

Once a year, the university's submersibles were sent out to make test runs, check out equipment, and train new pilots. Kerby saw this as the perfect opportunity to explore areas where the lost midget sub might be resting. As long as the submersibles were diving, he figured, he might as well also tackle the secondary mission of looking for a piece of history. After all, the primary restriction on searching for the sub was cost. Leasing a ship, taking out the submersibles, and paying the crew amounted to thousands of dollars a day, but the annual test and training runs were already part of the university's budget. Why not test and train in areas that might contain the long-lost sub?

Starting his search in 1992, Kerby, like Ballard, found all manner of military relics, but no sub. On one trip he ran across a Dauntless bomber (one of the early mainstays on U.S. carriers) sitting in very good condition on the bottom in 1,000 feet of water. The discovery led him to an encounter with what he refers to as two "warbird hunters." Gary Larkins and Dave Carter made a living finding war artifacts and selling them. Larkins had a business card with his title—"Air Pirate." Kerby had run across Larkins and Carter earlier in his career, and when he found the bomber, he notified the men. They became interested in what other salvageable loot might be there for the taking and persuaded Kerby to carry them along on a search. The fee they paid offset some of the university's submersible costs.

Searching at about 600 feet, they ran across what looked like a torpedo. No, it was too big. Then all three realized almost at once that it was the stern section of a midget submarine. Larkins and Carter went berserk. While the submersible's video recorder rolled on, they yelled, "Fucking A! Fucking A!" (All the missions on the submersibles are captured on videotape with sound.) They were sure they'd found the *Ward*'s midget sub.

Kerby had his doubts: The sub section looked as if it had been dismantled, not broken apart by an explosion, and nearby cables suggested that it might have been lowered overboard. Larkins and Carter wouldn't buy it. They were sure they'd found the sub. Back on shore, Kerby discovered that the two men had "borrowed" the tape of the trip and set off for the mainland. The next thing he heard was a news report from California that the *Ward*'s sub had been found by the two men, and that they'd made a salvage claim for it in the name of their company, Aeronautic Archaeological Institute. The matter finally ended up in court, and ultimately the rightful owner—the government of Japan—was awarded first rights to the sub. In the meantime, the National Park Service was given jurisdiction. A closer inspection also showed definitely that the sub had been discarded in pieces. It may have been a Japanese sub brought back from the Philippines, Guam, or Guadalcanal by the Navy in the latter part of the war; perhaps it had been dismantled, studied for intelligence purposes, and then dropped at sea. But it wasn't the *Ward*'s midget sub. Larkins and Carter went back to searching for war treasure, and Kerby kept looking for the sub.

As the 1990s passed, Kerby kept searching during his annual test runs, which had evolved into a systematic search of the historical defensive sea area, meaning the general vicinity where the *Ward* had patrolled. One frustration was the lack of good sonar equipment. He had what amounted to a "fish finder," which meant that he'd almost have to run into the sub in order to find it. In the late 1990s he picked up slightly better sonar equipment and later found the other two sections of the midget sub that Larkins and Carter had claimed as theirs. There remained no doubt it had been taken apart and thrown into the ocean as junk, though one section looked as if it might have been damaged by an explosion.

Kerby learned of Bob Ballard's assignment with *National Geographic* from Ballard himself. The two had met before, on the James Bond movie set, when Ballard dropped by to visit Al Giddings. Ballard told Kerby in early 2000 that he wanted to set up a conference call with *National Geographic* to discuss using the university's submersibles for the search. Kerby said he would need some specific dates, and Ballard said they'd talk soon. But no call came. Suspecting a change of plan, Kerby went to see a friend who leased out the *American Islander*, and that was how he learned that *National Geographic* had chartered the ship for the first half of November. His friend seemed a little sheepish when he said, "Yeah, they were here." He knew Kerby had been the victim of an end run.

Kerby wasn't overly surprised. A veteran of underwater explorations, he knew how complicated and competitive these missions could be: there were always conflicts about who would garner the glory and the financial reward. Finding the sub amounted to discovering a treasure ship. The publicity from a find like the midget sub would attract television documentary crews willing to pay large fees for footage of the long-lost craft, not to mention the positive publicity for the university.

What few people other than Kerby realized is that by cutting him out, *National Geographic* was taking a risk. Kerby would make his annual test run in September 2000, and there was a chance he and his crew could find the sub and upstage Ballard and *National Geographic* before their November search even began. Word of Kerby's scheduled dives finally filtered up to *National Geographic*. At last Kerby heard from them. "They said they wanted to send along a photographer with me in case we found the sub, and if we did find it, they wanted to keep it quiet," he said. "Bob Ballard had to have his name on it."

Kerby believed there were several reasons *National Geographic* pursued the course it did. One good one was that *American Islander* was cheaper. Ballard could get sixteen days of time on that ship for what he would have had to pay for a week's worth of search time with the university's submersibles. Also, Kerby believed Ballard's finding the sub was important to *National Geographic* for the media attention. Already famous, Ballard would draw publicity to *National Geographic*'s television show. The search would also increase public awareness about Pearl Harbor, another key but not so obvious point. The Disney Company, with a big movie, *Pearl Harbor*, scheduled for 2001 release, was intensely interested in creating a public buzz about the 1941 sneak attack and therefore Disney put money into Ballard's search.

In September Kerby began his annual test run as usual, but this time with a *National Geographic* photographer aboard. He showed the photographer the pieces of the midget sub he'd found, and the array of military hardware scattered over the ocean—three Army PBY airplanes were among the sightings. With just a few days to search, he again failed to find the *Ward*'s midget sub, but he believed Ballard would find it. With the help of the National Park Service, Ballad had a list of the best possible search targets and the time to systematically track down each lead. An official from the Park Service told Kerby, "That sub belongs to Bob Ballard." The official was probably right, Kerby thought.

But when Ballard struck out in November 2000, Kerby knew he would have another season for sub hunting. He talked to Ballard later, and they laughed about the impossible amount of debris scattered outside the harbor. Ballard asked, "Did you see the boat turned upside down on a trailer down there?" Kerby said, yes, he'd seen the same thing, but it wasn't a boat—it was an upside-down PBY airplane. They laughed some more. All the time and money spent by *National Geographic* proved how elusive the *Ward*'s midget sub could be. Kerby didn't buy Ballard's conclusion that the sub had imploded. They just hadn't looked in the right place yet.

In 2001, in conjunction with a survey of bottom fish habitats around Oahu, the National Oceanic and Atmospheric Administration (NOAA) arranged to lease HURL's two submersibles, *Pisces IV* and *Pisces V*. Both submersibles—one yellow, one white—were capable of depths up to 6,500 feet. The NOAA project would bring an unexpected upgrade to the midget sub search. One of the men joining the project was Chris Kelley, a 45-year-old biologist. He had a bottom-mapping and side-scan sonar system called a tow-fish, whose primary purpose for his project was to map the underwater terrain. The tow-fish sent sound images back to the boat that was pulling it, and the data were fed into a computer. The printed images that came out were called "shadows"; these appeared as dark blips that roughly matched the shapes of the objects on the ocean floor—similar to real shadows. When operated correctly, the tow-fish could give an extraordinarily accurate picture.

The trick for Terry Kerby was to interest Chris Kelley in looking for the midget sub as a side project to the biologist's main endeavor, which was to study red snapper habitat. Kerby showed Kelley photos of the sections of the midget sub he'd previously discovered, hoping a glimpse of what might be out there would fuel Kelley's adventurous side. Kelley was hooked. "I never hesitated," he later said.

The plan had a major flaw, however. A biologist, Kelley didn't really know how to use the sonar device. "I kind of inherited the thing," he said. "It came along with the department." Attached to a long cable, typically at least 1,000 feet long, the tow-fish, pulled along by a boat, "swam" near the bottom of the ocean. After a test run with the device, Kelley reviewed the results. "They were crap," he said. He called in reinforcements from his department, though they also lacked training for this task. Among the irregulars was Hal Richman, an animal endocrinologist, which meant he knew a lot more about hormones than tow-fish. He had some skill in tinkering with electronic gadgets and tried to figure out how to operate the device. They kept making sonar test runs but with little success. On one outing the fins came off the tow-fish, and it was doing 180-degree flip-flops as it was pulled. The readings were laughable.

They finally lassoed a graduate student from the mainland who had some experience with how the tow-fish was supposed to work. She stayed for a few weeks during the summer of 2001 and taught the biology team the basics of sonar technology. The results improved; they discovered they weren't towing the "fish" close enough to the bottom. The final improvement came when they upgraded to a sturdy "armored" cable more than 2,000 feet long, so they could methodically "stripe the ocean floor," as Richman put it.

In late February and early March 2002, Kelley and crew made a run on a 46-foot, two-hulled boat in some areas Kerby had asked them to survey. As always, the bottom was overly rich with targets. Kelley said they spotted thirty-nine "possibles," but two readings stood out. They evaluated one from three different angles. The object was clearly oblong, like a cucumber. It measured about 80 feet long and 5 feet wide. Because of Kerby's suggestion, they had taken the reading in an area "outside the box"—beyond the historical defensive perimeter. Few submersibles (if any) had ever systematically searched there.

There also was an image "inside the box" that looked promising. It was oblong and seemed to have something like a conning tower protruding from its center. The sonar readings were finished in March, but Kerby wasn't scheduled to go out until August. He said the wait through spring and summer "almost killed me." Would some new celebrity TV crew come along and make the find? Kelley and Kerby started to refer to the promising images with a code word—"canoes." (Kerby had years earlier spotted a canoe amid the debris on the ocean floor around Pearl Harbor.)

On the first day out, August 24, 2002, the submersibles headed straight for the most promising target—the one that had produced three cylindrical images. While the sonar readings themselves looked excellent, actually plotting the location on a grid and finding the exact spot on the ocean floor proved tricky. Two lines that looked close together on what's called a "small-scale large-area chart" could actually be several hundred feet apart. With only 30 feet or so of visibility, that distance might as well have been a thousand miles.

On day one, with Kerby piloting *Pisces IV* and Chris Holloway skippering *Pisces V*, they searched the area and came up with nothing. The crew believed the search was so thorough, "we just didn't see how we missed it," said Kelley. He suspected they had miscalculated the image's location. On day two, they decided to search for the second most promising target—the one with the "conning tower" sticking out. It lay within the defensive perimeter, and the submersibles found it without difficulty. It was indeed close to the right shape and size. Unfortunately, it was made of cement—a concrete piling with a rock protruding nearby. It wasn't a conning tower, and it wasn't a sub. Now they had one day left.

Debate that night centered on where to go next. Kelley and some others wanted to try the remaining "promising" targets within the perimeter. They believed they had searched the first areas as well as they could. Kerby had a different idea. He'd taken a grid and recharted the sonar reading on a large-scale chart. The cylindrical image was too good to give up on, and he had a new tack. He wanted to come in from a different direction. In the first attempt they had approached the area from the east. Now Kerby suggested they try from the north.

At 6-feet-7-inches tall, Al Kavaltis wasn't the ideal candidate for duty on a submersible. The underwater vessel's hatch is only 19 inches wide, and inside, it's about the size of a commercial jetliner cockpit. With Kavaltis and two other people aboard, the submersible had all the roominess of a tin of sardines. Also, Kavaltis, with thinning gray hair and a weather-beaten face, was entering the grandfatherly stage of his life. At age 62, he could already feel his stiff joints aching. He was the safety administrator for NOAA on Oahu and had asked many times to go along with the crew on one of its runs. NOAA, after all, was picking up part of the cost of the submersibles. In the past, it always seemed that "Al got bumped by some dignitary whenever there might be a chance to make the trip," Kerby said. Kavaltis was cleared to go out the last day of the three-day mission.

He rose at 4:00 A.M., ate a light breakfast, and drank one cup of coffee. Keeping liquids to a minimum was a must: the last dive of the season was scheduled for seven hours, and there are no bathrooms on submersibles. That morning HURL's research vessel *Kaimikai-Kanaloa* cruised out in the blue-green water of the Pacific. It was completely calm. Kerby, Kavaltis, and a trainee, Colin Wollerman, climbed aboard *Pisces IV*, as Chris Kelley, Chris Holloway, and Rachel Shackelford boarded the bright-yellow sister craft, *Pisces V*. The submersibles were lowered from an A-frame on the boat's stern and bobbed gently in the water. They started their descent, dropping about 85 feet a minute. After less than 10 minutes the *Pisces* team stopped at 800 feet, 30 feet from the bottom.

With their searchlights flipped on, they ran through phase one of the primary training exercises, to acquaint Wollerman with safety procedures. The first part of the session went without a hitch. The submersibles tested their tracking and communications gear and then did "entanglement exercises," in which they simulated the procedure they would use to cut away cable lines if they snagged the vessels' maneuvering arms or antennas.

Then the unexpected happened. Kerby's submersible actually caught on a 1-inch wire cable. When Kerby tried to move, the sub's propeller did nothing more than blow up a silt cloud. The submersible's starboard "arm," used for gathering items, was entangled. Kerby was stuck, and this was no exercise. Kavaltis began to wonder why the heck he'd come on this day. "Al was pretty upset," said Kerby. Shackelford, who'd crewed before on *Pisces V*, later explained, "Being caught on the bottom is the worst thing that can happen." Kerby's years of experience paid off. He maneuvered the arm away from the cable with a few moves and again headed for his target.

Then another problem: although the *Pisces* submersibles could communicate with each other, *Pisces V* lost communication with the mother ship that had brought them. Kerby thought it best for the two subs not to stray too far from each other, especially after he'd just escaped from a dangerous situation. Loose cables, twisted metal, and jagged edges all presented constant threats.

As they worked their way across the bottom, Terry Kerby at last believed he had a good grasp of where they were. He spotted a boulder sitting alone on a stretch of ocean floor and matched it with a sonar reading. It served as a landmark—an underwater positioning point from which to operate. The place they wanted to explore was a line of rocks about 90 feet away. Two days earlier they had approached the boulders from the east; now they were looking at the seascape from a different angle. The lights pierced the ocean depths, but the visibility was still limited. As they surveyed the area, Kerby in *Pisces IV* had to stop and change the CO_2-saturated air filter in the submersible. He told *Pisces V* to go ahead.

Then, three minutes later, at 12:20 P.M., pilot Holloway in *Pisces V* said, " . . . it's a . . . submarine." Kelley grabbed the communications microphone and said, "Terry, Terry we got it. . . ."

Kerby had been about 90 feet away. As he approached the sub, one of the first things he noticed was how hard it was to spot—almost like an optical illusion. "If you're abeam of it, you couldn't see it at all," he said. The sub had settled in the row of rocks so that from one angle, all that was visible was the end of the sub, and it blended into the seascape. From the new angle it sat there like a fat fish on a platter. The sub was in remarkably good condition. The currents had scoured the sand around the boat so it balanced on rocks as though it were on a pedestal. Almost upright, its torpedo guards remained intact, but the tail section had a broken propeller guard. Kerby speculated that the sub had dragged its aft section on the ocean floor sixty years ago before it laid itself to rest.

Proof that the sub was indeed the one sunk by the *Ward* came as Kerby and Holloway did their flyovers. "I could see the hole in the conning tower," Kerby said. He couldn't see through the hole, so it's likely the shell hadn't penetrated both sides of the tower. It's also likely that the pilot of the sub was killed instantly, since that was where he would have been standing to steer and look through the sub's periscope. The sub still carried both of its torpedoes. It never had a chance to fire them on December 7.

As it turns out, Al Kavaltis had picked the right day to take a dive in the Pacific. "I can't believe it," said Kavaltis. "It was like finding the *Titanic*." The Pisces team had been very, very close the first day, August 24. Kelley estimates they must have closed within 90 feet or so, but just couldn't see it. He credits Kerby with the find: "Terry made the right decisions. It's his discovery," Kelley said.

Word was radioed back to shore, and when the crew from the submersibles arrived, the media were waiting. The discovery elated Daniel Martinez, chief historian for the National Park Service at the USS *Arizona* Memorial. He told the press, "We've been talking about this incident that took place nearly an hour and a half before the attack on Pearl Harbor for nearly sixty years. Now we have the tangible evidence of what happened out there." Martinez was holding up a Park Service map and pointing to what had been a "highly probable" target during the Ballard search. Martinez in fact had been a big supporter of Bob Ballard's expedition. The place where he was pointing, of course, wasn't anywhere near where the *Pisces* team had found the midget sub. Kerby had long ago determined what Martinez's "highly probable" was. When he walked by, he said to Martinez, "It's a rock, Dan. A rock."

Kerby had a logical explanation for how the sub ended up about half a mile from where it was hit. The rudder was stuck and turned hard to starboard. The stern dive plates remained upright, and they would have helped the sub glide through the water. Kerby believed the sub went into a long, slow spiral. In water over 800 feet deep, it descended far beyond where anyone had previously guessed. Among his theories, Ballard, too, had speculated about whether the sub's skipper had been killed instantly, and the sub had drifted where no one could have anticipated. Ballard imagined seawater pouring into it as if blasted from a fire hose. The last minutes for the other crewman would have been horrific: batteries leaking caustic gas, the lights shorting out, the sub plunging deeper and deeper. What would someone think in those last moments: about a loved one, about the sacred mission to fight for his country, about the glory of dying for the emperor?

National news picked up the story right away. The *Washington Post* ran a special dispatch with the headline "Sea Yields a Story of Pearl Harbor, U.S. Fired First Shot, Sinking Enemy Sub" and interviewed surviving *Ward* crew members. U.S. Senator Daniel K. Inouye of Hawaii, a World War II hero, called it an important piece of history. Naval historians pitched in as op-ed columns speculated about the one-hour warning that was ignored and might have saved lives. People quickly revived the comparisons between the Pearl Harbor attack and the 9/11 terrorist attacks that destroyed the World Trade Center in New York and damaged the Pentagon in

Washington. The two events offered similar "what-ifs." What if the *Ward*'s report had received immediate attention? What if the ships at Pearl Harbor had sounded general quarters and most of the men below deck had come topside? What if airport security had done its job on 9/11? What if the World Trade Center buildings had been evacuated promptly?

Soon television crews from Fox Network, the Discovery Channel, and the History Channel descended on scenic Pearl Harbor to report the story of the first shot. As part of the Discovery Channel show, Kerby met Will Lehner, one of the *Ward* crewmembers who had accompanied Bob Ballard. The two men hit it off. Lehner was still disappointed that Ballard hadn't found the sub, but Kerby had a treat for him. He took the *Ward*'s cook down in the *Pisces IV* to see the midget sub. It was at that moment that all the years Kerby had spent searching for the sub seemed worth it. Lehner gazed at the sub through a porthole and marveled at it on the video screen—for him a window back in time. He commented on what great shape the little sub was in; there were a few shrapnel marks and one bullet hole. The *Ward* crew had done exactly what they said. This was where the Pacific War—arguably the worst conflict in history—had started. For the midget sub crew, of course, this was where it had ended. Kerby thought that if there were any remains inside the sub, they should be sent back to Japan for burial. The two-man Japanese crew, he said, had "been on patrol long enough."

In late 2004, a production crew for Asahi TV was in Hawaii to film the underwater wreck of what is thought to be *I-20-A*. Kerby was at the helm again for the dive. The documentary focuses on a Japanese sailor who says he shut the hatch on the little sub before it launched. He has been writing a long letter to the lost crewmen. He started it sixty years ago.

Sixty-three years passed before the sub shot and sunk by the USS *Ward* was seen again by Japanese eyes. The visitors literally dropped in on December 11, 2004. Terry Kerby and the Hawaii Undersea Research Laboratory crew (aka HURLers) signed on with a Japanese TV crew to take their cameras down. The same mother ship that had originally transported Kerby and crew on their original discovery mission, R/V *Kaimikai-Kanaloa*, and the same submersibles, *Pisces IV* and *V*, newly refurbished, were set to go.

Chris Kelley, who'd worked to master the side-scan sonar and who teamed with Kerby on the original midget sub discovery, was again on board. Rachel Shackelford, also a part of the historic *Pisces* crew in 2002, had joined them as well. She said they had the little sub's location so well plotted, "we had to be careful we didn't drop down directly on it." Kelley said they had set the mark for the submersible to enter directly on top of the sub about 1,000 feet below, with the idea that it was like shooting an arrow directly up in the sky: "There's almost no chance it will come back directly down." In fact, however, on one dive Kerby found himself right above the little sub's periscope. He almost hit it, but swerved off to the side just in time.

On board with Kerby was Kenji Ishidaka, who spearheaded the project for Asahi television. He'd brought with him the letter from a Japanese sailor who'd sealed the hatch on the little sub in 1941. Among the tasks for the *Pisces* crew was to collect a scoop of sediment from around the little sub; the sacred sand was to be taken back to Japan and parceled out to veterans. The idea was to give these Japanese men a sense of closure. "[It] would finally end the last chapter of the Pacific War for them," said Kerby.

The mission that day was typical: head out at 8:30 A.M., head back by 4:30 P.M. Before returning, the Japanese and Americans gathered on the stern of the mother ship, located above the little sub. Ishidaka read a poem, dropped a bouquet of flowers into the sea, and then, a few pages at a time, threw in the long letter written to the lost crew. "It was emotional," said Shackelford. For Kerby, the discovery and the interest in it "made me feel good [because it] touched so many people in so many ways. Some ways painful but good."

There is one sub left to be found. Whether it is *I-20-A* or *I-16-A*, no one knows for sure. When the subject of more searching is broached, Chris Kelley actually groans. There's literally no telling where the missing sub is. There are some educated guesses, however. Scheduled for some time in the future is a further exploration of the *Ward*'s sub first discovered by Kerby and Kelley. The two want to return to their find to take what Kerby calls a "video survey" and search for artifacts. Kelley said there's supposed to be a sword on board that will identify the sub—at long last—as either *I-20-A* or *I-16-A*, but even that might not be as easy is it sounds. Research shows that swords were pretty standard on the midget subs. In Australia, for example, a special wedding sword was on board one sub; the mother of the pilot retrieved the sword from an Australian museum fifty years later.

So where is the last little sub? If it is *I-16-A*, it's believed to have been operational enough to send a message back to its mother sub on the night of December 7. By then the sub had to be running low on power. If the little sub was heading as planned for a rendezvous, it would be in the expanse of ocean between Pearl Harbor and Lanai, the scheduled spot where the little sub was to be ditched and the crew recovered. If the sub sank in that vicinity, the task of finding it would require years of searching by sonar; also, as Kelley points out, it is probably only poking out of the seabed. The sub Kerby and he found was sitting up and conveniently cleaned by ocean currents. In other words, there was some pure luck involved in finding it so well preserved. The last sub likely "would be hard to spot," Kelley said. "I've talked to Terry, so who knows . . ." His voice trails off.

Still one to go.

Notes

Prologue

1 **Titanic, Bismarck:** Stephen Ambrose in Ballard, *Graveyards*, 7; also Ballard, *Graveyards*, 19.

1 **only 79 feet:** Measurement specs from original design, 78.8 feet, Sakamaki, 33; 78.5 according to Delgado, 1; 78.4 according to Kemp, 75

1 **"We have attacked":** Naval Historical Center; W. W. Outerbridge at Hewitt Inquiry, 138. July 12, 1945.

2 **hit scored by the Ward's No. 3 gun:** Naval Historical Center.

3 **"to write history":** Ballard, *Graveyards*, 66.

3 **"easy duty":** Ambrose in Ballard, *Graveyards*, 8.

3 **Early on November 6:** Ballard, *Graveyards*, 18.

3 **Russell Reetz (84):** Veslilind Dispatch #1, National Geographic.com. November 8, 2000.

4 **"No one ever believed":** *Pearl Harbor: Legacy of Attack.* DVD.

4 **"and close the book":** Ballard, *Graveyards*, 19.

5 **painted with black enamel:** Delgado, 1.

5 **24 knots:** Kemp, 70.

5 **more than 500 oblong:** Delgado, 1.

5 **"take care":** Ballard, *Graveyards*, 17.

5 **swam to safety:** Ibid.

6 **"middleman":** Ballard, *Graveyards*, 32.

6 **"junk":** *Pearl Harbor: Legacy of Attack.* DVD.

7 **"the *Ward* veterans were convinced":** Ballard, *Graveyards*, 37.
7 **another Nessie:** Ballard, *Graveyards*, 38, 67.

Chapter 1

9   **"he liked the country":** Agawa, 21.
10 **Crown Point Chalet register:** His signature is definitely on the Chalet register. The distinctive "I" and "Y" are matches with his signature when he registered at Harvard, as is the "J" when he wrote "Kobe Japan" as his residence.
10 **Phillips Brooks House:** *Harvard Crimson*, October 3, 1919.
10 **Hocking:** *Harvard Crimson*, September 22, 1919.
10 **"yellow race":** *Harvard Crimson*, April 1, 1919.
10 **Though recently married:** Yamamoto did not bring his wife because it was considered improper for her to go and be influenced by "Western" values.
10 **157 Naples Road:** Harvard application. Harvard University Archives UA III 15.88.101.
10 **Enrolled in English E:** Harvard transcript. Ibid., UA III 15.2.2.10
11 **"to take up":** Ibid., UA III 15.88.101 .
11 **life-long friends:** Harvard records confirm both applied to enter Harvard and that Morimura entered as a special student (like Yamamoto). Ibid., UA III 15.88.10; Oguma's transcript shows he took Economics and withdrew in February 1921. Ibid., UA 161-272.5.
11 **Rose Bowl:** Harvard won the game on January 1, 1920.
11 **Among them was James B. Conant:** Hershberg, 49. It's interesting to consider that on campus in 1919 the man who would plan and execute the attack on Pearl Harbor and draw America into war might have bumped into the man who helped plan and execute the final catastrophic blows that would bring the conflict to an end.
11 **Autumn leaves:** Brown, 13.
11 **"Winter is about":** Ames, 312.
11 **first paralyzing storm:** Ibid., 313.
11 **Yamamoto withdrew:** Harvard, VA III 15.2.10.
11 **hitchhike:** Roger Pineau to Harvard registrar, December 11, 1974. Harvard University Archives UA III 15.88.10.
12 **Yamamoto ventured:** Agawa, 74.
12 **"A man who claims":** Ibid.
12 **Some accounts:** Naval historian Roger Pineau believed Yamamoto returned to Washington after his trip to Mexico and then returned to

Japan on May 5, 1921. He had made inquiries in 1965. However, upon publication of his book about Yamamoto he received letters from Japan contending that Yamamoto returned to Harvard and finished a two-year term. He inquired in a letter dated December 11, 1974, if the Harvard registrar had further information; Mrs. J. N. Hillgarth replied that Yamamoto had in fact withdrawn on February 7, 1920, and, "There is no other record of his being enrolled at Harvard at all. I can only assume, if his embassy was vouching for him, that he was using Harvard as a front to cover other activities." Harvard University Archives UA III 15.88.10.

13 **a Japanese version of the American CIA:** Yamamoto's training in a CIA-type organization had always been part of his official service record, but apparently it was never translated from the Japanese. He entered the spy school in 1917. (Layton, 59). He notes that a spy ring involving two Americans passing secrets to two Japanese naval officers studying English in the United States was broken in 1936.

13 **he traveled with:** Agawa, 74.

13 **In December:** Ibid., 82, also 39.

13 **"If only you'd give me":** Ibid., 75.

13 **traveled cross-country:** *Time* magazine reported this and also noted that reporters thought Yamamoto was "short on English"; they'd later discover he was pretending to speak poorly to avoid questions (*Time*, December 22, 1941); a Yamamoto expert in Tokyo says it was to buy time to consider the question more carefully

14 *Life* **magazine:** Agawa, 233.

14 **"Born into poverty":** Ibid., 85.

14 **April 4, 1884:** On his Harvard application he wrote April 4, 1885, as his birth date. The error may be because converting the Japanese calendar to the Gregorian calendar off the top of one's head can be confusing.

14 **former samurai:** Agawa, 18.

15 **literally five ten six:** Hoyt, *Yamamoto*, 21.

15 **a missionary named Newall:** Agawa, 75.

15 **finished second:** Hoyt, *Yamamoto*, 21.

15 **"cold-water" school:** Ibid., 22.

15 **graduated seventh:** Ibid., 30.

15 **signed on as a gunnery officer:** Ibid., 27.

16 **". . .two fingers on my left hand":** Agawa, 2.

16 **name change came in 1916:** Hoyt, *Yamamoto*, 37.

17 **"it's Yamamoto who's beginning to have an edge on us."** Agawa, 38.

18 **"a bear's paw."** Ibid., 41.

18 **"If America's five":** Ibid., 37.

18 **The ships were twice as big:** Ibid., 91.

19 **"I'm afraid you'll be out":** Ibid., 93.

19 **"the three great follies":** Ibid., 93.

19 **previously worked for the Sopwith aircraft company:** Potter, 23.

20 **"avoid war with America":** Agawa, 189.

20 **"enemy is always America":** Potter, 33.

20 **The "February 26 Incident":** Agawa, 95.

21 **Navy vice minister:** Hoyt, 93; Agawa, chronology.

21 *farragoes:* Agawa, 161.

21 **100,000 yen:** Ibid., 163.

21 **interfered with his regular visits to a mistress:** Ibid., 162. One tactic the anti-Yamamoto groups considered was exposing publicly his relationship with his mistress. Yamamoto's relationship with several mistresses became public knowledge when Agawa's biography was published in 1969.

21 **"felt a sense of relief":** Ibid., 172.

21 **"Yamamoto's got no guts":** Ibid., 173.

22 **"(T)here'd have been a danger":** Ibid., 170.

23 **around April or May of 1940:** Ibid., 193.

23 **to attack the Philippines:** Ibid.,196.

23 **On January 7, 1941:** Ibid., 219–220.

23 **"obvious that the time":** Ibid.

23 **"outcome must be decided":** Ibid., 220.

24 **"there was no shortcut":** Ibid., 222.

24 **Kagoshima Bay:** Ibid., 227.

25 **"the other side has brought":** Ibid., 227–228.

26 **"give them hell":** Ibid., 233.

26 **"Why didn't Yamamoto":** Ibid., 233.

26 **"ready for distribution":** Ibid., 237.

27 **an appointment with Yamamoto:** Burlingame, 9.

27 **the sub's limited range:** Potter, 75.

27 **"can do so much more damage":** Burlingame, 90.

27 **a remote island of Niihau:** Burlingame, 51.

28 **unpredictable side:** Agawa, 50.

28 **throwing cooked beans:** Ibid., 56.

28 **handstands:** Ibid., 57.

28 **Little Tramp:** Ibid., 63.

29 **if they could bring some geishas:** Ibid., 205.

29 **Seals and walruses:** Potter, 78.

29 **"scratch their heads":** Agawa, 240.

29 **cup of sake:** Ibid., 241.

29 **ceremonial meal:** Hoyt, *Yamamoto*, 122.

30 **but did not speak:** Agawa, 243.

30 **"crossing the moat":** Hoyt, *Yamamoto*, 128.

30 **presence so out of the ordinary:** Hoyt, *Yamamoto*, 130;
Agawa, 246.

Chapter 2

33 **"the epitome of the":** Prange, 201.

33 **nitrogen and argon:** Thomareas and Craddock, # 84.

34 **didn't have ballast tanks:** Love and Craddock, Vol. 6.

34 **Successfully tested":** Ibid.

35 **holds the distinction:** Ibid.

35 **The second *Nautilus*:** Verne, chap. 10.

36 **the United States fleet of one:** Love and Craddock, vol. 6.

37 **Raffaele Rossetti:** Kemp, 17.

37 **at 6:20 the bomb:** Ibid., 19.

38 **"miniature submarine":** Elios Toschi, quoted in Kemp, 19.

39 **"That swine got away":** Teseo Tesei¡, quoted in Kemp, 21.

39 **sank after being depth-charged:** Ibid., 69.

40 **"Please report what":** Churchill, quoted in Kemp, 29.

40 **"If [the operation] only":** Commander Simpson, commanding officer
of the British 10th Submarine Flotilla, quoted in Kemp, 35.

41 **an upper-crust admirer:** Ibid., 41.

42 **German for "Moor":** Ibid., 43.

42 **"a singularly unsuccessful fashion":** Ibid, 49.

43 **came in early 1945. U-boats:** Ibid., 52.

45 **24.85 knots, probably:** Ibid, 70. He quotes Kaigun Zosen Gijitsu
Gaiyo (Survey of Naval Shipbuilding Technology), which speculates
the sub could hit 27.6 knots.

45 **Tests of the subs:** Sakamaki, 33.

46 **192 two-cell batteries:** Burlingame, 72. *National Geographic* reports
there were 224.

47 **As the war continued:** Kemp, 54.

Chapter 3

49 **The voyage of the USS *Antares*:** Attilio Edward Chiappari, interview by author; also *Sea Classics*, July 2003, 14.

50 **"I could see they weren't":** Chiappari, interview.

51 **"bread and water":** *Selfridge* deck logs. Naval Historical Center; also National Archives and Records.

51 **between Wake Island and Midway:** Sakamaki, 19.

51 ***Selfridge* rejoined:** *Selfridge, Antares* deck logs.

52 **"We were in rough seas":** William Ellis, interview in La Forte and Marcello, 3

52 ***Condor*:** Naval Historical Center.

52 ***Crossbill*:** Naval Historical Center.

53 **"That's a sub":** Chiappari, interview.

53 **"How do you know?":** Ibid.

53 **"The bridge just went":** Ellis, interview in La Forte and Marcello, 4.

54 **The first day of command:** Naval Historical Center.

54 **spotted by the *Condor* at 0342:** *Condor* deck logs.

54 **should have been in a scrap pile:** *Battle Report.* There's a question about how out of date the *Ward* really was. Besides hitting a midget sub in its first action on December 7, the *Ward* later was re-outfitted and posted an outstanding record in the South Pacific. Burlingame questions the critique of the four-stackers, *Advance Force*, 26.

55 **"It was 20 below zero:** Ken Swedberg, interview by author.

55 **like falling in behind:** There's another theory that the *I-20-A* was trying to sink the *Antares* rather than sneaking into Pearl Harbor in the ship's wake. Chiappari said he had long believed the *Antares* was the target for a torpedo. If *I-20-A* could sink the *Antares* at the harbor entrance, it would block the passage and bottle up the ships that might try to escape. Ellis said, "[The sub] looked very much like she was coming out of the water and was going to let us have it right there." Interview in La Forte and Marcello, 6.

55 **"Wild Willie was something":** Russell Knapp, interview, in *The Sun*, December 7, 1971.

56 **"Shoot first and ask":** Ibid.

56 **William Tanner and his crew:** Crocker, 3.

56 **blue-and-white kimono:** Robert Cressman, historian, Naval Historical Center, interview by author.

57 **"I believed this was":** Ellis, quoted in La Forte and Marcello, 5.

57 **"We have dropped depth charges":** Naval Historical Center.

57 **"We have attacked":** Naval Historical Center; see also W. W. Outer-bridge, testimony, Hewitt Inquiry, 138. July 12, 1945.

58 **According to the report:** Wohlstetter, 23.

58 **"This dispatch is to be considered":** National Archives and Records; reprinted in Layton, et al., 536.

59 **"This means war":** Layton, et al., 290.

60 **"Too much geography":** Ibid, 225.

60 **"Don't worry about it":** Wohlstetter, 111.

60 **"For Army bombardment":** Ibid, 18.

61 **"The brass":** Knapp, interview.

62 **"It would have been merciful had it had killed me":** Layton, 315. Kimmel was slightly wounded when a bullet grazed his chest.

62 **"the guys started running":** Ellis, interview in La Forte and Marcello, 8.

62 **"then I hung up my towel":** Chiappari, interview.

62 **"They are making a lot":** Naval Historical Center.

62 **"I had no idea":** Ibid.

63 **"We expected the whole":** Knapp, interview.

63 **the gun sits today:** *St. Paul Pioneer Press*, August 30, 2002.

64 **"It had to be done":** Warner and Seno, 181.

64 **"I asked the captain":** Chiappari, interview.

65 **"You don't know":** Layton, et al., 18.

66 **"Wake up, America!":** Ibid., , 299.

67 **"Dear Eddie":** Ibid., 91.

67 **Yardley:** Ibid., 41.

68 *Captain Midnight:* Singh, 125.

69 **$684.65:** Ibid., 81.

69 **736:** quoted in Wohlstetter, 187.

69 **"The fact remains":** Ibid., 200.

70 **"Remain calm.":** Ibid., 206.

70 **"come quicker than anyone dreams.":** Ibid., 208.

71 **"wharves and buoys":** Ibid., 374.

71 **disbelief:** Prados, 165.

72 **"had enough information":** Layton, et al., 20.

73 **Tomomasa Emura pen name:** Ibid., 71.

73 **Grew:** Ibid., 74.

73 **"kicked himself":** Ibid., 18.

73 **Bywater:** Burlingame, 19.

73 *Fantasy on the Outbreak of a Japanese-American War:* Ibid., 20.

74 **"attitude that there":** Biard, video.

Chapter 4

75 **"we'd done it at last":** Takao Okuna, quoted in Buruma, 111.

75 **fictional newspaper serial . . . and a movie:** *Kaigun*, translated by Masato Fukushima and Yukiko Fukushima; the movie *Kaigun*, released in 1943, directed by Tasaka Tomotaka,was criticized as "disjointed" and failing to "sustain a consistent narrative." William B. Hauser in Lee, 145.

76 **"discipline, training":** five aspects of the Navy, essentially the code the Navy followed, translated from *Kaigun*.

77 **twenty midget subs:** Shigeru Fukudome, in Stillwell, 70.

77 ***Taiyo Maru:*** Hart Inquiry, page 353. April 15, 1944.

77 **On November 18:** Sakamaki, 15.

77 **was swept overboard:** Sakamaki, 19.

78 **clipped a fingernail:** Fukudome, in Stillwell, 71.

79 ***1-16* and *I-20* positioned:** Watabe, 166.

79 **harbor entrance:** Warner, 48; also Watabe, 150–152.

80 ***Curtiss* opened fire:** Naval Historical Center.

80 ***Monaghan's* first reaction:** Naval Historical Center.

81 **"Lucky Lou":** Stillwell, 185; also Naval Historical Center.

81 **Howard French:** Burlingame, 225; also Stillwell, 185.

81 **"If you want to see":** George A. Rood, quoted in Burlingame, 226.

82 **which sub is which:** If the midget subs had markings at all, they were part of the class known as HA, the third letter in the Japanese alphabet (I and Ro are the first two letters and represent two other sub classes.) *I-24-A* has the marking HA 19, meaning it was the nineteenth midget sub off the assembly line. (Burlingame, 66). Also, Watabe, 27, likens the markings to vehicle identification numbers.

83 **"became sick and had to drop out":** Sakamaki, 27.

84 **"On to Pearl Harbor!":** Ibid., 21.

84 **"my submarine nearly toppled over":** Ibid., 37.

84 **see ships patrolling the entrance:** Ibid., 39.

85 **"old destroyer":** Ibid., 40.

85 **"They've done":** Ibid., 41.

86 **"The only thing":** Ibid., 43

86 **"Yes, sir":** Ibid.

86 **go under the waves:** Ibid., 46.

87 **5-foot-3½-inch, 131-pound:** Interned Alien Enemy card. Admiral Nimitz Museum, National Museum of the Pacific War, Fredericksburg, TX.

87 **"Where in the hell":** Burlingame, 251.

87 **"looked like a prune":** Ibid., 251.

87 **"secret":** Doris Lama, office of the Chief of Naval Operations interview by author.

87 **killed by a self-inflicted:** Burlingame, 278; also Thomas Unger, interview, *Honolulu Advertiser*, December 7, 2001.

88 **Weiner figured:** Burlingame, 252.

88 **18-year-old high school football player:** *Honolulu Advertiser*, December 7, 2001.

88 **"seemed like":** Ibid.

89 **Radioman Charles Jackson:** Burlingame, 274.

89 **a few taps:** Ibid., 283.

89 **likes of Lana Turner and Frank Sinatra:** Samuel, 58.

89 **"The Bonds" photo:** Burlingame, 421.

90 **"In accordance":** Burlingame, 306.

90 **his picture:** Interned Alien Enemy card, Nimitz Museum.

90 **height and weight, his color:** Ibid.

90 **Arrived March 9, 1942:** Sakamaki, 50.

91 **April 9, April 18:** Ibid., 53–54.

91 **22,000 prisoners:** Cowley: 12.

91 **about one third of the population:** Ibid., 8.

92 **about $19:** Ibid. 21.

92 **if a German escaped:** Ibid., 43.

92 **"[H]e was always":** Sakamaki, 75.

93 **his midget on display:** Ibid., 67.

94 **June 8, 1943:** *Rochester Democrat and Chronicle*, February 17, 2003.

94 **arrived on January 4, 1946:** Sakamaki, 108.

94 **"No wonder we lost":** Ibid., 109.

94 **"newspaper writer":** Ibid., 110.

95 **"You have had":** Ibid., 111.

95 **"supreme in name and fact":** Ibid, 113.

95 **"I was walking":** Ibid., 129.

96 **Sakamaki wept:** *Honolulu Star-Bulletin*, May 11, 2002.

97 **Actually, Sakamaki had made:** Burlingame, xii.

97 **It was not uncommon:** This happened in Sydney Harbor; Warner and Seno, 127.

Chapter 5

99   "What possible good": Prange, 338.
99   "the victories outpaced": Dull, 133.
100 "he had been caught": Agawa, 300
100 "just enough of a taste": Ibid.
100 "The idea": Ibid, 299.
101 "do-nothing": Ibid.
101 five harbors: Sakamaki, 34.
101 Three American ships: Dull, 129.
101 The *Yorktown*'s skilled crew: Layton, et al., 403.
102 homeland waters: Layton, et al., 18.
102 Cracking the code: Biard, video.
103 Typical would be: Layton, et al,. 538.
103 "hot shot": Biard, video.
103 "highly intelligent": Ibid.
103 Rochefort: Ibid.
103 Finnegan: Ibid.
104 "the man with the blue eyes": Layton, et al., 411.
104 "whatever you heard": Biard video. Biard apparently despised Fletcher, who had chewed Biard out during the Battle of the Coral Sea for a coding error that wasn't his fault. Layton, 399.
104 "any particular": Layton et al., 412.
104 "If we listen": Ibid., 409.
104 The Battle of the Coral Sea proved so significant: Ibid., 406.
105 "wiped the floor": Agawa, 86.
105 "still being wrongly": Layton et al., 414.
106 AK was a place: Ibid., 406.
106 it would convince Washington: Ibid, 421.
107 Layton would later: Ibid., 435.
108 they were now joined: Warner and Seno, 100.
108 reported it to the patrol boat *Yarroma*: Ibid., 111.
109 It hit the wall: Ibid., 115.
110 around 5:00 A.M.: Ibid., 118.
110 "The question of": Wiliam J. Dunn, quoted in Burlingame, 390.
111 No. 5 battalion: Dower, 14.
111 send in the midget submarines: Warner and Seno, 144–145.
112 the battleship: Ibid., 147.
112 sank it on the spot: Ibid., 149.

112 **armed with swords and pistols:** Ibid., 150.
113 **"knew too much about Yamamoto's operation":** Layton, et al., 436.
113 **concentrate your fire power:** Ibid., 391.
114 **Midway consists of two:** Dull, 133.
115 **Nimitz reminded Layton:** Layton, et al., 438.
116 **"hell divers":** Ibid., 441.
116 **Yamaguchi, refused:** Ibid.
117 **the Aleutian chain's:** Potter, 183.
118 **Sent to attack on June 4:** Hoyt, *Yamamoto*, 162.
118 **"Midway Operation Cancelled":** Layton, et al., 446.
118 **"In battle as in *shogi*":** Ibid.
119 **On that Sunday morning:** Ibid., 448.
119 **"The Battle of Midway":** Ibid.
120 **One was hit in the:** Prados, 333.
120 **an amazing 4,947:** Ibid., 334.
121 **a good indicator:** Ambrose, *To America*, 94.

Chapter 6

123 **The loss at Midway:** Dull writes that the "loss of four precious first-line carriers stunned the naval section of Imperial Headquarters,"175.
123 **Laurel and Hardy:** Ballard, *Graveyards*, 21.
124 **The long, hard-fought Japanese retreat:** Americans ended fighting on February 7. By then the Japanese Army had already evacuated; Frank, 240.
124 **"bawling":** Agawa, 324; also considered "effete" and cowardly, Hoyt, *Yamamoto*, 229.
124 **"the magnitude of the stakes":** *New York Herald-Tribune*, October 16, 1942, as quoted in Frank, 332.
124 **Book-of-the-Month Club selection:** Tregaskis, 233.
125 **Iwo Jima:** Newcomb, 261.
125 **"I was scared":** Elliott, paper.
125 **Yamamoto's death:** Glines, 90.
125 **He was irreplaceable:** Layton, et al., 474.
125 **"all up for Japan":** Agawa, 389.
126 **"Blue-green mountains":** Dyer, 328.
126 **Mendaña:** Morison, *The Struggle for Guadalcanal*, 5.
126 **"rediscovered":** Ibid., 7.

127 **Colgate-Palmolive-Peet:** Ernest E, Lycan, USMC, interview by author. He bivouacked on Guadalcanal. Morison writes that Lever Brothers was owner, too; Morison, 7.

127 **the way they were planted:** Lycan interview by author.

127 **"we have had":** Dyer, 316.

128 **"Hotel Yamato":** Agawa, 328.

128 **Iron Bottom Sound:** Morison, 4.

128 **six road rollers, four generators:** Frank, 127.

128 **180-foot gap . . . By August 12:** Ibid.

129 **the personal plane of Admiral John S. McCain:** Ibid.

129 **The First Battle of the Solomon Sea:** Dull, 187.

129 **Japanese sailors drilled for night battles:** Frank, 84–86.

130 **"we took one hell of a beating":** Dyer, 358.

130 **"It was a peculiar":** Dull, 197.

130 **It didn't work because the pressure:** Hashimoto, 69.

131 **Imperial Navy reports show that:** Morison, 150.

131 **"a heartening victory":** Ibid., 147.

131 **"I want to pass along to you":** Frank, 321.

132 **"I now have confidence":** Hoyt, *Yamamoto*, 205.

132 **Soldiers slogged:** Frank, 352.

132 **"captured the airfield":** Hoyt, 213.

132 **Marine Sergeant Mitchell Paige:** Frank, 363–364.

132 **Sergeant John Basilone:** Ibid., 355.

133 **Basilone would die:** Newcomb, 99.

133 **"ga-to":** Agawa, 338.

133 **1,800-ton Navy cargo ship *Majaba*:** Morison, 226–227.

133 **_Alchiba_ had been hit:** Morison, 292.

134 **over a 20-day period:** Frank, 523–524.

134 **"All the balls of any man":** Brokaw, 118.

135 **"but we got shot up":** Tregaskis, 167.

135 **some island natives:** Frank, 223.

136 **duck-hunting weekend:** Layton, et al., 64.

137 **Knox took a look:** Potter, 302.

139 **ON 18 APRIL:** Layton, et al., 538.

139 **"We've hit the jackpot!":** Glines, 2.

140 **"I dozed off":** Ibid., 59.

140 **Mitchell divided the mission into five "legs":** Ibid., 32–33.

141 **A note came back:** Agawa, 348.

142 **Their tanks dropped:** Glines, 59.

143 **and wore white gloves:** Agawa, 358.

143   **"I definitely can't":** Glines, 80.
144   POP GOES THE WEASEL: Ibid., 86.
144   **"lucky" targets:** Agawa, 371.
145   **"The only better news":** *Time*, May 31, 1943.
146   **Chopin's "Funeral March":** Agawa, 390.
147   **"the beginning of the end":** Ibid., 388.

Chapter 7

149   **"Gentlemen, start":** Jim Murray, *Los Angeles Times*, May 29, 1966.
149   ***"bonzai":*** Straus, 51.
149   **"Rather than live":** Warner and Seno, 1.
149   **"Great Japan . . . the land of the Gods":** Hashimoto, 126.
150   **In 1274 . . . 1281:** Kemp, 54.
150   **also translated:** Hashimoto, 117.
151   **A big sub:** Ibid., drawing, 115.
151   **Ulithi Atoll:** Ibid., 118.
151   **The blast knocked:** Naval Historical Center.
152   **On the morning of the 20th:** Ibid.
152   **The Japanese lost:** Kemp, 57.
153   **"The unpredictable Kaiten":** Hashimoto, 118.
153   **drinking alcohol on board was prohibited:** Ibid., 120.
154   **"I wanted all the details":** Ibid., 123.
155   **"Three cheers for":** Ibid., 125.
156   **By March 27 all except:** Newcomb, 254.
156   **A new replenished submarine:** Hashimoto, 131.
156   **"complete control by sea and in the air":** Ibid.
156   **"go in and fight":** Ibid., 133.
157   **"hypnotic fascination":** Yoshida, xix.
158   **"a heaven-sent opportunity":** Ibid., 6.
158   **"The tracks of the torpedoes":** Ibid., 66.
158   **"We die for sovereign and country":** Ibid., 41.
158   **exploded April 7:** Spurr, 119.
159   **"With the sinking":** Dull, 335.
161   **"it would have been difficult to score":** Hashimoto, 144.
161   **In about 12 seconds:** Ibid., 146
161   **The doctor noticed:** Graves, 39.
162   **"there's no doubt":** Naval Historical Center.
162   **One of the ship's doctors:** Ibid.

163 **"I've seen men":** Dick Theland, interview, *Toledo Blade*, June 23, 2002.

165 **He was called as:** Naval Historical Center.

165 **"I hear that":** Mochitsura Hashimoto to Senate Armed Services Committee, November 24, 1999.

166 **One was the Koryu:** Kemp, 58.

167 **Intelligence analyst:** Prados, 712.

167 **"had the paradoxical effect":** Spector, 543.

167 **7,000 aircraft:** Prados, 723.

168 **767,000:** Spector, 543.

168 **The losses from the atomic blasts:** Ibid., 555.

168 **268,000:** Spector, 543.

168 **One last suicide:** Warner and Seno, 194.

169 ***Antares*:** Naval Historical Center.

Chapter 8

171 **"Before, the militarists":** Sakamaki, 112.

171 **"It's their fault":** Ibid.

171 **Under the supreme commander:** Piccigallo, 6.

171 **"It is a trial of us all":** Sakamaki, 125.

172 **"shattered jewels":** Straus, 51.

172 **By the time of the Russo-Japanese War:** Ibid., 19.

172 **By 1939, an incident:** Ibid., 25.

173 **The Field Service Code:** Ibid., 38.

173 **Japan eventually refused to take:** Ibid., 19.

174 **In 1972 a soldier:** Reuters, September 23, 1997.

174 **A picture ran:** Straus, 63.

175 **"white pigs":** Tanaka, 114.

175 **Chinese captives were used:** Piccigallo, 135.

175 **"were committed in all theaters":** Ibid., 27.

176 **Of the group:** Tanaka, 2. Altogether there were 474 war trials in the Philippines, China, the Pacific Islands, and Japan. Piccigallo, 48.

177 **MacArthur wrote that "the principle":** Ibid., 7.

177 **Admiral Nagano:** Ibid., 20.

178 **Some military men:** Prados, 732.

178 **Watanabe . . . later transitioned:** Ibid.

179 **Hull believed the Japanese representatives:** Layton, 314.

180 **Keenan. . . "strictly legally":** Piccigallo, 16.

180 **"[t]o tell the truth":** Agawa, 389.

181 **Historian Stephen Ambrose wrote:** Ambrose, 112.

182 **"A beast is an animal":** Ibid.

182 **"If we do not respect them":** *New York Times,* October 30, 2002.

Chapter 9

183 **"What if a Navy dredging":** Ballard, *Graveyards,* 38.

183 **and was stored there:** Delgado, 2.

184 **The National Park Service:** Ibid., 7.

184 **"Vulgar disregard of":** Burlingame, 422.

185 **One person asked:** Ibid., 70.

185 **"Today we went over to":** Ibid., 429–430.

185 **In 1952, a dragline:** Stillwell, 195–196.

186 **The museum downplays:** *New York Times,* October 30, 2002.

186 **according to a museum official:** Masato Fukushima, interview by author.

186 **A diving instructor:** Warner and Seno, 179–180; Burlingame, 425.

187 **"They were either drowned":** Warner and Seno, 180.

187 **even after twenty years:** Burlingame, 428.

187 **The Japanese workers found:** Watabe, 28–33.

188 **When Bob Ballard:** Ballard, *Graveyards,* 67.

189 **Around 1990, another theory:** Burlingame, 198–199.

190 **To prove the point:** "Unsolved History: Myths of Pearl Harbor." DVD. Discovery Channel, 2003.

191 **A problem with the theory:** Naval Historical Center.

192 **The subs from Sydney:** Warner and Seno, 169.

192 **the sub was painted:** Ibid., 184.

192 **A marker was erected:** Watabe, 38.

193 **Either way, they were buried:** Ibid.

Epilogue

195 **"We found a bunch":** *Pearl Harbor: Legacy,* DVD.

196 **"They almost certainly":** Ambrose in Ballard, *Graveyards,* 9.

196 **"Terry's an adventurer":** Rachel Shackelford, interview by author.

196 **"I always loved":** Terry Kerby, interview by author.

196 ***Star 2:*** Ibid.

197 **Al Giddings:** Giddings would also be the director of underwater photography for the movies *The Abyss* and *Titanic.*

197 **"not to harm":** Kerby, interview.

200 **"They said they wanted":** Ibid.
201 **"That sub belongs":** Daniel Martinez, quoted in Kerby, interview.
201 **They just hadn't:** Ibid.
202 **"I never hesitated":** Chris Kelley, interview by author,
202 **"They were crap":** Ibid.
202 **"stripe the ocean floor":** Hal Richman, interview by author.
203 **"almost killed me":** Kerby, interview.
203 **"canoes":** Ibid.
203 **"we just didn't see":** Kelley, interview.
204 **At 6-feet-7-inches:** Al Kavaltis, NOAA newsletter, and interview by author.
204 **"Al got bumped":** Kerby, interview.
205 **"Being caught on":** Shackelford, in "Deep Sea Detectives: Japanese Sub at Pearl Harbor," Video. The History Channel. 2004.
206 **"Terry, Terry":** Kelley, interview.
206 **"I could see the hole":** Kerby, interview.
206 **"Terry made the":** Kelley, interview.
207 **"It's a rock":** Kerby, interview.
207 **"blasted from a fire hose":** Ballard, *Graveyards*, 66.
207 **important piece of history:** Daniel K. Inouye, *Washington Post*, August 31, 2002.
208 **Lehner gazed:** "Unsolved History: Myths of Pearl Harbor."
208 **"been on patrol":** Kerby, interview.
209 **"It was emotional":** Shackelford, quoted in Kerby, interview.
210 **"would be hard to spot":** Kelley, interview.

Bilbliography

Agawa, Hiroyuki. *Reluctant Admiral: Yamamoto and the Imperial Navy.* Translated by John Bester. Tokyo: Kodansha International, 1979; dist. in U.S. by Harper & Row.

Ambrose, Stephen E. *To America.* New York: Simon & Schuster, 2002.

Ames, Oakes. *Oakes Ames: Jottings of a Harvard Botanist, 1874–1950.* Cambridge, MA: Botanical Museum of Harvard University, 1979; dist. by Harvard University Press.

Andrieu d'Albas, Emmanuel M. F. *Death of a Navy: Japanese Naval Action in World War II.* Translated by Anthony Rippon. New York: Devin-Adair, 1957.

Ballard, Robert D. *The Eternal Darkness: A Personal History of Deep-Sea Exploration.* Princeton, NJ: Princeton University Press, 2000.

———. *Graveyards of the Pacific: From Pearl Harbor to Bikini Atoll.* Washington: National Geographic, 2001.

Beasley, W. G. *Japanese Imperialism, 1894–1945.* Oxford: Clarendon Press; New York: Oxford University Press, 1987.

Biard, Forrest R. "Tex." *Breaking of Japanese Naval Codes.* Video. Fort Meade, MD: National Cryptologic Foundation, 2002.

Brokaw, Tom. *The Greatest Generation.* New York: Delta/Dell Publishing, 2001.

Brown, Rollo W. *Harvard Yard in the Golden Age.* New York: Current Books, 1948.

Burlingame, Burl. *Advance Force Pearl Harbor.* Annapolis, MD: Naval Institute Press, 2002.

Buruma, Ian. *Inventing Japan, 1853–1964.* New York: Modern Library, 2003.

Carr, Caleb. *The Lessons of Terror: A History of Warfare Against Civilians: Why It Has Always Failed and Why It Will Fail Again.* New York: Random House Trade Paperbacks, 2003.

Chang, Iris. *The Rape of Nanking: The Forgotten Holocaust of World War II.* New York: Penguin Books, 1997.

Clancy, Tom. *Submarine: A Guided Tour Inside a Nuclear Warship.* New York: Berkley Books, 1993.

Cowley, Betty. *Stalag Wisconsin: Inside World War II Prisoner-of-War Camps.* Oregon, WI: Badger Books, 2002.

Crocker, Gary. "Day of Infamy." Unpublished manuscipt.

Delgado, James P. *Japanese Midget Submarine "HA-19."* Washington: National Park Service, Historic Landmark Study, 1988.

Divine, Robert A. *The Reluctant Belligerent: American Entry into World War II.* New York: Wiley, 1979.

Dower, Gandar K. C. *Into Madagascar.* Harmondsworth, Middlesex: Penguin Books, 1943.

Dull, Paul S. *A Battle History of the Imperial Japanese Navy, 1941–1945.* Annapolis, MD: Naval Institute Press, 1978.

Dyer, George C. *The Amphibians Came to Conquer: The Story of Admiral Richmond Kelly Turner.* Washington: U.S. Department of the Navy, 2 vols., 1972.

Elliott, Ray. "James Jones: The Evolution of a Soldier and a Writer." Paper presented at Illinois Authors Book Fair, 2004.

Frank, Richard. *Guadalcanal: The Definitive Account of the Landmark Battle.* New York: Random House, 1990.

Genat, Robert, and Robin Genat. *Modern U.S. Navy Submarines.* Osceola, WI: Motorbooks International, 1997.

Glines, Carroll V. *Attack on Yamamoto.* New York: Jove Books, 1990.

Graves, Richard W. *Men of Poseidon: Life at Sea Aboard the USS Rall.* Nevada City, California: Willow Valley Press, 2000.

Harris, Brayton. *The Navy Times Book of Submarines: A Political, Social, and Military History.* New York: Berkley Books, 1997.

Hart Inquiry. *Pearl Harbor Attack.* Hearings before the United States Joint Committee on the Investigation of the Pearl Harbor Attack, Seventy-Ninth Congress. Washington, D.C.: United States Government Printing Office, 1946.

Hashimoto, Mochitsura. *Sunk: The Story of the Japanese Submarine Fleet, 1941–1945.* Translated by E. H. M. Colegrave. New York: Avon Publications, East Gate Book, 1954.

Hein, Laura, and Mark Seldon, eds. *Censoring History: Citizenship and Memory in Japan, Germany, and the United States.* Armonk, NY: M. E. Sharpe, 2000.

Hersey, John. *Hiroshima.* New York: Knopf, 1946.

Hershberg, James G. *James B. Conant: Harvard to Hiroshima and the Making of the Nuclear Age.* New York: Knopf, 1993.

Hewitt Inquiry. *Pearl Harbor Attack.* Hearings before the United States Joint Committee on the Investigation of the Pearl Harbor Attack, Seventy-Ninth Congress. Washington, D.C.: United States Government Printing Office, 1946.

Hoyt, Edwin P. *Japan's War: The Great Pacific Conflict, 1853 to 1952.* New York: McGraw-Hill, 1986.

———. *Three Military Leaders: Heihachiro Togo, Isoroku Yamamoto, Tomoyuki Yamashita.* Tokyo, New York: Kodansha International, 1993.

———. *Yamamoto: The Man Who Planned Pearl Harbor.* Guilford, CT: Lyons Press, 2001.

Iriye, Akira. *Pearl Harbor and the Coming of the Pacific War: A Brief History with Documents and Essays.* Boston: Bedford/St. Martin's, 1999.

Iwata, Toyoo. *Kaigun.* Tokyo: Shinchosha, 1943.

Jones, Don. *Oba, the Last Samurai: Saipan 1944–45.* Novato, CA: Presidio Press, 1986.

Jones, James. *The Thin Red Line.* New York: Delta/Dell, 1998.

Kemp, Paul. *Midget Submarines of the Second World War.* London: Chatham, 1999.

La Forte, Robert S., and Ronald E. Marcello, eds. *Remembering Pearl Harbor: Eyewitness Accounts by U.S. Military Men and Women.* Wilmington, DE: Scholarly Resources, 1991.

Layton, Edwin T., with Roger Pineau and John Costello. *"And I Was There": Pearl Harbor and Midway—Breaking the Secrets.* New York: Morrow, 1985.

Lee, Loyd E., ed. *World War II in Asia and the Pacific and the War's Aftermath, with General Themes.* Westport, CT: Greenwood Press, 1998.

Lord, Walter. *Day of Infamy.* New York: Holt, 1957.

Love, Paul , and John Craddock. *Secrets of the Sea.* Stamford, Connecticut: International Masters Publishers. 2001.

McCullough, David. *Truman.* New York: Touchstone, 1993.

Montgomery, Michael. *Imperialist Japan: The Yen to Dominate.* New York: St. Martin's, 1988.

Morison, Samuel Eliot. *Coral Sea, Midway and Submarine Actions: May 1941–August 1942.* Vol. 4 of Samuel Eliot Morison, *History of United States Naval Operations in World War II.* 15 vols. Boston: Little, Brown, 1947–1962.

———. *The Liberation of the Philippines.* Vol. 13 of *History of U.S. Naval Operations.*

———. *The Struggle for Guadalcanal: August 1942–February 1943.* Vol. 5 of *History of U.S. Naval Operations.*

National Archives and Records: College Park, Maryland. Deck logs, action reports and other miscellaneous documents.

Naval Historical Center. Washington: Department of the Navy. *Includes ship information, deck logs and other documents related to individual ships.*

Newcomb, Richard F. *Iwo Jima.* Garden City, NY: Doubleday, 1983.

Pearl Harbor: Legacy of Attack. DVD. National Geographic, 2001.

Piccigallo, Philip R. *The Japanese on Trial: Allied War Crimes Operations in the East, 1945 – 1951,* Austin: University of Texas Press, 1979.

Pineau, Roger, coauthor with Masanori Ito. *End of the Imperial Japanese Navy.* Translated by Andrew Y. Kuroda and Roger Pineau. Westport, CT: Greenwood Press, 1984.

Potter, John Deane. *Yamamoto: The Man Who Menaced America.* New York: Viking, 1965.

Prados, John. *Combined Fleet Decoded: The Secret History of American Intelligence and the Japanese Navy in World War II.* New York: Random House, 1995.

Prange, Gordon W. *At Dawn We Slept: The Untold Story of Pearl Harbor.* New York: McGraw-Hill, 1981.

Rusbridger, James, and Eric Nave. *Betrayal at Pearl Harbor: How Churchill Lured Roosevelt into World War II.* New York: Summit Books, 1991.

Russell, Henry Dozier. *Pearl Harbor Story.* Macon, GA: Mercer University Press, 2001.

Sakamaki, Kazuo. *I Attacked Pearl Harbor.* Translated by Toru Matsumoto. New York: Association Press, 1949.

Samuel, Lawrence R. *Pledging Allegiance: American Identity and the Bond Drive of World War II.* Washington: Smithsonian Institution Press, 1997.

Singh, Simon. *The Code Book: The Evolution of Secrecy from Mary, Queen of Scots, to Quantum Cryptography.* New York: Doubleday, 1999.

"Special Attack Flotilla." Monograph. Japanese Imperial Navy, 1942.

Spector, Ronald H. *Eagle Against the Sun: The American War with Japan.* New York: Free Press, 1985.

Spurr, Russell. *A Glorious Way to Die: The Kamikaze Mission of the Battleship "Yamato,"April 1945.* New York: Newmarket Press, 1981.

Stillwell, Paul, ed. *Air Raid, Pearl Harbor!: Recollections of a Day of Infamy.* Annapolis, MD: Naval Institute Press, 1981.

Stinnett, Robert B. *Day of Deceit: The Truth About FDR and Pearl Harbor.* New York: Free Press, 2000.

Straus, Ulrich. *The Anguish of Surrender: Japanese POW's of World War II.* Seattle: University of Washington Press, 2003.

Tanaka, Yuki. *Hidden Horrors: Japanese War Crimes in World War II.* Boulder, CO: Westview Press, 1996.

Thomareas, Michelle, and John Craddock. *Wildlife Explorer.* Stamford, Connecticut: International Masters Publishers. 1999.

Tregaskis, Richard. *Guadalcanal Diary.* New York: Random House, 1943.

Unsolved History: Myths of Pearl Harbor. DVD. Discovery Channel, 2003.

Vesilind, Pritt. "J. Dispatch #1-#6." NationalGeographic.com. November 8–16, 2000.

Verne, Jules. *20,000 Leagues Under the Sea.* Many editions.

Vyborny, Lee, and Don Davis. *Dark Waters: An Insider's Account of the NR-1, the Cold War's Undercover Nuclear Sub.* New York: New American Library, 2003.

Warner, Peggy, and Sadao Seno. *The Coffin Boats: Japanese Midget Submarine Operations in the Second World War.* London: L. Cooper/ Secker & Warburg, 1986.

Watabe, Yoshiuki. *Unknown Japanese Imperial Navy Secrets.* Tokyo: Tetsuro Koike, 2003.

Wohlstetter, Roberta. *Pearl Harbor: Warning and Decision.* Stanford, CA: Stanford University Press, 1962.

Yoshida, Mitsuru. *Requiem for Battleship "Yamato."* Translated by Richard Minear. Seattle: University of Washington Press, 1985.

ACKNOWLEDGMENTS

THERE ARE BEDROCK BOOKS about the war that began so suddenly one December morning in Hawaii in 1941. Gordon Prange's *At Dawn We Slept*, Walter Lord's *Day of Infamy*, Paul Dull's *A Battle History of the Imperial Japanese Navy*, Richard Frank's *Guadalcanal: The Definitive Account of the Landmark Battle*, and Samuel E. Morison's multi-volume series *History of United States Naval Operations in World War II*—all were basic to the research for this book. Add to that list some relative newcomers: Burl Burlingame's *Advance Force Pearl Harbor* is like a museum filled with unexpected artifacts. Peggy Warner and Sadao Seno's *The Coffin Boats* provides key details about midget subs and their crews in Australia and Madagascar. If someone asked me to "pick a favorite," it would be *"And I Was There,"* the remembrances of Rear Admiral Edwin T. Layton, aided by ace collaborators Navy Captain Roger Pineau and John Costello. Layton was the Navy intelligence officer at Pearl Harbor on December 7, 1941. Despite not predicting the sneak attack, he kept his job and for the rest of the war had a unique vantage point.

Other contributions to this book came from a variety of sources: Masato Fukushima, Mrs. Yukiko Fukushima, and Junya Katsume translated books and a variety of documents from Japanese to English. Their work on *Kaigun* was exceptional.

The dedicated people at the Hawaii Undersea Research Laboratory spent countless hours explaining their underwater missions; special thanks to Terry Kerby and Chris Kelley.

Also providing valuable assistance were the staff members at the National Crytologic Museum, the National Museum of the Pacific War/Admiral Nimitz Museum, and the Harvard University Archives.

Dozens of veterans consented to interviews and contributed many of their own papers and documents. A special thanks goes to those sailors from the *Antares* and *Ward*, in particular "Til" Chiappari of the *Antares* and Ken Swedberg of the *Ward*. Also thanks to Ernest E. Lycan, a Marine who fought at Guam and Iwo Jima.

At International Marine, thanks to Jon Eaton and his talented colleagues. At Progressive Media, Paul Love helped in the initial research for this book, and John Craddock III dug out two helpful books from his library. Special thanks to Nancy Lycan and Sissy Lycan for their inspiration.

Index